Supervising Paraeducators in Educational Settings

Supervising Paraeducators in Educational Settings

A Team Approach

SECOND EDITION

Edited by

Anna Lou Pickett
Kent Gerlach

pro·ed
An International Publisher
8700 Shoal Creek Boulevard
Austin, Texas 78757-6897
800/897-3202 Fax 800/397-7633
www.proedinc.com

pro·ed
An International Publisher

8700 Shoal Creek Boulevard
Austin, Texas 78757-6897
800/897-3202 Fax 800/397-7633
www.proedinc.com

Library of Congress Cataloging-in-Publication Data

Supervising paraeducators in educational settings : a team approach / edited by Anna Lou Pickett, Kent Gerlach.—2nd ed.
p. cm.
Includes bibliographical references and index.
ISBN-13: 978-089079899-7
ISBN-10: 0-89079-899-0
1. Teachers' assistants—Training of—United States. 2. Special education teachers—Training of—United States. 3. Teaching teams—United States. I. Pickett, Anna Lou. II. Gerlach, Kent.

LB2844.1.A8 S86 2003
371.2'02—dc21 2002036723

This book is designed in Italia and New Century Schoolbook.

Printed in the United States of America

4 5 6 7 8 9 10 11 10

To Hugh Pickett
and
Laurence Gerlach,
who encouraged us
to accept challenges

Contents

Foreword

We are educators employed by the Board of Cooperative Education Services (BOCES) located in Suffolk County on the eastern end of Long Island in New York. We, along with other colleagues, have provided leadership in the development of a district-wide teacher/paraeducator trainer and mentor program. Our initial efforts were concerned with the need to find effective methods for preparing more than 700 paraeducators for their emerging roles as key participants in all aspects of the learning process. We soon learned that, to strengthen the work of teacher and paraeducator teams, we needed to train teachers for their roles as supervisors of paraeducators as well.

The BOCES inservice training program for paraeducators, developed in collaboration with the local affiliate of the New York State United Teacher, was launched in 1990. Over the years it has proven to be flexible enough to train paraeducators working in general, special, compensatory, and early childhood education. Therefore, when administrators, teachers, and paraeducators recognized the need to prepare teachers to direct and work effectively with paraeducators, it made sense to incorporate teacher training into the model. Fortunately for us, we discovered the first edition of this text, *Supervising Paraeducators in School Settings: A Team Approach.* It provided us with guidelines we used to expand our inservice training program to enhance opportunities for professional development of new and experienced teachers. The range of issues discussed in the text, along with what we learned from teachers who participated in the inservice training, raised our consciousness about the critical need for teacher educators to prepare graduates to plan for, direct, and monitor the day-to-day performance of pareducators.

As a result, we reached out to the school of education at the State University of New York (SUNY) at Stony Brook, and the faculty agreed to work in concert with us to develop a competency-based course. This text served as a valuable resource as we developed the syllabus, and is the text for the class now offered at the SUNY at Stony Brook campus.

James Fogarty
Associate Executive Director of Phi Delta Kappa International for Leadership and Development (formerly Executive Director of Instructional Service, Eastern Suffolk BOCES)

Arlene Barresi
Coordinator of the BOCES Teacher / Paraeducator Training and Mentoring Program

Kathy Sweezy and Sam Palmer
BOCES Teachers and Adjunct Instructors, State University of New York at Stony Brook

Preface

Teachers and other school professionals are responsible for supervising paraeducators and other support personnel. The term *paraeducators* is defined in this text as school or agency employees (1) who work under the supervision of teachers or other professional practitioners who are responsible for (a) the design, implementation, and assessment of learner progress, and (b) the evaluation of the effectiveness of learning programs and related services for children and youth and their families, and (2) whose positions are either instructional in nature or who provide other direct services to children and youth and their families (Pickett, 1989). Other job titles used to identify these employees may include, among others, paraprofessionals, teacher aides or assistants, education assistants, instructional assistants, education technicians, transition trainers, job coaches, therapy assistants, and home visitors. This second edition of *Supervising Paraeducators in Educational Settings: A Team Approach* is intended to provide administrators, teachers, and related services personnel, including physical and occupational therapists and speech–language pathologists, with the skills and knowledge necessary to work more effectively with paraeducators. It also serves as a prompt for policymakers in local education agencies (LEAs) and state education agencies (SEAs) to recognize the need for standards and guidelines to prepare teachers and other school professionals to supervise paraeducators. It will also assist SEAs, LEAs, and other education provider agencies to identify knowledge and skill competencies required by teachers and paraeducators as members of education teams.

Although several texts have been written about collaboration and communication in the schools, this book differs in that it concerns issues associated with the management and supervision of paraeducators. It provides guidelines and methods to prepare school professionals to understand (a) the contributions that paraeducators make to the delivery of education services and (b) the need for role clarification, effective supervision and management, good communication, and teamwork.

We wrote this text for a broad audience. Our goal is to provide teacher educators and other personnel developers, policymakers, administrators, general and special educators, and related services practitioners with information they can build on to address the issues and practices surrounding the employment, supervision, and preparation of paraprofessionals.

Overview

Over the years, we have worked with many dedicated teachers, paraeducators, parents, administrators, and providers of related services who have encouraged us to create this book. We have tried to make the contents clear and practical. The information you will read is the outgrowth of many years of experience working with paraeducators and the teachers or therapists who supervise them.

Chapter 1 begins with a historical perspective and overview of paraeducators working in today's schools. It provides the framework for the issues that school administrators and practitioners are facing today. Chapter 2 focuses on team roles in classrooms and learning environments and examines the roles of teachers, other professionals, and paraeducators. The management of paraeducators and paratherapists is discussed in Chapter 3. The topic of Chapter 4 is team roles in therapy services. This chapter is devoted to speech–language pathology, physical and occupational therapy, and the paratherapist's role in the delivery of these services. The importance of team building and effective communication is the focus of Chapter 5. Administrative issues are examined in Chapter 6, and Chapter 7 deals with the professional and ethical responsibilities of team members.

Our primary objective was to produce a reader-friendly, thoughtful guide that would enable education personnel to work effectively with paraeducators. Each chapter consists of instructional objectives, discussion questions, and suggested exercises, and some chapters include case studies. We hope that the information provided in this text will address your needs and help improve the productivity of education teams.

Acknowledgments

We are indebted to many colleagues who assisted with the writing, reviewing, and preparation of this text. First and foremost we want to thank the chapter authors for their commitment to this text. Their individual and collective contributions provide insight into current best practices associated with the roles, supervision, and preparation of paraeducators and paratherapists.

Special thanks to Patty Lee, University of Northern Colorado at Greeley, who assisted in the development of Chapter 5, and Lynn Beck, dean of the School of Education at Pacific Lutheran University, who assisted in reviewing Chapter 7.

Carroll Ferguson assisted in editing the first draft and the final copy and provided word processing services. Charlotte Fisk, the administrative assistant at City University of New York, deserves our special thanks. Her patience and sense of humor remained constant throughout the process.

The staff of PRO-ED has given us guidance, encouragement, and advice. We especially appreciate the support received from Jim Patton, Chris Anne Worsham, Kathy Synatschk, Martin Wilson, and Jason Crosier.

We also want to recognize the thousands of paraeducators and their teacher partners who inspired and motivated us to write this text.

Reference

Pickett, A. L. (1989). *Restructuring the schools. The role of paraprofessionals.* Washington, DC: Center for Policy Research, National Governors' Association.

Contributors

Nancy K. French
University of Colorado at Denver
Denver, Colorado

Kent Gerlach
Pacific Lutheran University
Tacoma, Washington

William Heller
University of South Florida
St. Petersburg, Florida

Thomas M Longhurst
Idaho State University
Pocatello, Idaho

Anna Lou Pickett
City University of New York
New York, New York

Lynn Safarik
Colorado State University at
Fort Collins
Fort Collins, Colorado

Allen Steckelberg
University of Nebraska–Lincoln
Lincoln, Nebraska

Stan Vasa
University of Nebraska–Lincoln
Lincoln, Nebraska

Paraeducators in Educational Settings: Framing the Issues

1

Anna Lou Pickett

Setting the Stage

Rose, an instructional assistant with 20 years of experience in elementary and special education, has been assigned to work with Ruth, a first-year teacher. Ruth decided to go on for her master's degree in special education immediately after she received her baccalaureate in elementary education. She feels confident that she has the necessary skills for planning, teaching the students, and working collaboratively with other licensed and certified professional staff. Because she was not prepared at the undergraduate or graduate level to plan and assign tasks to other adults and to monitor their performances, Ruth is uncertain about her ability to integrate Rose into instructional and other classroom activities. During her career Rose has assisted teachers in all aspects of the instructional process. Rose is becoming increasingly unhappy because she feels that Ruth does not appreciate her or the skills she has learned over the past 20 years. Ruth, too, is not pleased with how things are going because she keeps hearing rumors that Rose complains about her and the program changes she has made to the teachers she worked with previously. Further complicating the situation is that no time is set aside in the weekly schedule for them to meet to discuss their concerns or to plan together.

For the first time in her 10-year career as a speech–language pathologist, Perri is working with a therapy aide. She is pleased that Maria, who speaks Spanish, has been added to the team because many students in her caseload are English language learners. Perri feels strongly that it is her responsibility as the speech–language pathologist to involve parents in all aspects of their child's treatment. Recently Perri has become aware that many parents seem to feel more comfortable speaking with Maria about their children than with her. She recognizes that this may be because Maria lives in the neighborhood where the school is located, understands their language, and is familiar with their culture. While she and Maria work well together, Perri is afraid she will offend Maria if she asks her not to communicate with the parents.

John is a teacher's assistant who was employed to facilitate the inclusion of five students with disabilities into general education programs. He works with several teachers and all of them have different expectations about what he should do in "their" classrooms. The duties assigned to John by the different teachers range from being fully responsible for teaching "the special education kids" in one class; to assisting *all* students the teacher thinks will benefit from personalized attention in another classroom; to escorting students from one class to another, and then sitting in the back of the room and doing routine record keeping, preparing instructional materials, and occasionally scoring papers. Because of their schedules, John and the special education teacher to whom he is assigned have been able to meet only once during the first month of school. John is confused about what his role and responsibilities are supposed to be. Of even greater importance to him is the fact that he was hired and sent into the classroom immediately without any training. This is of great concern to him because he does not feel that he has the skills needed to work with students who have so many different needs. He has asked other assistants about job descriptions and training opportunities and has been told that neither exist. He does not know to whom he should speak regarding his concerns. Should it be the principal, the special education teacher, the general education teachers?

Josie is the new coordinator of human resources and personnel development for a local school district. The district serves children and youth in various programs from birth through 21 years of age. One of her first calls was from Mark and Aiyong, the directors of special education and related services, Title I, and migrant education programs. They have identified a critical need to prepare teachers and paraeducators to work together more effectively as members of instructional teams. Josie suggests that they meet to discuss their concerns.

During the meeting, Mark and Aiyong share with Josie several problems and issues that have an impact on the performance of teacher–paraeducator teams. For example, they have found that the district's job descriptions for paraeducators have not been revised since the early 1970s. They also have discovered that the language in the teacher's contract does not clearly define the teacher's supervisory responsibilities. Further compounding the problem, teachers are reporting that they feel unprepared to direct and monitor paraeducator performance. In addition, although the district is committed to and making progress toward providing ongoing professional development for teachers, opportunities for paraeducator training are not part of the program.

Josie agrees to explore the availability of resources at the state and local levels that could address some of these issues. Her first call is to a member of the task force that is drafting new statewide standards for teacher preparation and licensure in different programs and grade levels. In response to her question about whether the standards will recognize the emerging roles of teachers as supervisors of paraeducators, she is told, "That's an interesting question, but it is not one of our agenda items."

A second call, to the state education agency, found that there are no statewide policies or regulatory procedures concerned with paraeducator roles, supervision, and preparation in any programs. In fact, the state leaves it totally up to the districts to decide what skills and training paraeducators need. Her contact did say, however, that the commissioner is beginning to assess the need for the state to take a more active role in addressing issues that surround the supervision and training of education assistants due to recent mandates from the federal government.

During her investigative efforts, Josie also discovered that the local community college offers an associate's degree in early childhood education for paraeducators. Because of recent changes in the Individuals with Disabilities Education Act (IDEA) of 1997, the curriculum may be expanded to meet the needs of paraeducators who work in home- and center-based programs serving infants, toddlers, and young children and their families. She also learned that an associate's degree program for paraeducators employed in elementary and special education programs for school-age learners was discontinued at that college several years earlier. When Josie asked why the program was dropped, she was told that the district's salary scale and the lack of a career ladder for paraeducators were barriers to recruiting paraeducators.

As Josie reported all of this to Mark and Aiyong, they were stunned to learn that there were so few resources they could build on to strengthen the performance of teacher–paraeducator teams. Moreover, they knew that it would be almost impossible for them to develop and maintain programs to prepare paraeducators and teachers for their team roles without the assistance and support of other stakeholders. Their first question was, "Where do we go from here?" The second was, "How do we get there?"

OVERVIEW

These scenarios, like others that occur daily in schools and other education settings across the country, reflect the emerging but underrecognized management roles of teachers and other school professionals who are responsible for directing and monitoring paraeducator performance. They are also indicative of the growing need for policymakers and administrators in state and local education agencies (SEAs and LEAs) to join forces with their colleagues in institutions of higher education

(IHEs), professional organizations representing different disciplines, and unions to (a) improve policies, procedures, and personnel practices that influence the roles, supervision, and performance of paraeducators; (b) prepare school professionals to supervise paraeducators; and (c) develop standardized, ongoing opportunities for training and career development for paraeducators.

The purpose of this text is to provide personnel developers, administrators, and practitioners with information they can build on to strengthen the performance of education and related services teams that work in schools and other learning environments. This chapter identifies the broad range of issues connected with paraeducator supervision, roles, and preparation, and lays the foundation for the six chapters that follow.

Instructional Objectives

After studying this chapter and participating in class discussions and the exercises, the reader will be able to do the following:

1. Describe the historical basis for the employment of paraeducators in schools and other learning environments.
2. Discuss contemporary factors that contribute to continued reliance on paraeducators.
3. Explain why development of standards, policies, and mechanisms for improving paraeducator supervision and preparation is important.
4. Describe the unique role of SEAs in promulgating and implementing standards for paraeducator roles, supervision, and preparation.
5. Explain why it is important for SEAs, LEAs, IHEs, and other stakeholders to work together to ensure that professional development opportunities are available to prepare teachers and other professional practitioners to supervise paraeducators.
6. Discuss why it is important for SEAs, LEAs, and IHEs to collaborate in the design of ongoing, seamless, comprehensive systems of training and career development for paraeducators.

Introduction

The 20th century was a time of continual ferment that led to dramatic changes in political, economic, social, health care, and education systems and transformations in the ways human services are delivered in the United States. As a result of our country's involvement in two world wars, the emergence of a global economy, and other events, our country has moved from being in a period of isolationism and internal expansion to having a dominant position in the international community. We completed our passage through the industrial and manufacturing era and have entered the age of high technology, personal computers, space exploration, and a service-driven economy. The population moved from small towns and family farms to great urban centers and from there to suburbs. Increasing numbers of immigrants created a multiracial, multicultural, and multilingual society. Advances in medical science enabled more children with disabilities and life-threatening health care needs to survive and to thrive. An expanding economy led to higher standards of living for many families and improved education for their children, while at the same time the numbers of children and youth living in poverty and coming from educationally disadvantaged backgrounds were increasing.

Changes in our nation's history and personal lives of our citizens are constant. The events that occurred on September 11, 2001, have ensured that changes will take place that will have a profound impact on individuals' lives and the country's political, social, health care, economic, and human services systems. We cannot know what the ultimate outcomes of these events will be; they will no doubt present challenges to stakeholders at all levels of the education community as they continue short-term and long-term efforts to improve the quality of education for all learners and prepare them to live, work, and actively participate in a diverse society and a changing world.

Defining the Term

The factors mentioned in the preceding paragraphs, as well as a multitude of other factors, including critical shortages of teachers and related services professionals that have existed for the better part of 50 years, have had a profound impact on the nation's schools and other education provider agencies. They have caused policymakers and administrators at the federal, state, and local levels to develop and test different methods for improving the quality of education for all children and youth. One of the many strategies has been the introduction of new staffing arrangements, including increased reliance on paraeducators and paraprofessionals to assist teachers and other licensed and certified practitioners with their expanding program and classroom management roles.

Local school districts and other education provider agencies use many titles to describe employees (a) who work under the supervision of teachers and other licensed and certified professionals who are responsible for identifying learner needs, designing and implementing programs to meet learner needs, and assessing learner performance, and (b) who assist with the delivery of instructional or other direct services for learners and their families developed by and assigned by professional practitioners (Pickett, 1989). Paraeducator, paraprofessional, paratherapist, instructional assistant, teacher aide, occupational and physical therapy assistant or aide, speech–language pathology aide or assistant, education technician, transition trainer, job coach, and home visitor are some of the titles assigned to support personnel who work in early childhood programs and elementary, middle, and secondary schools.

To reduce wordiness, throughout the different chapters, we will use primarily the term *paraeducator.* There are times, however, when other titles are more appropriate to maintain historical accuracy or to identify a specific discipline. In addition, although supervisors of paraeducators may include teachers, occupational and physical therapists, speech–language pathologists, early childhood and transition specialists, nurses, and other licensed and certificated practitioners, we refer to all supervisors as *teachers*, unless we are discussing specific disciplines. Finally, we use the terms *learners, children and youth*, and *students* interchangeably because this text may be used to prepare supervisory personnel who work in early childhood; elementary, middle, and secondary schools; and other education provider agencies.

Historical Perspective: A Legacy of Promise and Problems

The employment of paraprofessionals throughout education, health, mental health, and other human services delivery systems is not a modern phenomenon. Paraprofessionals have become an integral part of the workforce as policymakers and advocates have sought ways to meet the needs of learners created by changes in society and the country's demographics. Paraprofessional auxiliary workers were first employed in the great settlement house projects established by social reformers in the early 1900s in response to a surge of new immigrants who settled in major urban centers. Three of the most prominent sites were Henry Street and Greenwich House in New York City and Hull House in Chicago. The mission of these and other settlement houses was to improve living conditions and help new arrivals adjust to their new world. They provided social and basic health care services, created nursery schools, offered English classes and other adult learning opportunities, and produced some of the first publications designed to help tenants understand their rights. Later, various New Deal programs, initiated during the Great Depression, used "nonprofessional" workers to provide services. Chief among these programs were the Social Security Act of 1935, the Works Progress Administration, and the National Youth Administration. Little attention was paid to retaining and enhancing the status of these workers through the war years of the 1940s, and only the Social Security program survived after World War II ended (Gartner, 1971).

The 1950s

In the mid-1950s, a need to alleviate post–World War II shortages of licensed educators, and the fledgling efforts of parents of children with disabilities to develop community-based services as alternatives to institutions stimulated interest in the employment of teacher aides. Two significant research projects were undertaken to assess the appropriateness and effectiveness of employing teacher aides as one way to enable teachers to spend more time in planning and implementing instructional activities. The first, sponsored by the Ford Foundation, took place in the Bay City, Michigan, schools. College-educated women who were not licensed teachers were recruited and trained to provide clerical, monitoring, and other routine classroom tasks (Fund for the Advancement of Education, 1961). Acceptance of this approach was not automatic. A primary concern of critics was that teachers would be replaced by unqualified "cheap labor." By the time the project was concluded, reactions were cautiously optimistic, and to a limited extent a few districts in Michigan and other states began to adopt the program. At about the same time, Cruickshank and Herring (1957) documented the results of a project conducted at Syracuse University designed to evaluate the efficacy of using teacher aides in special education programs that were beginning to spring up across the country. Although the results, like those in Bay City, showed promise, it would be almost 10 years before the benefits of employing teacher aides to work alongside teachers in both general and special education would be more fully tested and realized.

The 1960s and 1970s

The 1960s and early 1970s were a time of social and political turmoil. Many significant events occurred that touched the lives of most Americans in one way or another. Challenges to long-standing governmental policies and practices, and demands for social and institutional change came from many sources. They included efforts that began in the 1950s to achieve educational equality for African American children; the expansion of the civil rights movement to obtain social and judicial justice and to end racial segregation in public and private facilities; efforts of women and senior citizens to achieve financial and political equity; the campaign to provide public education and other community-based services to children and adults with disabilities and to ensure their human and legal rights; emergence of strong antiwar feelings sparked by U.S. participation in the Vietnam War; and more.

Separately and together, advocates for different constituencies pressured public officials to reorder social, political, and fiscal priorities and to reassess the roles of the executive, legislative, and judicial branches of federal and state governments in providing increased and improved education, health care, and other human services. As a result, under the leadership of President

Lyndon Johnson, several Great Society initiatives came into being: A war on poverty was launched; Medicare and Medicaid were created; Head Start was established; Congress amended the Elementary and Secondary Education Act (ESEA) of 1965 to incorporate Title I and other compensatory programs to increase education and support services for economically and educationally disadvantaged children and youth, and those who came from homes where English was not the primary language; and several community action programs were initiated to help restore neglected neighborhoods and provide workforce development training for individuals who were underemployed or not prepared for jobs that did exist.

In addition, advocacy organizations representing people with disabilities became more assertive in their efforts to convince governors and legislators to undertake the closing of state institutions that all too frequently served as nothing more than warehouses for children and adults with mental retardation, mental illness, and other disabilities. One of the primary goals of parents and other advocates was the reallocation of funds to create new programs and services that would enable children and adults with disabilities to stay at home or live near their families and to work or go to school in their local communities. Their efforts paid off when Congress enacted Public Law (P.L.) 94-142, the Education for all Handicapped Children Act of 1975. This landmark legislation, renamed the Individuals with Disabilities Education Act (IDEA) in 1990, required LEAs and SEAs to ensure the availability of a free, appropriate education for all children and youth with disabilities.

At the heart of each of the various laws enacted by Congress in the 1960s and 1970s was a recognition of the importance of learner-centered instructional services to meet the needs of children and youth with diverse ability levels, learning preferences, and other special needs, although only P.L. 94-142 specifically mandated Individualized Education Programs for learners who were identified as requiring special education services. Thus, to provide teachers in both general and special education with the support they required to develop and carry out individualized or personalized education services for all learners who could benefit from them, the employment of paraprofessionals gained momentum.

During this period, a few researchers assessed the effect of paraprofessionals on the delivery of education services. Bowman and Klopf (1967, 1968), reporting on two in-depth studies conducted by the Bank Street School of Education, identified various benefits derived from the presence of paraprofessionals in classrooms. One of the most significant findings was that teacher time was increasingly redirected toward the central goal of instructional improvement because more time was available for

- one-to-one and small group instruction,
- cooperative planning among faculty and other professional practitioners,
- program and learner assessment,
- attention to learners' personal–social needs,
- increased on-task learner performance, and
- increased innovation in teaching.

Gartner and Riessman (1974) reported other factors that were instrumental in increasing the employment of paraprofessionals. Foremost among them was a growing lack of confidence on the part of parents and policymakers in the ability of traditional educational delivery systems to meet the needs of growing numbers of learners from diverse racial, cultural, and language heritages, and economic backgrounds. To bridge the widening gap between families and schools in which teachers and administrators were predominantly White and middle class, policymakers began to recruit indigenous workers who, because they understood the cultural and ethnic heritages of the community, could facilitate better communication with learners and their parents. As a result, the role of teacher aides began to evolve from being primarily clerical and monitoring in nature to one in which they served as liaisons between schools and communities and provided instructional and other direct services to learners and their parents.

At the same time that employment of paraprofessionals began to expand, an awareness began to emerge of the need to reduce barriers that prevented workers from racial and language minority heritages, young people from disadvantaged backgrounds, and women from achieving professional status. In *New Careers for the Poor*, Arthur Pearl and Frank Riessman (1965) charted a course for developing programs in higher education that would reach out to paraprofessionals and encourage them to enter the professional ranks. They also provided the expanding movement with a name—*New Careers*. The career development efforts undertaken during the 1960s and 1970s were based on several assumptions. Among the most important were the following (Cohen, 1976; Gartner & Riessman, 1974; Jackson & Acosta, 1971; Kaplan, 1977):

- Belief that paraprofessionals *appropriately trained* to carry out their assigned tasks would help to reduce the impact of ongoing shortages of professional practitioners and help to improve the quality of education and other human services
- Recognition that it is possible to differentiate tasks performed by personnel in different positions and separate them into different functions, some that must be performed by licensed and certified professionals and others that can be shared with paraprofessionals
- Recognition that providing access to higher education for individuals who needed to work and carry out family responsibilities while they were earning academic credentials would open up opportunities for career advancement for African Americans, Latinos, Native Americans, and others who were underrepresented in the professional workforce

Throughout the 1970s, the federal government was a major facilitator of the New Careers movement. Support for professional development opportunities for paraprofessionals and other nontraditional students came primarily through federal legislative actions. In *From Aide to Teacher: The Story of the Career Opportunities Program,* George Kaplan (1977) analyzed and reported on one of the most comprehensive programs undertaken during that time period: the Career Opportunities Program (COP). Established in 1970 by the U.S. Office of Education, COP successfully involved more than 20,000 people nationwide in career advancement programs. The mission of COP was to enable community residents, working as teacher aides in the nation's low-income urban and rural areas, to advance within various education disciplines. One of the most creative aspects of COP was that programs were developed locally by school districts and teacher education programs to support committed, talented paraprofessionals who wanted to become teachers. The COP design for teacher preparation represented a sharp break from established teacher education programs. Participating school districts helped the IHEs plan and conduct the program. The schools selected the people who would be trained and described the skills that would enable them to become more effective teachers. The colleges and universities adapted their baccalaureate programs to the needs of prospective teachers by removing potential barriers to participants' successful completion. They scheduled required coursework at night and on weekends, conducted classes off campus near participants' homes, provided financial assistance, tutored candidates for high school equivalency tests, and helped participants learn study techniques that would facilitate academic success.

In his analysis of the 7-year program, Kaplan (1977) found that the COP was an effective way to provide an alternative route to teacher certification for paraprofessionals and other school employees without weakening the programs. His conclusions were based on the following:

- Individual COP training models were generally shaped to address the personal needs of the participants.
- Introduction to and immersion in classrooms was a natural method of career selection. (On-the-job experiences helped participants decide whether they preferred to remain in the field as paraprofessionals or to move into other careers in education before the investment of time and money had become irretrievable.)
- Participants found that the combination of career ladders and lattices (i.e., upward mobility or movement laterally across program positions), which were part of many COP programs, worked for individuals who wanted to enter the professional ranks or those who chose to remain in the field as paraprofessionals.
- COP's recognition of the value of recruiting participants from within a community contributed to accountability.

(The paraprofessionals were part of the community, and their children or their neighbors' children attended the schools where they lived.)

- LEA personnel and building principals liked the COP model. (They could draw from a pool of experienced practitioners they knew both personally and professionally and in whose training they had taken an active interest.)
- Participants liked the COP formula. (Although it demanded sacrifice, it rewarded hard work and commitment.)

At the same time that these collaborative efforts to develop flexible degree programs designed to recruit and support paraprofessionals were getting started, a few SEAs began to create credentialing procedures with guidelines for paraprofessional roles. Some of these systems included criteria for career advancement; however, most did not. States that developed paraprofessional credentialing systems in the late 1960s and early 1970s included Delaware, Georgia, Illinois, Kansas, New Hampshire, New York, Ohio, Vermont, and Wisconsin. Rather than develop regulatory procedures, most states chose to establish administrative guidelines. These guidelines loosely defined appropriate duties for paraprofessionals; they were not, however, mandates that LEAs were required to follow.

Moreover, only in rare cases were teacher supervisory responsibilities delineated in either SEA teacher or paraprofessional credentialing systems or the administrative guidelines. Also, although the roles of paraprofessionals were evolving and the paraprofessionals were increasingly participating in all phases of the instructional process, principals were usually their designated supervisors. Thus, the emerging roles of teachers as planners, schedulers, directors, and monitors of the day-to-day performance of paraprofessionals were not recognized. For the most part in today's schools, contracts, job descriptions, and other personnel practices are still based on this system (Pickett, Likins, & Wallace, 2002).

Despite COP's apparent success in opening doors to professional advancement for paraprofessionals, when the federal funding ended, most of the programs ended. Thus, most of the lessons learned through various COP models about the recruitment and preparation of paraprofessionals who were nontraditional students disappeared and were lost to those who could benefit from them—that is, employers who are still confronted with finding methods to reduce ongoing shortfalls of skilled, committed teachers and related services practitioners; personnel developers in IHEs who are searching for effective methods to attract candidates into teacher education programs; and paraprofessionals who are interested in moving up a career ladder, but must continue to work and require support to achieve their goals (Haselkorn & Fideler, 1996; Pickett, 1989).

The 1980s

In the annals of education history, the decade of the 1980s will be remembered as a time of vigorous debate about how to stem a perceived decline in the quality and accountability of U.S. schools. Initially concerns centered on two issues: (a) the need to raise learning standards in order to improve student achievement and (b) the need to attract and prepare a highly competent teaching force (Lieberman & Miller, 2000; National Board for Professional Teaching Standards, 1989; National Commission for Excellence in Teacher Education, 1985; National Commission on Excellence in Education, 1983).

Later in the decade, educators and other advocates for more effective schools added another item to the agenda. It was connected to the growing realization that, by enabling educators and parents to be actively engaged in identifying the learning needs of the children and youth in "their school," deciding which programs would best meet the identified needs, and determining how to allocate human and fiscal resources to meet the needs, the performance and quality of schools could be improved. As a result, advocates for education reform began to reassess the practice of governing schools from a central office, and the concept of creating opportunities for site-based management and problem solving was born (Bauch & Goldring, 1998; Carnegie Forum on Education and the Economy, 1987; David, 1996; Pipho, 2000; Wall & Rinehart, 1998).

Reports issued throughout the 1980s by governmental agencies, IHEs, and stakeholders in the private and public sectors, stressed the need for significant changes in education policies and practices to improve learner and teacher performance. *A Nation at Risk: The Imperative for Education Reform* (National

Commission on Excellence in Education, 1983) was the first report to focus attention on the need for increased standards and accountability for learning outcomes. While encouraging administrators to explore new options for organizing classrooms, the commission assumed that the traditionally recognized roles of teachers as planners and deliverers of instruction would remain unchanged. Concerned primarily with the recruitment, competence, and preparation of the teaching force, the commission championed higher standards for recruitment to the profession, for the preparation and performance of teachers, and of accountability for learner achievement.

A Nation Prepared: Teachers for the 21st Century (Carnegie Forum on Education and the Economy, 1987) generated another round of intense debate among different stakeholders. A great deal of the debate was concerned with a call for teachers to assume expanded leadership roles that included coordinating the work of instructional teams comprised of volunteers and "teacher aides" who would assist with routine classroom management tasks, aligning curriculum content with instructional activities, assessing instructional strategies, and participating in school-based governance and decision-making activities with principals and parents to determine how best to meet the needs of learners. The report also emphasized the critical need for continuing efforts to improve the quality and performance of the teaching force as an important method for meeting higher standards for learner achievement in a time when global competition was emerging and employers were demanding a highly skilled workforce.

Time for Results (National Governors' Association, 1986) supported many of the proposals made by the Carnegie Forum (1986). It also emphasized the need for the sustained support of governors for seeing to it that (a) higher state standards for teacher preparation and licensure were established and (b) personnel practices and incentives that contribute to the recruitment and retention of a skilled teaching force were created and sustained.

Recommendations contained in these reports and the work of other researchers and advocates for education reform served as catalysts for bringing administrators in SEAs and LEAs together with elected officials, business executives, teacher educators, parents, professional organizations, and unions to ensure that standards for teacher preparation and performance were established (California Commission on the Teaching Profession, 1985; Committee for Economic Development, 1985; Holmes Group, 1986; National Commission for Excellence in Teacher Education, 1985). One of the most important responses to the calls for action from the various groups was the creation of the National Board for Professional Teaching Standards (NBPTS). In 1989, the board issued its first set of standards that identified what teachers need to know, what they need to be able to do, and methods for certifying that candidates could meet the standards. The ongoing work of the board has refined and expanded the standards for 26 areas of specialization. Currently, the board administers assessments and certification in the 19 fields taught by 95% of teachers. This process enables teachers to demonstrate skill mastery within their areas of specialization (NBPTS, 1994a, 1994b).

Although these various efforts laid the groundwork for contemporary activities to empower teachers and improve their performance, they virtually ignored the growing reliance on paraprofessionals in general and special education, multilingual, Title I, and other compensatory programs as one method of helping teachers to carry out these new roles and responsibilities. Thus, provisions requiring teachers to be prepared to supervise and work effectively with paraprofessionals are found in teacher certification and licensure systems in only two states, Minnesota and Washington. As a result, curriculum content in the majority of teacher education programs has not been modified to prepare teachers for their new roles as supervisors of paraeducators (French & Pickett, 1997; Lindemann & Beegle, 1988; Pickett et al., 2002; Pickett, Vasa, & Steckelberg, 1993; Salzberg & Morgan, 1995; Wallace, Jongho, Bartholomay, & Stahl, 2001). Moreover, the federal support for the professional development programs for paraprofessionals that existed during the 1970s all but evaporated in the 1980s, and Pickett (1994) reported that, by the end of that decade, paraprofessionals had become the forgotten members of education teams, even though their roles and responsibilities had continued to expand and become more complex and challenging. As a result, by the beginning of the 1990s, in most states and locales guidelines or standards for paraprofessional roles and supervision, as well as infrastructures for their preparation, either were nonexistent or did not reflect the changes that were occurring in both teacher and paraprofessional roles (Pickett, 1986, 1989, 1994, 1999; Pickett et al., 2002).

The 1990s to the Present

Despite the lack of attention to paraeducator issues in the 1980s, paraeducators continued to grow in number and their responsibilities in the delivery of instruction and other education services increased. Once again, one of the most important factors that contributed to a resurgence of interest in a range of issues linked to the paraprofessional workforce was and continues to be federal legislation. New laws enacted in the late 1980s and early 1990s did two things. First, in many cases they brought about a surge in the employment of paraprofessionals; second, amendments to the various laws stressed the need for SEAs and LEAs to strengthen and expand professional development opportunities to ensure the availability of highly skilled personnel at all levels, including paraprofessionals. This trend has continued with the 2001 reauthorization of the Elementary and Secondary Education Act (ESEA), referred to as the No Child Left Behind Act (NCLB Act; P.L. 107-110).

The legislative actions that caused education provider systems to employ paraeducators and paratherapists in greater numbers included the mandates in P.L. 99-457, the Education of the Handicapped Act Amendments of 1986. Provisions in the act required public schools to provide services to children ages 3 through 5 who have disabilities or chronic health needs that place them at risk. Schools and other provider agencies were also encouraged to create programs to serve infants and toddlers with disabilities and their families; they were not, however, required to provide these services. IDEA 1990 acknowledged the need for transitional and school-to-work programs for teenagers. To provide these new programs, LEAs and other provider agencies once again turned to paraeducators to support teachers and other licensed and certified professional staff.

Goals 2000: Educate America Act of 1994, which amended and reauthorized the ESEA, urged states to establish higher professional development standards for preparing all personnel. To achieve this goal, Title I of ESEA contained new guidelines for the employment and preparation of teacher aides and assistants. Title II of the same act authorized school districts to use program funds to train both teachers and paraprofessionals. In recognition of the ongoing shortfalls of teachers, ESEA also allowed LEAs to use funds to develop career ladder programs to assist paraprofessionals to become licensed and certified teachers in all core subject areas. Amendments to Title VII of ESEA contained several provisions that supported employment and professional development opportunities for paraprofessionals who work in programs serving learners from diverse linguistic backgrounds.

One of the most significant legislative actions that occurred in the 1990s that had a major impact on paraeducator preparation and supervision was the 1997 reauthorization of IDEA. For the first time, IDEA specifically recognized the increasing reliance on paraeducators by placing greater emphasis on their learner support roles and participation in the instructional process. In the personnel standards section of Part B, paraprofessionals and assistants who are appropriately trained and supervised in accordance with state law, regulations, or written policy are allowed to assist in the provision of special education and related services for school-age children and youth with disabilities [Section 612(a)(15)]. Part C, concerned with personnel who work with infants, toddlers, and their families, mandates the preparation of professionals and paraprofessionals in the areas of early intervention with the content knowledge and collaborative skills needed to meet the needs of infants and toddlers with disabilities in accordance with state-approved or -recognized certification, licensing, or regulations [Section 635(a)(8)]. Part D Section 635 requires a state, as part of its comprehensive system of personnel development, to ensure that all personnel (including both professionals and paraprofessionals who provide special and general education, as well as related and early intervention services) have the skills and knowledge necessary to meet the needs of children and youth with disabilities.

An independent assessment of Title I programs, mandated by Congress, brought about increased scrutiny to a wide range of issues connected with paraeducator roles in the instructional process, and the skills and levels of education they require (U.S. Department of Education, 1999). Based on the findings of the commission that conducted the assessment and the work of other researchers, Title I of the NCLB Act identifies duties that may be performed by paraeducators, sets higher standards for paraeducator employment and preparation, and places greater emphasis on establishing opportunities for career advancement for paraeducators who want to join the ranks of the licensed and certified teaching force. Although for the first time amendments to Title I require paraprofessionals to work under the direct supervision of a teacher, SEAs and LEAs are not compelled to set standards for preparing teachers to plan for, direct, monitor, and assess paraeducator performance. There are several amendments that address paraeducator issues in various titles throughout the NCLB Act; the most significant and relevant to the goals of this book are found in Section 1119 and are summarized in Table 1.1.

In addition to these legislative actions, other factors have brought about a need for increased attention to developing and maintaining standards for paraeducator supervision, roles, preparation, and performance. They include, but are not limited to, the following:

- Efforts to more effectively serve children and youth with disabilities in learning environments that increasingly are centered on their inclusion in early childhood settings, general education classrooms, and community-based school-to-work programs (Blalock, 1991; Daniels & McBride, 2001; Downing, Ryndak, & Clark, 2000; Giangreco, Edelman, Luiselli, & McFarland, 1997; Killoran, Templeman, Peters, & Udell, 2001; Marks, Schrader, & Levine, 1999; Morehouse & Albright, 1991; Pickett, 1999; Riggs, 2001; Riggs & Mueller, 2001; Rogan & Held, 1999)
- Increasing needs for occupational and physical therapy and speech–language pathology services for children and youth of all ages (American Occupational Therapy Association [AOTA], 1990, 1999; American Physical Therapy Association [APTA], 2000; American Speech-Language-Hearing Association [ASHA], 2000; Council for Exceptional Children [CEC], 1996; Fenichel & Eggbeer, 1990; Killoran et al., 2001; Radaszewski-Byrne, 1997)
- Growing numbers of children and youth nationwide, who come from diverse cultural and linguistic heritages (Ebenstein & Gooler, 1993; Genzuk & Baca, 1998; Haselkorn & Fideler, 1996; National Center for Education Statistics [NCES],

Table 1.1

Paraeducator Employment, Preparation, and Supervision

Section 1119. Qualifications for Teachers and Paraprofessionals

Subsection (1)(c) requires LEAs receiving Title I assistance to ensure that all new paraeducators employed after the date of enactment of ESEA 2001 have

- a secondary school diploma or its equivalent, and
- completed at least 2 years of study at an institution of higher education; or
- obtained an associate's (or higher) degree; or
- met a rigorous standard of quality and can demonstrate, through a formal state or local academic assessment: (i) knowledge of and the ability to assist in instructing reading, writing, and mathematics; or (ii) knowledge of and the ability to assist in instructing reading readiness, writing readiness, and mathematics readiness, as appropriate.

Subsection (1)(d) requires LEAs to ensure that all currently employed paraeducators shall

- not later than 4 years after the date of enactment satisfy the requirements of subsection (1)(c).

Subsection (1)(g) describes appropriate duties for paraeducators. Paraeducators may

- provide one-to-one tutoring for eligible students at a time when students would not otherwise receive instruction from a teacher;
- assist with classroom management;
- assist in a computer laboratory;
- conduct parental involvement activities;
- provide support in a library or media center;
- act as a translator.

The final item in subsection (1)(g) addresses supervision of paraeducators:

- Paraeducators may not provide any instructional service to a learner unless they work under the direct supervision of a teacher.

Note. Adapted from Title I, Section 1119, subsections (1)(c), (d), and (g) (pp. 128–133), Qualifications for Teachers and Paraprofessionals in the No Child Left Behind Act of 2001, reauthorizing the Elementary and Secondary Education Act.

1995, 2000; Office of Special Education Programs and Rehabilitative Services [OSEPRS], 2000; Rueda & Monzo, 2000; U.S. Bureau of the Census, 2001)

- Continuing shortages of teachers and related services personnel in all program areas and disciplines (American Association for Employment in Education, 1998; Haselkorn & Fideler, 1996; NCES, 1995, 2000; OSEPRS, 2000; Recruiting New Teachers, 1997)
- Emerging roles of school professionals as classroom and program managers (Drecktrah, 2000; French, 1998, 2001; French & Pickett, 1997; Pickett, 1999; Pickett et al., 1993; Putnam, 1993; Snodgrass, 1991; Wallace et al., 2001)

Changing Roles of Teachers

Although all of the previously discussed issues and concerns have contributed to renewed interest in the employment of paraeducators to work alongside teachers, the continuing evolution in teacher roles to include greater responsibility for program management and team leadership is one of the most significant but underrecognized reasons for increased reliance on paraprofessionals. The introduction, in the 1980s, of various initiatives concerned with reforming education systems and practices had a profound impact on teachers' roles and professional development needs. Many of these efforts, which are continuing to be assessed and refined, are linked to two interrelated sets of issues. The first is connected to the changes that have occurred in school governance and administration. The second is concerned with empowering teachers and other school professionals by involving them more directly in setting education priorities (Bauch & Goldring, 1998; Carnegie Forum on Education and the Economy, 1987; Darling-Hammond, 1997; Darling-Hammond & McLaughlin, 1995; Lieberman, 1995; Lieberman & Miller, 2000; Pipho, 2000).

Approaches used by many LEAs to restructure and improve the quality of schools have centered on moving to systems that place greater responsibility for managing education programs and determining how best to meet the needs of learners into the hands of building staff and parents. The shift from centralized, district-level management of all aspects of the education process has contributed to redefining and reshaping teacher roles (Bauch & Goldring, 1998; Lieberman & Miller, 2000; Pipho, 2000). In addition to their traditionally recognized responsibilities as diagnosticians of learners' educational needs, lesson planners, instructors, and assessors of learner progress, teachers increasingly are becoming frontline managers. These new responsibilities for teachers require them to work in partnership with principals, parents, and other members of shared decision-making teams to identify the needs of learners in their school and to allocate human, fiscal, and technological resources to meet those needs. Moreover, the roles of school professionals are becoming more collaborative in nature, particularly for teachers and related services personnel who are responsible for facilitating the inclusion of learners with disabilities in general education. Thus, more time is required for multidisciplinary planning of individualized instructional and therapeutic treatment plans (French & Pickett, 1997; Friend & Cook, 1996; Pickett, 1999; Putnam, 1993; Wallace et al., 2001). Other new dimensions added to the scopes of responsibilities for teachers are increased leadership in aligning curriculum content with instructional activities, modifying instructional methods to meet the needs of individual learners, and assessing the impact of the instructional strategies on the ability of all learners to solve real-world problems, think conceptually and creatively, and work cooperatively (Alper, Fendel, Fraser, & Resek, 1996; Carnegie Forum on Education and the Economy, 1987; Darling-Hammond, 1994, 1997; David, 1996; Pickett, 1999; Simpson, Whelan, & Zabel, 1993).

Changing Roles of Paraeducators

The evolution of teacher and other professional practitioner roles in education and related services has also affected paraeducator roles. Since paraeducators were introduced into classrooms almost 5 decades ago as teacher aides, their roles have changed dramatically. In contemporary schools teacher aides are technicians who indeed are accurately described as paraeducators, just as their counterparts in law and medicine are designated as paralegals and paramedics (Pickett, 1989). Although they still perform clerical tasks, photocopy materials, prepare learning centers, and monitor learners in nonacademic settings, paraeducators increasingly work at higher levels of independence and assist in all phases of the instructional process and the delivery of related services. Under the direction of teachers, licensed and certified early childhood educators, and transition or school-to-work specialists, paraeducators instruct individuals and small groups of learners; assist with functional assessment activities; carry out behavior management and disciplinary programs developed by teachers; document learner behavior and performance; and help engage families in all aspects of their children's education (Blalock, 1991; Downing et al., 2000; Killoran et al., 2001; Marks et al., 1999; Miramontes, 1990; Passaro, Pickett, Latham, & HongBo, 1994; Moshoyannis, Pickett, & Granik, 1999; Pickett, 1999; Riggs, 2001; Riggs & Mueller, 2001; Rogan & Held, 1999; Safarik, 1999; Snodgrass, 1991).

In schools and other learning environments, speech–language pathologists, occupational and physical therapists, and nurses are also supervisors of paratherapists, therapy aides and assistants, and health aides and assistants. The paratherapists carry out therapeutic treatment plans developed by the supervising therapists and nurses for children and youth who have developmental, sensory, physical, and speech–language disabilities, and those who have health or medical needs that place them at risk (AOTA, 1999; APTA, 2000; ASHA, 2000; Coufal, Steckelberg, & Vasa, 1991; CEC, 2000; Fenichel & Eggbeer, 1990; Killoran et al., 2001; Longhurst & Witmer, 1994; Radaszewski-Byrne, 1997). Duties assigned to paratherapists and health aides and assistants range from performing clerical tasks, to observing and documenting learner needs, to maintaining adaptive equipment and safe and healthy environments, to providing treatment under the direction of licensed professionals.

Distinctions in the scopes of responsibilities of teachers and paraeducators are discussed more fully in Chapter 2. Comparisons of differences in the roles of paratherapists working with occupational and physical therapists and speech–language pathologists are presented in Chapter 4.

Policy Questions and Systemic Issues

Despite increased reliance on paraeducators and increased emphasis on the instructional nature of their jobs, many states still do not have legislative requirements, regulatory procedures, or written policies that set standards for their roles, supervision, and preparation. Where policies and systems do exist, many have not been revised since the late 1960s or early 1970s when interest in paraeducator employment and preparation was at its peak (Pickett, 1989, 1999, 2001). The most critical issues confronting policymakers and implementers in SEAs, LEAs, and IHEs can be summarized as follows:

- The vast majority of paraeducators and paratherapists, no matter whether they work in early childhood, general, special, compensatory, or transitional education, spend all or part of their time assisting teachers or licensed related services professionals with the delivery of instructional and other direct services to children, youth, and their families (AOTA, 1999; APTA, 2000; ASHA, 2000; Blalock, 1991; CEC, 1996, 2000; Fenichel & Eggbeer, 1990; Killoran et al., 2001; Lyons, 1995; Moshoyannis et al., 1999; Passaro et al., 1994; Riggs & Mueller, 2001; Snodgrass, 1991).
- During the last 20 years, SEAs, LEAs, and IHEs have paid scant attention, either on their own or together, to (a) determining core skills and knowledge for all paraeducators, and the specialized skills required by the program or position to which they are assigned; (b) defining experiential and education qualifications for paraeducator employment; (c) establishing criteria for advancement to different levels of paraeducator positions; and (d) setting standards for evaluating paraeducator performance (Pickett, 1999; Pickett et al., 2002).
- Training for paraeducators, when it is available, is usually highly parochial and is rarely competency based or part of seamless comprehensive systems of career development that include (a) systematic on-the-job coaching, (b) standardized opportunities for preservice and inservice training, and (c) access to flexible academic degree programs that enable paraeducators to earn professional certification or licensure while they continue to work (Pickett, 1999; Pickett et al., 2002).
- At the present time, a little over half of the 50 states, and the District of Columbia, the Commonwealth of Puerto Rico, and the territories of the U.S. Virgin Islands, Guam, American Samoa, and Saipan, have established standards or regulatory procedures for roles, supervision, and preparation of paraeducators. Thirteen states have credentialing mechanisms. These systems range from multilevel certification or permit systems that define roles, training, and career advancement criteria to

one-dimensional systems that do not specify appropriate responsibilities or training requirements (Pickett et al., 2002). Eleven states have established standards for paraeducator roles and training, and in some cases those states provide support to LEAs with the development of training models. Most, but not all, of the remaining states have written policies that allow LEAs to implement the policies voluntarily.

- Contemporary education reform efforts emphasize team and management functions of teachers. These efforts, however, have overlooked the roles of teachers as leaders of instructional teams and supervisors of paraeducators. Currently two states, Minnesota and Washington, require as part of their licensure and certification procedures that special education teachers be trained to supervise and work effectively with paraeducators. Four states, California, Rhode Island, Utah, and Iowa, have established standards for teacher roles in supervising paraeducators; they are not, however, incorporated into the licensure systems. As a result, most teacher education programs do not offer courses to prepare teachers to (a) determine which tasks may appropriately be performed by paraeducators, (b) plan and schedule paraeducator assignments, (c) provide on-the-job training to paraeducators, (d) monitor the performance of paraeducators, and (e) share relevant information about paraeducator performance and training needs with principals (Drecktrah, 2000; French, 1998; French & Pickett, 1997; Lindemann & Beegle, 1988; Pickett, 1999; Pickett et al., 1993; Wallace et al., 2001).
- Teacher shortages that began in the 1950s have continued into the 21st century. Shortfalls are particularly acute among teachers and other professional practitioners who come from diverse cultural, racial, and language minority backgrounds. Although paraeducators are usually highly representative of the racial, ethnic, cultural, and language populations in their communities, they are frequently overlooked as resources for recruitment into teacher education and other professional preparation programs (Drecktrah, 2000; French & Pickett, 1997; Genzuk & Baca, 1998; Genzuk, Lavadenz, & Krashen, 1994; Haselkorn & Fideler, 1996; Macais & Kelly, 1996; McDonnell & Hill, 1993; NCES, 1995, 2000; OSEPRS, 2000).

Addressing the Issues and Establishing Systems

Establishing standards for paraeducator supervision and roles and for comprehensive systems of personnel development to ensure that both teachers and paraeducators are prepared for their roles as team members is not an easy task. The broad range of issues linked to paraeducator roles, professional development, and supervision cannot be addressed in isolation. One of the keys to successfully focusing attention on these issues is to establish partnerships among the SEA, LEAs, 2- and 4-year IHEs, professional organizations representing different disciplines, unions, and parents—all of which have different responsibilities for improving the performance and preparation of paraeducators and their supervising professionals.

In this section, the important roles of SEAs in developing standards and systems for paraeducator supervision and preparation are discussed. The emerging interest in paraeducator and paratherapist issues by various professional organizations and unions is outlined. Also discussed is the need for standardized, comprehensive systems of personnel development, including curriculum content and instructional strategies that are part of practicum and student teaching experiences to prepare teachers for their supervisory roles and paraeducators for their roles as key members of education teams.

The Role of State Education Agencies

Each of the policy, systemic, and personnel development issues described in the previous sections needs to be explored by SEA personnel in concert with LEAs, other education provider agencies, IHEs, professional organizations representing different disciplines, unions, and parents. A primary role for SEA personnel is to establish partnerships and spearhead efforts among the different players, with responsibility for establishing and implementing policies, standards, and infrastructures to assure that teachers and paraeducators are appropriately and systematically prepared for their evolving roles.

Statewide standards that clearly define distinctions in teacher and paraeducator roles, along with technical assistance and support for creating and maintaining infrastructures to achieve the standards, help build the capacity of LEAs and other education provider agencies to strengthen education and related services teams. This creation of standards is achieved by providing administrators and personnel developers in LEAs and other education agencies with information they can use to (a) identify local needs, (b) develop personnel practices and job descriptions that recognize the distinctions in teacher and paraeducator roles, (c) provide opportunities for ongoing pre- and inservice competency-based training and professional development for paraeducators, and (d) develop policies and procedures for improving the supervision of paraeducators. (The roles and responsibilities of district and building administrators are addressed in greater detail in Chapter 6.)

In addition, statewide standards provide policymakers and IHE faculty with guidelines they can build on to develop new or revise existing curriculum content to prepare teachers and other supervising professionals to more fully tap the resources of the paraeducator workforce. The standards will also provide a basis for teacher educators and community college faculty to develop articulated agreements that will facilitate the transfer from one system to another, and will, therefore, be more student friendly.

For partnerships to find viable solutions to policy questions, they must have access to accurate data about paraeducator employment in their state. SEAs have the responsibility for collecting data that identify who paraeducators are in their state, where they work, what they do, and who supervises them in different programs and educational settings. In far too many cases, SEAs do not collect these data, and when they do, they are fragmented because they are not maintained in a centralized database (Pickett et al., 2002). Without this information, stakeholders do not have the tools they require to systematically address policy issues that cross program lines and include

- delineating teacher responsibilities that may not be delegated or assigned to paraeducators, and those that may be shared with paraeducators;
- determining similarities and distinctions in the roles and responsibilities of paraeducators working in different programs or position levels;
- identifying a common core of skills required by all paraeducators, as well as hierarchies of skills and the knowledge base needed by paraeducators working in programs where they have greater independence and require more advanced or complex skills;

- establishing standards for paraeducator supervision and performance evaluations;
- developing and implementing ongoing comprehensive systems of pre- and inservice training for paraeducators that are tied to opportunities for career advancement;
- identifying the knowledge and skill competencies required by teachers who supervise paraeducators; and
- establishing standards for preparing teachers to carry out these responsibilities.

Teacher Licensure and Certification Systems

Traditional approaches to professional development for teachers are beginning to change. These changes are occurring in response to the growing recognition that various reform initiatives cannot succeed unless teachers are prepared for the multitude of challenges that confront them in schools and other learning environments. The efforts that have taken place over the last 2 decades to empower teachers and develop more effective practices and standards for preparing teachers have overlooked their emerging roles as supervisors of paraeducators. These initiatives do not recognize the value of differentiated staffing arrangements in classrooms and other learning environments that can provide teachers with human resources necessary to support their expanding program management and administrative functions. Administrators of teacher licensure systems must join forces with personnel in SEAs, LEAs, teacher preparation programs, and professional organizations to establish and incorporate standards into their state's credentialing process to certify that teachers are prepared to (a) identify tasks that may appropriately be shared with paraeducators, (b) plan paraeducator assignments, (c) direct and monitor paraeducator performance, (d) provide on-the-job coaching to strengthen paraeducator performance, and (e) share relevant information about paraeducator strengths and training needs with principals (Pickett, 1999).

Paraeducator Credentialing

In addition to issues surrounding the supervision of paraeducators, there is a growing awareness among various constituencies of the need to explore the importance of creating paraeducator credentialing systems or other regulatory procedures to ensure that paraeducators have the skills and knowledge necessary to meet role requirements. Paraeducator credentialing is not a new idea; it is, however, highly controversial. As noted previously, only 12 states have criteria for paraeducator hiring, training, and career advancement that they regard as a credentialing system. Eleven states have chosen to develop standards for paraeducator roles and preparation rather than more formal credentialing procedures. The majority of the states and territories have not established either a paraeducator certification system or standards for their roles, preparation, and supervision (Pickett, 1999).

Pickett (1999, p. 55) identified five benefits that will accrue from developing new or strengthening current credentialing systems for paraeducators:

1. All learners will be better served and the quality of education will improve with the availability of an appropriately prepared paraeducator workforce.
2. Credentialing will ensure that paraeducators have mastered skills that are required to support and assist teachers with their program and administrative functions.
3. Credentialing will establish clear distinctions in the roles and levels of responsibilities and competencies for paraeducators who work in different programs.
4. Credentialing will establish opportunities for upward mobility through different paraeducator position levels.
5. Credentialing will serve as a method for providing recognition and respect for the contributions that paraeducators make to the delivery of instructional and other direct services for all learners.

Roles of Professional Organizations and Unions

Until recently, professional organizations representing teachers in different education disciplines have not been actively engaged in assessing the need to differentiate distinctions in teacher and paraeducator roles, or to establish supervisory responsibility. Changes are beginning to occur, primarily in organizations concerned with improving the quality of special education services for learners with disabilities, and even these organizations are moving slowly.

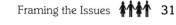

In 1995, the CEC's board of directors approved a resolution prepared by the Teacher Education Division calling on IHEs, SEAs, and LEAs to work together to develop standards and guidelines that address

1. role distinctions among teachers, therapists, or other credentialed and licensed specialists and paraeducators and other support staff;
2. supervision of paraeducators and other support staff;
3. preservice training, inservice training, and professional development combined with career advancement opportunities for paraeducators;
4. job descriptions that articulate the knowledge and skills required by paraeducators to perform their assigned tasks;
5. strategies for structured, systematic management and supervision of paraeducators; and
6. ethical and legal responsibilities for paraeducators working in a variety of positions.

In response to the resolution, CEC has published skill and knowledge competencies for paraeducators who work in programs serving learners with disabilities. In the same document, CEC also began the process of assessing knowledge and skill standards for preparing teachers to plan for and monitor paraeducators (CEC, 2000). The National Joint Committee on Learning Disabilities (1999) has also established guidelines for the supervision and appropriate roles for paraeducators. The National Association for the Education of Young Children (1994) and the International Reading Association (1998) have issued position papers that provide guidance for establishing standards for paraeducator roles and preparation.

Professional organizations representing occupational and physical therapists and speech–language pathologists have been at the forefront of efforts to set standards for the supervisory roles of licensed and certified practitioners who work with paratherapists. These organizations have targeted the need to ensure that distinctions in the roles and responsibilities of licensed professionals and paratherapists are clearly delineated. AOTA, APTA, and ASHA have also provided leadership in the development of certification systems for therapy assistants. These mechanisms clearly establish differences in the roles and responsibilities of therapy aides and therapy assistants. For several years, AOTA and APTA have recognized standards for community college associate's degree programs for certified occupational and certified physical therapy assistants (AOTA, 1990, 1999; APTA, 2000). Although ASHA has delineated distinctions in speech–language pathologist roles and those of speech–language pathology assistants and has established guidelines for the supervision and training of assistants (ASHA, 1999, 2000), only a few associate's degree programs for SLP assistants are currently in place. (Chapter 4 contains a more in-depth discussion of systems and strategies used by AOTA, APTA, and ASHA to ensure that paratherapists are appropriately supervised and well prepared.)

It is important that, in addition to professional organizations, the roles of unions in supporting the development of standards for the roles and preparation of paraeducators not be overlooked. In many cases, unions fulfill the role of a professional organization for paraeducators who work in educational settings. In addition to their concern with collective bargaining issues, including salaries, pensions, health coverage, and working conditions, the American Federation of Teachers (AFT), the National Education Association (NEA), and other unions increasingly are concerned with issues that affect the roles, performance, preparation, and status of paraeducators as team members. Nationwide, unions have encouraged the development of standards for paraeducator roles, their training, and infrastructures to ensure that paraeducators are appropriately prepared (AFT, 1998; NEA, 2001). The AFT has completed a project of national significance that establishes standards and performance indicators for paraeducators who work in childcare settings; preschool, elementary, middle, and secondary education programs; and transition services.

The Roles of Institutions of Higher Education

Some of the most underappreciated support systems available to SEAs and LEAs are the expertise and resources available from colleges and universities. Three issues are connected with paraeducator employment, supervision, and preparation that directly concern administrators and faculty in 2- and 4-year colleges and universities. The first (and the primary focus of this text) is related to strengthening and improving the quality of education practices by preparing teachers and other professional practitioners to supervise and work effectively with paraeducators. The second is the role of IHEs in the preparation of paraeducators and paratherapists. The third is linked to the continuing shortages of teachers and related services personnel that exist in all disciplines and program areas across the country. The shortages are particularly acute in science and mathematics, special education, and related services, and among teachers from diverse racial, ethnic, cultural, and linguistic heritages (Genzuk & Baca, 1998; Haselkorn & Fideler, 1996; McDonnell & Hill, 1993; NCES, 1995, 2000; OSERS, 2000).

Although there is mounting evidence that the supervisory roles of teachers are expanding, analysis of several research efforts indicates that for the most part teachers are not prepared at either the undergraduate or graduate level to supervise and work effectively with paraeducators (Drecktrah, 2000; French, 2001; French & Pickett, 1997; Lindemann & Beegle, 1988; Pickett, 1999; Pickett et al., 1993; Salzberg & Morgan, 1995; Wallace et al., 2001). These reports found that few teacher educators were working in concert with SEAs, LEAs, and state agencies responsible for teacher licensure to develop standards that will ensure that teachers are prepared for their emerging roles as team leaders and supervisors of paraeducators.

French and Pickett (1997) identified eight policy questions that require the attention of teacher educators and administrators in SEAs and LEAs related to preparing teachers and other school professionals to supervise paraeducators:

1. Are both entry-level and experienced professionals receiving preparation for their supervisory roles?
2. If so, is the information that prospective professionals get from their preservice programs accurate and current?
3. What knowledge, attitudes, and skills should professionals demonstrate regarding paraeducator supervision?

4. Is the reluctance to supervise paraeducators that was found in one study a generalizable phenomenon? If so, to what can it be attributed? How should it be managed?
5. Are there differences in the ways that supervisory responsibilities are carried out by professionals who have and have not had preservice or inservice training regarding paraeducator supervision?
6. How does the type of supervision provided to paraeducators affect their performance of assigned duties?
7. What role should teacher educators play in staff development provided by LEAs to improve professionals' skills regarding paraeducator supervision?
8. Should standards be established regarding the amount or type of experience and preparation required for professionals to supervise paraeducators?

In addition to these questions, faculty and curriculum developers in IHEs and policymakers and staff developers in SEAs and LEAs must be concerned about ethical issues. What ethical issues emerge when distinctions in the roles of school professionals and paraeducators are not clear, when tasks are assigned or delegated inappropriately to paraeducators, when opportunities for systematic staff development for paraeducators do not exist, and when school professionals are not adequately prepared to supervise paraeducators?

The second issue connected with personnel preparation that requires the attention of all stakeholders is the role of community colleges in providing systematic standardized preservice and inservice training and opportunities for career advancement for paraeducators. The dilemma confronting policymakers in SEAs, LEAs, and IHEs is how to develop systems that interface and are flexible enough to meet the needs of (a) school employees whose career choices are to remain in the field as skilled paraeducators and (b) those who want to move into the professional ranks.

Since the beginning of the New Careers movement that began with the advent of Title I and Head Start, and the passage of P.L. 94-142, community colleges have offered associate's degrees and 1-year certificate programs for paraeducators and paraprofessionals in education and other human services programs. Traditionally, these programs have been designed to prepare paraeducators to work in early childhood education, special education, and school-to-work transition programs and adult services. In all too many cases, however, community colleges are not acknowledged in state initiatives to develop training programs for paraeducators or LEA policies and practices concerned with paraeducator training and, therefore, such training programs do not achieve permanency. The reasons are related to the fact that most LEAs do not recognize a set of core competencies required by all paraeducators or a hierarchy of skills and knowledge required by paraeducators who work in programs where they have greater independence or require more complex skills for other reasons. As a result, associate's degrees are not viewed as being important for advancement on a career ladder or for steps on salary scales. Further compounding the problems for community colleges is the lack of articulated systems with teacher preparation programs that support transfers between the systems, especially for paraeducators who are taking courses because they want to improve their on-the-job skills. Thus, community colleges find it difficult to attract and retain paraeducators when there are so few incentives for them to earn these degrees (Pickett, 1989, 1999). It is, however, highly likely that this situation will change as LEAs and SEAs establish standards for paraeducator preparation mandated by Title I. Indeed, it is possible that community colleges may become the primary source of paraeducator training.

Finally, the third significant issue that confronts policymakers in our nation's schools, colleges, and universities is the need to attract individuals into most areas of teacher education and to expand efforts to recruit more women and men from diverse racial, cultural, and language heritages. Paraeducators are an important but underrecognized resource for teacher recruitment. The vast majority of paraeducators are women entering or reentering the workforce who work in programs located near their homes. They are generally representative of the ethnic, cultural, and language populations in their community. They are familiar with both community and school concerns and, therefore, can help to bridge gaps in trust and communication between schools, homes, and the wider community just as they did in the 1960s and 1970s. Moreover, because their roots are in the community, they are likely to remain or return there after they have completed their education (Emig, 1986; Gartner, 1971; Genzuk & Baca, 1998; Genzuk et al., 1994; Haselkorn & Fideler, 1996; Kaplan, 1977; Miramontes, 1990; Moshoyannis et al., 1999).

Haselkorn and Fideler (1996) pointed out that the strategies developed and tested by different Career Opportunities Programs in the 1970s are still relevant to the field today. In *Breaking the Class Ceiling: Paraeducator Pathways to Teaching,* they describe examples of reemerging efforts between schools and IHEs to recruit paraeducators and support their career advancement. To a limited degree, personnel preparation programs across the country once again have started to reach out to paraeducators and to provide the support that will help them to succeed. These efforts are not part of traditional teacher education programs and cannot meet the almost insatiable demands of employers in major urban centers and rural areas.

Because of the complexity of the issues described throughout this chapter, none of them can be addressed in a vacuum or by a single agency. Finding effective solutions to issues requires active participation of LEAs, other education provider agencies, IHEs, professional organizations, unions, and other stakeholders. Because of their relationships that cross jurisdictions, SEAs are in the unique position to develop and nurture these partnerships.

Summary

As always, our nation's schools are respondents to and agents for change. Policymakers and implementers in SEAs and LEAs are confronted with a multitude of issues as they grapple with finding effective methods for improving the quality and performance of schools and other education provider agencies. One of the most critical areas of need is preparing professionals and paraeducators to work together as effective instructional and related services teams.

Over the last 20 years, SEAs, LEAs, IHEs, and other stakeholders have joined forces to forge systems that empower teachers, by involving them more directly in establishing education priorities, determining how best to allocate fiscal and human resources, and aligning curriculum content with instructional strategies to improve learner performance and achievement. These same partners also have worked together to establish new standards for teacher education that recognize the redefined and restructured roles of teachers.

These efforts have not recognized the need to prepare teachers and other school professionals to supervise paraeducators and paratherapists. The current resurgence of interest in issues surrounding the employment, roles, preparation, and supervision of paraeducators is fairly limited, and the issues remain "afterthoughts" in the public policy arena. To ensure that teachers and paraeducators are adequately and appropriately prepared for their new, more demanding roles, it is important that these issues be more closely tied to major education reform initiatives that are currently being tested and assessed.

Various agencies and organizations with responsibility for and interest in improving the quality and performance of education for all learners must work together to develop policies, standards, and permanent infrastructures for the employment, roles, preparation, and supervision of paraeducators. This includes gathering and assessing information they can use to

1. clearly delineate distinctions in teacher and paraeducator roles;
2. identify similarities and differences in the roles of paraeducators who are assigned to all programs administered by LEAs and other education provider agencies;
3. identify core knowledge and skill competencies required by all paraeducators and hierarchies of competencies required by paraeducators who work in programs and learning environments that require more advanced levels of skills and knowledge;
4. establish standards for comprehensive, ongoing systems of paraeducator preparation that include pre- and inservice training, structured on-the-job training, and access to postsecondary education programs that will support and facilitate career advancement;

5. develop credentialing systems or other mechanisms that will ensure that paraeducators have mastered the skills required to carry out tasks that comprise their scopes of responsibilities;
6. set standards for paraeducator supervision and indicators for evaluating their performance;
7. develop standards for preparing teachers and related services personnel, who supervise paraeducators to plan for, direct, and monitor their performance; and
8. develop curriculum content that addresses these standards and, when appropriate, incorporate the standards into teacher licensure requirements.

Each of these issues is addressed in greater depth in the chapters that follow.

Discussion Questions

1. What were the most significant reasons that caused school districts to test the efficacy of paraprofessional utilization in the 1950s?
2. Why did the "paraprofessional movement" expand in the 1960s and 1970s?
3. What was the impact of reform initiatives that occurred in the 1980s on teacher roles?
4. Why did interest in issues surrounding paraeducators recede in the 1980s? How could this have been avoided?
5. How have changes in teacher roles, which began in the 1980s, influenced paraeducator roles?
6. In addition to the changing roles of teachers, what are other major factors that are contributing to continued and growing reliance on paraeducators in today's schools and other learning environments?
7. What are the current practices in your state with regard to the employment, placement, supervision, and preparation of paraeducators?

8. In your state, what are the most significant barriers to developing standards and systems for improving the performance of teacher–paraeducator teams?

9. In your state, are organized efforts under way to develop policies, standards, and infrastructures to improve the performance of teacher–paraeducator teams?

EXERCISES

1. Obtain copies of your state's written policies, guidelines, or regulatory procedures for the employment, supervision, roles, and preparation of paraeducators. Divide into groups of five or six. Working together, analyze the documents to determine if your state has (a) established standards for paraeducator supervision; (b) established standards for preparing teachers to supervise paraeducators; (c) identified appropriate roles and duties for paraeducators; (d) established criteria or guidelines for education and experiential qualifications for paraeducator employment; (e) established standards for paraeducator training; and (f) developed a comprehensive plan that includes inservice staff development and opportunities for professional advancement for paraeducators. (To obtain this information, it may be necessary to contact the state departments of education, human services, and health, or other agencies responsible for the licensure and credentialing of education and related services personnel. In some states, you may be able to access the information on the SEA's Web site. In other states, you may have to request the information by calling or writing.)

2. Working in small groups, identify agencies and organizations that should be members of partnerships to address policy questions and develop systems to meet your state's needs. Discuss methods that the SEA, working in partnership with stakeholders you have identified, might use to strengthen current policies and procedures or to develop new systems to improve the overall performance of teacher–paraeducator teams.

References

Alper, L., Fendel, D., Fraser, S., & Resek, D. (1996). Problem-based mathematics: Not just for the college-bound. *Educational Leadership, 53*(6), 18–25.

American Association for Employment in Education. (1998). *Teacher supply and demand in the United States: A research report from AAEE.* Evanston, IL: Author.

American Federation of Teachers. (1998). *Standards for a profession.* Washington, DC: Author.

American Occupational Therapy Association. (1990). Entry-level role delineation for registered occupational therapists (OTRs) and certified occupational therapy assistants (COTAs). *American Journal of Occupational Therapy, 44,* 1091–1102.

American Occupational Therapy Association. (1999). *Guidelines for the use of aides in occupational therapy practice.* Bethesda, MD: Author.

American Physical Therapy Association. (2000). *Providing physical therapy services under parts B and C of the Individuals with Disabilities Education Act (IDEA).* Alexandria, VA: Author.

American Speech-Language-Hearing Association. (1999). *Practical tools and forms for supervising speech–language pathology assistants.* Rockville, MD: Author.

American Speech-Language-Hearing Association Information Services. (2000). *Speech–language pathology assistants.* Rockville, MD: Author.

Bauch, P. A., & Goldring, E. B. (1998). Parent–teacher participation in the context of school governance. *Peabody Journal of Education, 73,* 15–35.

Blalock, G. (1991). Paraprofessionals: Critical team members in our special education programs. *Intervention in School and Clinic, 26*(4), 200–214.

Bowman, G. W., & Klopf, G. J. (1967). *Auxiliary school personnel: Their roles, training and institutionalization.* New York: Bank Street College of Education.

Bowman, G. W., & Klopf, G. J. (1968). *New careers and roles in the American school: A study of auxiliary personnel in education.* New York: Bank Street College of Education.

California Commission on the Teaching Profession. (1985). *Who will teach our children? A strategy for improving California schools.* Sacramento: Author.

Carnegie Forum on Education and the Economy. (1987). *A nation prepared: Teachers for the 21st century—The report on the Task Force on Teaching as a Profession.* New York: Carnegie Corporation of New York.

Cohen, R. (1976). *New careers grow older: A perspective on the paraprofessional experience, 1965–75.* Baltimore: Johns Hopkins University Press.

Committee for Economic Development. (1985). *Investing in our children.* New York: Research and Policy Committee for Economic Development.

Coufal, K. L., Steckelberg, A. L., & Vasa, S. F. (1991). Current trends in the training and utilization of paraprofessionals in speech and language programs: A report of an eleven state survey. *Language, Speech, and Hearing Services in Schools, 22*(1), 51–59.

Council for Exceptional Children. (1996). *Report of the Consortium of Organizations on the preparation and use of speech–language paraprofessionals in early intervention and education settings.* Reston, VA: Author.

Council for Exceptional Children. (2000). *What every special educator must know: The international standards for the preparation and licensure of special educators.* Reston, VA: Author.

Cruickshank, W., & Herring, N. (1957). *Assistants for teachers of exceptional children.* Syracuse, NY: Syracuse University Press.

Daniels, V. I., & McBride, A. (2001, March). Paraeducators as critical team members: Redefining roles and responsibilities. *National Association of Secondary School Principals Bulletin, 85*(623), 66–74.

Darling-Hammond, L. (1994). *The current status of teaching and teacher development in the United States.* Background paper prepared for the National Commission on Teaching and America's Future. New York: Teachers College–Columbia.

Darling-Hammond, L. (1997). *The right to learn: A blueprint for creating schools that work.* San Francisco: Jossey-Bass.

Darling-Hammond, L., & McLaughlin, M. W. (1995). Policies that support professional development in an era of reform. *Phi Delta Kappan, 76,* 597–604.

David, J. L. (1996). The who, what and why of site-based management. *Education Leadership, 53*(4), 4–9.

Downing, J. E., Ryndak, D. L., & Clark, D. (2000). Paraeducators in inclusive classrooms: Their own perspectives. *Remedial and Special Education, 21,* 171–181.

Drecktrah, M. E. (2000). Preservice teacher preparation to work with paraeducators. *Teacher Education and Special Education, 23,* 157–164.

Ebenstein, W., & Gooler, L. (1993). *Cultural diversity and developmental disabilities workforce issues.* New York: Consortium for the Study of Disabilities, City University of New York.

Education for All Handicapped Children Act of 1975, 20 U.S.C. § 1400 *et seq.*

Education of the Handicapped Act Amendments of 1986, 20 U.S.C. § 1400 *et seq.*

Elementary and Secondary Education Act of 1965, 79 Stat. 27.

Emig, C. (1986). *A report on certification of paraprofessionals in education.* Washington, DC: Paraprofessional and School Related Personnel Committee, American Federation of Teachers.

Fenichel, E., & Eggbeer, L. (1990). *Preparing practitioners to work with infants, toddlers and their families: Issues and recommendations for educators and trainers.* Arlington, VA: National Center for Clinical Infant Toddler Programs, Zero to Three.

French, N. K. (1998). Working together: Resource teachers and paraeducators. *Remedial and Special Education, 19,* 357–368.

French, N. K. (2001). Supervising paraprofessionals: A survey of teacher practices. *Journal of Special Education, 35,* 41–53.

French, N. K., & Pickett, A. L. (1997). The utilization of paraprofessionals in special education: Issues for teacher educators. *Teacher Education and Special Education, 20*(1), 61–73.

Friend, M., & Cook, L. (1996). *Interactions: Collaboration skills for school professionals* (2nd ed.). White Plains, NY: Longman.

Fund for the Advancement of Education, 1951–61. (1961). *Decade of experiment.* New York: Ford Foundation.

Gartner, A. (1971). *Paraprofessionals and their performance: A survey of education, health and social services programs.* New York: Praeger.

Gartner, A., & Riessman, F. (1974). The paraprofessional movement in perspective. *Personnel and Guidance Journal, 53,* 253–256.

Genzuk, M., & Baca, R. (1998). The paraeducator to teacher pipeline. *Education and Urban Society, 32*(1), 73–88.

Genzuk, M., Lavadenz, M., & Krashen, S. (1994). Paraeducators: A source for remedying the shortage of teachers for limited–English-proficient students. *The Journal of Educational Issues of Language Minority Students, 14,* 211–222.

Giangreco, M. F., Edelman, S. W., Luiselli, T. E., & McFarland, S. Z. C. (1997). Helping or hovering? Effects of instructional assistant proximity on students with disabilities. *Exceptional Children, 64,* 7–18.

Goals 2000: Educate America Act of 1994, 20 U.S.C. § 5801 *et seq.*

Haselkorn, D., & Fideler, E. (1996). *Breaking the class ceiling: Paraeducator pathways to teaching.* Belmont, MA: Recruiting New Teachers.

Holmes Group. (1986). *Tomorrow's teachers.* East Lansing, MI: Author.

Individuals with Disabilities Education Act of 1990, 20 U.S.C. § 1400 *et seq.*

Individuals with Disabilities Education Act Amendments of 1997, 20 U.S.C. § 1400 *et seq.*

International Reading Association. (1998). *Standards for reading professionals.* Newark, DE: Author.

Jackson,V. C., & Acosta, R. (1971). *Task analysis: A systematic approach to designing new career programs.* New York: New Careers Training Laboratory, New York University.

Kaplan, G. (1977). *From aide to teacher: The story of the Career Opportunities Program.* Washington, DC: U.S. Government Printing Office.

Killoran, J., Templeman, T. P., Peters, J., & Udell, T. (2001). Identifying paraprofessional competencies for early intervention and early childhood special education. *Teaching Exceptional Children, 34*(1), 68–73.

Lieberman, A. (1995). *The work of restructuring schools.* New York: Teachers College Press.

Lieberman, A., & Miller, L. (2000). A new synthesis for a new century. In R. S. Brandt (Ed.), *Education in a new era* (pp. 47–66). Alexandria, VA: Association for Supervision and Curriculum Development.

Lindemann, D. P., & Beegle, G. P. (1988). Pre-service teacher training and the use of the classroom paraprofessional. *Teacher Education and Special Education, 11*(4), 183–186.

Longhurst, T. M, & Witmer, D. M. (1994, April). *Initiating therapy aide/assistant training in a rural state.* Paper presented at the 13th annual conference on the Training of Paraprofessionals in Education and Rehabilitative Services, Albuquerque, NM.

Lyons, D. (1995). *Training for special education funded paraprofessionals: A report on the education and responsibility study.* Federal Way: Washington Education Association.

Macais, R. F., & Kelly, C. (1996). *Summary report of the survey of the states' limited English proficient students and available educational programs and services, 1994–1995.* Washington, DC: National Clearinghouse for Bilingual Education.

Marks, S. U., Schrader, C., & Levine, M. (1999). Paraeducator experiences in inclusive settings: Helping, hovering or holding their own? *Exceptional Children, 65*, 315–328.

McDonnell, L., & Hill, P. (1993). *Newcomers in American schools: Meeting the needs of immigrant youth.* Santa Monica, CA: RAND Corp.

Miramontes, O. B. (1990). Organizing for effective paraprofessional services in special education: A multilingual/multiethnic instructional service team model. *Remedial and Special Education, 12,* 29–36.

Morehouse, J. A., & Albright, L. (1991). Training trends and needs of paraprofessionals in transition services delivery agencies. *Teacher Education and Special Education, 14,* 248–256.

Moshoyannis, T., Pickett, A. L., & Granick, L. (1999). *The evolving roles and education/training needs of paraprofessionals and teachers in the New York City public schools: Results of survey research and focus groups.* New York: City University of New York, Paraprofessional Academy, Center for Advanced Study in Education.

National Association for the Education of Young Children. (1994). NAEYC position statement: A conceptual framework for early childhood professional development. *Young Children, 49*(3), 68–77.

National Board for Professional Teaching Standards. (1989). *Toward high and rigorous standards for the teaching profession (1989).* Washington, DC: Author.

National Board for Professional Teaching Standards. (1994a). *How we plan to achieve our vision.* Southfield, MI: Author.

National Board for Professional Teaching Standards. (1994b). *What teachers should know and be able to do.* Southfield, MI: Author.

National Center for Education Statistics. (1995). *Projections of education statistics to 2005.* Washington, DC: U.S. Department of Education, Office of Education Research.

National Center for Education Statistics. (2000). *Education statistics: Elementary and secondary schools and staffing survey.* Washington, DC: U.S. Department of Education, Office of Education Research.

National Commission for Excellence in Teacher Education. (1985). *A call for change in teacher education.* American Association for Colleges of Teacher Education.

National Commission on Excellence in Education. (1983). *A nation at risk: The imperative for education reform.* Washington, DC: U.S. Government Printing Office.

National Education Association. (2001). *Pareducators and IDEA: What paraeducators need to know to advocate for themselves.* Washington, DC: Author.

National Governors' Association. (1986). *Time for results.* Washington, DC: Center for Policy, Research and Analysis, National Governors' Association.

National Joint Committee on Learning Disabilities. (1999, Winter). Learning disabilities: Use of paraprofessionals. *Learning Disability Quarterly, 22,* 23–28.

No Child Left Behind Act of 2002, P.L. 107-110.

Office of Special Education Programs and Rehabilitative Services. (2000). *22nd annual report to Congress on the implementation of the Individuals with Disabilities Education Act.* Washington, DC: U.S. Department of Education.

Passaro, P., Pickett, A. L., Latham, G., & HongBo, W. (1994). The training and support needs of paraprofessionals in rural special education settings. *Rural Special Education Quarterly, 13*(4), 3–9.

Pearl, A., & Riessman, F. (1965). *New careers for the poor: The non-professional in human services.* New York: Free Press.

Pickett, A. L. (1986). *Paraprofessionals in education: The state of the art.* New York: National Resource Center for Paraprofessionals, Center for Advanced Study in Education, Graduate Center, City University of New York.

Pickett, A. L. (1989). *Restructuring the schools: The role of paraprofessionals.* Washington, DC: Center for Policy Research, National Governors' Association.

Pickett, A. L. (1994). *Paraprofessionals in the education workforce.* Washington, DC: National Education Association.

Pickett, A. L. (1999). *Strengthening and supporting teacher/provider–paraeducator teams: Guidelines for paraeducator roles, supervision, and preparation.* New York: National Resource Center for Paraprofessionals, Center for Advanced Study in Education, Graduate School, City University of New York.

Pickett, A. L., Likens, M., & Wallace, T. (2002). *A state of the art report on paraeducators in education and related services.* Logan, UT: National Resource Center for Paraprofessionals in Education, Utah State University and the University of Minnesota.

Pickett, A. L., Vasa, S. F., & Steckelberg, A. L. (1993). *Using paraeducators effectively in the classroom* [Fastback No. 358]. Bloomington, IN: Phi Delta Kappa Educational Foundation.

Pipho, C. (2000). Governing the American dream of universal public education. In R. S. Brandt (Ed.), *Education in a new era* (pp. 5–19). Alexandria, VA: Association for Supervision and Curriculum Development.

Putnam, J. W. (1993). *Cooperative learning and strategies for inclusion: Celebrating diversity in the classroom.* Baltimore: Brookes.

Radaszewski-Byrne, M. (1997). Issues in the development of guidelines for preparation of speech–language paraprofessionals and their SL supervisors working in education settings. *Journal of Children's Communication Development, 18,* 5–21.

Recruiting New Teachers. (1997). *The urban teacher challenge.* Belmont, MA: Author.

Riggs, C. G. (2001). Paraprofessionals' perceptions of their training needs. *Teaching Exceptional Children, 33*(3), 78–83.

Riggs, C. G., & Mueller, P. H. (2001). Employment and utilization of paraeducators in inclusive settings. *Journal of Special Education, 35*(1), 54–62.

Rogan, P. M., & Held, M. (1999). Paraprofessionals in job coach roles. *Journal of the Association for Persons with Severe Handicaps, 24,* 273–280.

Rueda, R. S., & Monzo, L. D. (2000). *Apprentices for teaching: Professional development issues surrounding the collaborative relationship between teachers and paraeducators.* Washington, DC: Center for Research on Education, Diversity, and Excellence.

Safarik, L. (1999). *Lives in transition.* Retrieved from the National Resource Center for Paraprofessionals Web site: http://www.nrcpara.org

Salzberg, C. L., & Morgan, J. (1995). Preparing teachers to work with paraeducators. *Teacher Education and Special Education, 18*(1), 49–55.

Simpson, R. L., Whelan, R. J., & Zabel, R. H. (1993). Special education personnel preparation in the 21st century: Issues and strategies. *Remedial and Special Education, 14*(2), 7–22.

Snodgrass, A. S. (1991). *Actual and preferred practices of employment, placement, supervision, and evaluation of teacher aides in Idaho school districts.* Unpublished doctoral dissertation, University of Idaho, Moscow.

Social Security Act of 1935, 49 Stat. 147.

U.S. Bureau of the Census. (2001). *Population 2000: State profiles.* Washington, DC: U.S. Department of Commerce.

U.S. Department of Education. (1999). *Promising results, continuing challenges: Final report of the national assessment of Title I.* Washington, DC: Author.

Wall, R., & Rinehart, J. R. (1998). School based decision making and the empowerment of secondary school teachers. *Journal of School Leadership, 59*(8), 49–64.

Wallace, T., Jongho, S., Bartholomay, T., & Stahl, B. J. (2001). Knowledge and skills for teachers supervising the work of paraprofessionals. *Exceptional Children, 67,* 520–533.

Team Roles in Classrooms and Other Learning Environments

2

Anna Lou Pickett and Lynn Safarik

OVERVIEW

Educators are increasingly challenged to provide instruction and other services to children and youth who are diverse in terms of cultural background, primary language, and special learning needs, often with scarce resources. Most licensed and certified professional practitioners (e.g., teachers, early childhood educators, transition specialists), administrators, and parents recognize the critical role of the paraeducator in contributing to learner success and well-being. The problem is that paraeducators' roles are not always clearly delineated in different staffing arrangements and learning environments, and the training they need to meet the needs of these roles is rarely defined. In many state and local education agencies (SEAs and LEAs), there are discrepancies between policies, regulatory procedures, job descriptions, teacher expectations, and learner needs. Paraeducator skill levels and the extent of formal education can also be disparate. Training options for paraeducators are rarely standardized or competency based, are usually piecemeal, and are not necessarily based on accurate assessments of the evolving roles of teachers and paraeducators.

Paraeducators provide services, under the supervision of teachers, that are usually technical, concrete, and routine in nature. It is not uncommon for paraeducators to be assigned to a position and then to perform tasks that go well beyond the parameters of that position, often with no preservice or inservice training or adequate supervision. This situation is particularly likely for paraeducators working with learners who have special needs, including those with disabilities or limited English proficiency (Downing, Ryndak, & Clark, 2000; Giangreco,

Edelman, Luiselli, & McFarland, 1997; Miramontes, 1990; Pickett, Safarik, & Echiverria, 1998; Riggs & Mueller, 2001; Rueda & Monzo, 2000; Snodgrass, 1991). Throughout general, special, compensatory, and transitional education programs, from preschool through high school, the primary duties of most paraeducators are to assist with the delivery of instruction (Downing et al., 2000; French, 1998; Killoran, Templeman, Peters, & Udell, 2001; Miramontes, 1990; Moshoyannis, Pickett, & Granick, 1999; Passaro, Pickett, Latham, & HongBo, 1994; Riggs & Mueller, 2001; Rogan & Held, 1999; Safarik, 1999; Snodgrass, 1991). In areas such as inclusive education programs for children and youth with disabilities, transition and school-to-work programs, early childhood education, and multilingual education, paraeducators, like their professional colleagues, have experienced role transformations as the lines between school, home, and community have become blurred. The trend toward education and human services integration for infants, young children, teenagers, and adults has broadened the scope of paraeducator roles to include job titles such as job coach, transition trainer, technology assistant, case aide, outreach worker, home visitor, health aide or assistant, therapy aide or assistant, and community liaison, in addition to the traditional titles of instructional or teacher aide or assistant.

The goal of this chapter is to provide better understanding of responsibilities that may be assigned or delegated to paraeducators to (a) ensure the integrity of teacher and paraeducator roles and (b) provide information that personnel in SEAs, LEAs, other provider systems, and institutions of higher education (IHEs) can build on to establish well-conceived policies and practices for the supervision and preparation of teachers and paraeducators. Current literature on paraeducator supervision, roles, and competencies is synthesized, and offers a conceptual framework that administrators, supervisors, personnel developers, and professional practitioners can build on to develop standards and infrastructures that will strengthen the performance of education teams. Topics discussed are (a) a scope of responsibilities and standards for skill and knowledge competencies required by teachers as team leaders and supervisors of paraeducators; (b) scopes of responsibilities for paraeducators and standards for core competencies required by all paraeducators and for competencies required by paraeducators working in programs and positions that require more complex skills and knowledge; (c) training models for paraeducators working in different programs and learning environments; and (d) a core curriculum for preparing paraeducators working in different programs and position levels.

Instructional Objectives

After studying this chapter and participating in discussions and activities, the reader will be able to do the following:

1. Describe educational settings and programs where paraeducators are employed.
2. Describe a scope of responsibilities for teachers as team leaders and supervisors of paraeducators.
3. Delineate teacher responsibilities that may not be delegated or assigned to paraeducators, and those responsibilities that may be shared with and performed by paraeducators.
4. Describe scopes of responsibilities for paraeducators as members of education teams.
5. Describe similarities and distinctions in the roles and duties of paraeducators working in general and special education, multilingual programs, Title I and other compensatory (remedial) education programs, early childhood education, and transitional services.
6. Identify competencies required by teachers as leaders of education teams and supervisors of paraeducators.
7. Identify a common core of competencies required by all paraeducators, and competencies needed by paraeducators who work in programs and learning environments that require more advanced or complex skills and knowledge.

Introduction

Nationwide there is a lack of uniformity in the roles, supervision, and training of paraeducators across state lines and often within states. There are signs, however, of renewed interest in determining how roles and responsibilities of paraeducators who work in early childhood, elementary, middle, and secondary school programs are evolving (Downing et al., 2000; Killoran et al., 2001; Marks, Schrader, & Levine, 1999; Miramontes, 1990; Moshoyannis et al., 1999; Pickett, 1999; Riggs & Mueller, 2001; Rueda & Monzo, 2000; Snodgrass, 1991). Reports indicate a growing awareness of the need to pay attention to emerging roles of teachers as team leaders and supervisors of paraeducators (Drecktrah, 2000; French, 2001; French & Pickett, 1997; Pickett, 1999; Pickett, Vasa, & Steckelberg, 1993; Wallace, Jongho, Bartholomay, & Stahl, 2001). Other reports have focused on professionals and paraprofessionals employed in transition services (deFur & Taymans, 1995; Rogan & Held, 1999; Safarik, 1999; Safarik et al., 1991).

Position papers that establish guidelines for paraeducator utilization have been developed by the following professional organizations: Council for Exceptional Children (CEC, 2000), National Association for the Education of Young Children (NAEYC, 1994), International Reading Association (IRA, 1998), National Joint Committee on Learning Disabilities (NJCLD, 1999), and Association for Education and Rehabilitation of the Blind and Visually Impaired (AERBVI; Wiener et al., 1990). Some of the papers provide guidance for developing paraeducator roles, competencies, supervision, and systems of training and career advancement; some are more limited in their scope and discuss only roles and competencies required by paraeducators.

Federal legislative actions that began in the 1960s have led to increased reliance on paraeducators, with greater emphasis on their learner support roles. The surge in paraeducator employment began with the introduction of Title I and other compensatory programs and continued into the 1970s with the passage of P.L. 94-142, the Education for All Handicapped Children Act of 1975. Passage of the Education of the Handicapped Act Amendments of 1986 and of the Individuals with Disabilities Education Act (IDEA) of 1990 required LEAs to provide services to (a) children ages 3 to 5 who have disabilities or chronic health needs that place them at risk and (b) teenagers with disabilities who require assistance in making the transition from school to work and independent living. Related legislation in the areas of vocational education, rehabilitative human services, and employment and training (Americans with Disabilities Act of 1990,

Carl D. Perkins Vocational and Applied Technology Education Act of 1990, Job Training Partnership Act of 1982 and its Reform Amendments of 1992, School-to-Work Opportunities Act of 1994) have expanded the services that schools are required to provide and the need to establish systematic mechanisms for linking schools with other agencies providing early childhood and adult education.

The 1997 IDEA amendments allow LEAs to employ paraeducators and therapy assistants who are *appropriately trained and supervised* in accordance with state law, regulations, or written policies to assist in the provision of special education and related services for children and youth with disabilities. The No Child Left Behind Act of 2001, which reauthorized the Elementary and Secondary Education Act of 1965, calls for higher standards for both the employment and training of paraeducators assigned to Title I programs. Although the NCLB Act mandates that paraeducators who assist with instruction are to be supervised by teachers, it does not require states to develop standards for teacher preparation that will ensure that paraeducators are effectively supervised. If teachers are not prepared for these supervisory responsibilities, the work of teacher–paraeducator teams will be adversely affected.

Supervising Paraeducators: A Team Approach

The value of a team approach in the delivery of education and related services is gaining acceptance. This is particularly true in programs serving children and youth who have sensory, physical, learning, developmental, emotional, and health-related disabilities, as well as English language learners, and those who come from educationally disadvantaged backgrounds that may place them at risk. The teaming process is increasingly divided into three categories.

- 1. **School or site-based governance teams** make overall decisions about how to achieve higher learning standards for all learners and address the needs of individual learners, their families, and building staff. Among the tasks performed by these teams are assessing programs and strategies to meet mutually agreed upon needs and determining how best to allocate human, fiscal, and technological resources to achieve short-term and long-range goals. Members of these teams may include building principals and representatives of other administrative and related services personnel, teachers, paraeducators, support staff, and parents. The two additional categories of teams work under the umbrella of the site-based governance team and contribute to implementing decisions made by that team as well as carrying out responsibilities related to their specific missions.

▶ 2. **Program planning teams** are mandated by IDEA. Members are responsible for (a) identifying education and related services needs and goals for individual learners of all ages who have disabilities and (b) developing Individualized Education Programs (IEPs), Individualized Transition Plans (ITPs), and Individualized Family Service Plans (IFSPs) to meet learner and family needs. Participants on these teams represent administrative personnel, education and related services practitioners, and parents or other caregivers. Membership on these teams depends on the learner's needs and may include, but is not limited to, principals or program administrators, general and special education teachers, early childhood educators, transition specialists, parents, paraeducators, occupational therapists, physical therapists, speech–language pathologists, psychologists, social workers, physicians, nurses, and interpreters. Leadership of program planning teams may rotate or be assumed by a person representing the discipline with the primary responsibility for achieving the learner's goals and objectives (Pickett, 1999). Although no legislative mandates or regulatory procedures require individualized programs for learners from diverse linguistic heritages, or those who may be at risk because they come from educationally and economically disadvantaged backgrounds, formal and informal consultation among teachers and other professional practitioners to develop instructional strategies for supporting these students is becoming more common.

- **3. Program implementation teams** are smaller than the other teams and have day-to-day responsibility for providing education and other direct services to children, youth, and sometimes their families. Program implementation teams may be deployed in inclusive general and special education classrooms at all levels, and early childhood, transition or school-to-work, compensatory or remedial, multilingual, and other programs administered by LEAs or other education provider agencies. Typically, program implementation team members include general and/or special education or resource teachers, and one or more paraeducators. Depending on the program or the setting, a teacher, an early childhood educator, or a transition specialist usually assumes the role of team leader and supervisor of paraeducators. Based on identified learner needs, other personnel who may be part of these teams are occupational and physical therapists, speech–language pathologists, nurses, and reading and other content specialists; however, these personnel rarely serve as leaders of program implementation teams (Pickett, 1999).

Although teachers' program management and supervisory functions have expanded, teachers do not have sole responsibility for the management of paraeducators. District or agency and building administrators also play key roles in the management and supervision of paraeducators. Administrators at the district or agency and building levels have operational responsibility for establishing and carrying out policies and personnel practices connected with paraeducator employment, supervision, evaluation, preparation, and dismissal. Their responsibilities include (a) developing job descriptions for paraeducators that recognize their team roles and contain entry-level educational and experiential requirements and criteria for advancement to different positions; (b) establishing performance standards for all members of program implementation teams; (c) conducting annual performance reviews and evaluations of all team members; (d) providing time for teachers and paraeducators to meet regularly with one another and, when necessary, other team members for planning and on-the-job coaching; (e) ensuring that teachers are aware of and prepared for their roles as supervisors of paraeducators;

and (f) providing standardized, systematic opportunities for preservice and inservice preparation for paraeducators as part of the professional development program (Pickett, 1999).

Developing Standards for Paraeducator Responsibilities, Supervision, and Preparation

Although it may appear to casual observers in various learning environments that the roles and functions of teachers and paraeducators are more alike than different, nothing could be further from the truth. Although they do share some tasks and work together to achieve program and learner goals, team members have their own scopes of responsibility that need to be clearly defined by policymakers and administrators in SEAs, LEAs, and other education provider systems.

The suggested guidelines and standards proposed in position papers prepared by professional organizations and the individual researchers cited throughout this chapter are only that—suggestions. They do not have the same weight as state law or regulatory procedures. Although LEAs and other providers of education services increasingly utilize paraeducators to support the program and administrative functions of teachers and to expand the availability of individualized services for learners, standards for paraeducator roles and preparation are not always established at either state or local levels. Also, the vast majority of SEAs and LEAs have not established standards for paraeducator supervision. Moreover, for the most part, only minimal references are made to teacher supervisory roles in written policies and job descriptions (e.g., "teacher aides/assistants work under the supervision of licensed/certified teachers"). Although a small number of researchers recognize the need to prepare teachers for their supervisory roles, only a limited number of professional organizations are systematically addressing these issues, and further major ongoing reform initiatives have not yet recognized the need for standards to prepare teachers for their supervisory roles. Thus, teacher preparation programs at the undergraduate and graduate levels have few if any incentives to develop courses and curriculum content to prepare teachers for their supervisory roles.

Other professions, however, have come to recognize the value of differentiated staffing arrangements and the contributions that well-trained and effectively supervised paraprofessionals and assistants make to improving and expanding services. Different disciplines, including occupational and physical therapy, speech–language pathology, law, medicine and related health occupations, and their state licensure systems, have (a) defined distinctions in professional and paraprofessional scopes of practice and responsibilities in the delivery of services, (b) determined supervisory responsibility, (c) developed standards for knowledge and skill competencies for paraprofessionals working in different positions and settings, and (d) recognized a continuum of career development opportunities that prepare paraprofessionals for their team roles and, in some cases, may facilitate advancement for paraprofessionals who want to move to the professional ranks.

The models developed by the American Occupational Therapy Association (AOTA, 1999), the American Physical Therapy Association (APTA, 2000), and the American Speech-Language-Hearing Association (ASHA, 2000) are addressed in greater depth in Chapter 4. Professionals in these disciplines can provide guidance on which educators in SEAs, LEAs, IHEs, and other stakeholders can build to develop and set standards for differentiated staffing arrangements that include the teacher–paraeducator team.

Efforts to clarify paraeducator roles and establish standards for their supervision and preparation begin with defining teacher responsibilities in the education process that cannot be assigned or delegated to paraeducators, and those that may be shared with paraeducators who are appropriately trained and supervised. The National Resource Center for Paraprofessionals in Education and Related Services (NRCP) has developed and assessed scopes of responsibilities and standards for skill and knowledge competencies required by teachers and paraeducators who work in different programs and levels of education, ranging from early childhood programs through high school (Pickett, 1999). The standards and scopes of responsibilities developed by NRCP, through a grant of national significance, from the U.S. Department of Education, recognize the similarities and differences in programs administered by LEAs that have different missions, including home- and center-based early childhood education; inclusive general and special education; and multilingual, Title I, and transition programs for learners. The primary objectives of the NRCP project were to develop guidelines for use in (a) clarifying distinctions in the parameters of teacher and paraeducator responsibilities in the delivery of instructional and other services to learners and their parents, (b) establishing standards for knowledge and skill competencies required by teachers to supervise paraeducators, (c) setting standards for knowledge and skill competencies required by all paraeducators and hierarchies of competencies needed by paraeducators who work in programs or positions that require more complex skills and knowledge, and (d) establishing performance indicators for teacher and paraeducator team members. The following are definitions used by the project.

- **Scopes of responsibilities** are agreed-upon standards of practice for a profession or occupation. Because education services are provided by professional practitioners representing different education disciplines and occur in different program areas, there may not always be total agreement on all standards of practice. In general, however, scopes of responsibilities for teachers, early childhood educators, and transition specialists, who are usually the leaders of program implementation teams, fall into the following general categories: identifying learner needs, establishing learner-centered environments, developing lessons and modifying plans to meet individual learner needs, implementing the plans, evaluating learner progress, and assessing the effectiveness of the plans. These professionals also have responsibility for involving parents and other caregivers in all aspects of the child's education. The differences in teacher and paraeducator scopes of responsibilities are that paraeducators assist teachers by carrying out tasks developed, directed, and monitored by teachers that help children and youth achieve learning goals (Pickett, 1999).

- **Competencies** are the knowledge base and skills required for employment and advancement within different professions or occupations, programs, or positions.

- **Standards** are statements that describe job functions and responsibilities related to competency areas for a profession or occupation. The standards include knowledge and skill competencies and performance indicators to ensure that individuals have mastered the required skills.

To develop and test scopes of responsibilities and standards for teacher and paraeducator skill and knowledge competencies and performance indicators, the NRCP used the following process. A task force representing SEAs, LEAs, 2- and 4-year IHEs, professional organizations, unions, parents, and paraeducators was convened. Members were selected for their expertise and understanding of factors that influence the employment, performance, and preparation of teacher–paraeducator teams. To assist the process, the following resources were assembled: (a) current policies, regulatory procedures, and standards for licensure and credentialing concerned with the roles, supervision, and preparation of paraeducators in SEAs and (b) lists of paraeducator and teacher competencies developed by SEAs, LEAs, 2- and 4-year IHEs, researchers, and professional organizations representing different programs and disciplines.

A comparison of SEA policies, regulations, and licensure systems and the guidelines established by professional organizations provided information required to develop scopes of responsibilities for teachers and paraeducators. Teacher scopes of responsibilities are divided into six functional areas:

1. Teachers are leaders of program implementation teams with supervisory responsibility for paraeducators.
2. Teachers create and maintain learner-centered, supportive, inclusive environments.
3. Teachers develop and plan learning experiences.
4. Teachers engage children and youth in learning experiences.
5. Teachers assess learner needs.
6. Teachers practice standards of professional and ethical conduct.

The same six functional areas are used for paraeducators' responsibilities, the difference being that *assist* is inserted into the first five areas:

1. Paraeducators *assist* teachers with building and maintaining effective teams.
2. Paraeducators *assist* teachers with maintaining learner-centered supportive environments.
3. Paraeducators *assist* teachers with organizing learning experiences.
4. Paraeducators *assist* teachers with engaging children and youth in learning experiences.
5. Paraeducators *assist* teachers with activities that assess learner achievement.

The final area is exactly the same as the one for teachers:

6. Paraeducators meet standards of professional and ethical conduct.

To complete the first phase of the NRCP project and access the proposed standards for scopes and responsibilities and knowledge and skill competencies for teachers and paraeducators, a nationwide mail survey was conducted. Survey respondents included a broad representation of SEA personnel, individuals employed in various LEAs and other agencies that provide education services, members of organizations representing different disciplines and education specialties, faculty in 2- and 4-year IHEs, unions, and other stakeholders. Respondents provided valuable information needed to refine and finalize the scopes of responsibilities and competency standards.

To complete the process, an analysis by the NRCP task force of teacher and paraeducator roles and competencies took place at two levels. The purpose of the Level 1 analysis was to determine whether there were enough similarities in the roles and responsibilities of teachers and paraeducators in different education fields that parameters for scopes of responsibilities could apply to the following: inclusive general and special education, multilingual, compensatory and remedial, early childhood, and transition and school-to-work programs. In the Level 2 analysis, a cross-disciplinary analysis was used to (a) identify leadership and supervisory competencies for teachers, early childhood educators, and transition specialists; (b) derive a set of core competencies shared by all paraeducators; and (c) establish hierarchies of skill and knowledge competencies for paraeducators working in programs and environments where responsibilities are more complex and demanding.

A series of research questions helped identify distinctions and similarities in teacher and paraeducator functional capacities and knowledge and skill competencies recognized by different agencies, professional organizations, researchers, and survey respondents. The questions are as follows:

1. What are the primary functions and responsibilities of teachers in different education disciplines and program areas? How are they alike? How do they differ?
2. What are teacher functions and responsibilities that may not be assigned or delegated to paraeducators?
3. What teacher responsibilities may be shared with paraeducators?
4. Are there any tasks for which paraeducators have sole responsibility?
5. How do the levels of the knowledge and skill competencies required by teacher and paraeducator differ?

Teacher and Paraeducator Roles: The Differences

To finalize scopes of responsibilities for teachers as team leaders and supervisors of paraeducators, similarities and differences in their roles in various education discipline or program areas were identified. To accomplish this, the survey results were compared and contrasted with current SEA policies and practices, guidelines established by professional organizations representing the different areas, and recommendations made by various research efforts that assessed teacher and paraeducator roles, supervision, and preparation. Responsibilities that are similar to and connected with teachers' team leadership and supervisory functions in different disciplines and programs were collapsed and assigned to one of the six responsibility areas described previously.

Parameters for a Scope of Responsibilities for Teachers

The comparison of the survey with responsibilities established by the various agencies and organizations and those recommended by researchers indicated general agreement across all disciplines and program areas that teacher functions include responsibility for managing all phases of the instructional process: interpreting the results of formal and informal assessment instruments, diagnosing learner needs, planning lessons, aligning curriculum content with instructional activities to meet needs of individual learners, facilitating learning, and evaluating learning outcomes. In addition, there is also general agreement that teachers have primary responsibility for including parents or other caregivers in all aspects of their child's education.

Significant agreement was found among respondents to the survey from IHEs, professional organizations, and the results of investigative efforts that the following are teachers' responsibilities: planning paraeducator assignments; directing, monitoring, and assessing their day-to-day performance; and providing on-the-job coaching to improve their performance. However, some teachers, paraeducators, and LEA administrators were less certain that assessment tasks should be the responsibility of teachers. Their concerns centered on the roles of teachers in evaluating the performance of paraeducators. The reason for the concern seems to be attributable to the practice that began in the 1960s of designating the building principal or a program administrator as the primary supervisor of paraeducators. The practice has continued to the present, thus creating situations where the importance of teacher involvement in directing and monitoring paraeducator performance is not fully understood or appreciated (Pickett, Likins, & Wallace, 2002). Respondents to the survey also mentioned two other factors that contribute to this concern. The first is that the policies and practices of many SEAs and LEAs do not clearly specify the components of the instructional process that teachers must perform and those that may be performed by paraeducators with teacher supervision. The second factor is that teachers are not prepared for these supervisory tasks. (Specific teacher supervisory responsibilities are discussed more fully in Chapters 3 and 6.)

Almost unanimous agreement among the different stakeholders also occurred for two other significant functional areas. The first is associated with the responsibilities of teachers for creating and maintaining learner-centered, supportive, and safe environments that respect differences among learners, families, and staff, and protect everyone's legal and human rights. The second is related to the professional, ethical, and legal responsibilities of both teachers and paraeducators. The need for teachers to be aware of the distinctions between their roles and the roles of paraeducators, and to have the ability to apply this knowledge to all aspects of diagnosing learner needs, planning and providing learning programs, and assessing programs and learner performance is a recurring theme throughout the various resources used to help establish the scope of responsibilities for teachers. (Table 2.1 is a model scope of responsibilities for teachers.)

Teacher Functions that May Not Be Delegated or Assigned to Paraeducators

There was almost total agreement among the respondents to the survey, the SEA policy statements and regulatory procedures, the guidelines developed by professional organizations, and the research efforts, that in all matters associated with the learning process, such as assessment, diagnosing learner needs, planning and modifying curriculum and instructional methods, implementing learning activities, and managing behavior, teachers function as interpreters, prescribers, developers, managers, facilitators, and decision makers. Although some of the tasks may be shared with paraeducators, the overall responsibility cannot be delegated or assigned to them.

Parameters for Paraeducator Scopes of Responsibilities

The scopes of responsibilities for paraeducators apply to school or agency employees (a) who work under the supervision of teachers and other licensed or certified professional practitioners who are responsible for identifying learner needs, developing programs to meet the needs, and assessing learner performance and achievement, and (b) who assist with the delivery of instructional and

Table 2.1

Model Scope of Responsibilities for Teachers

Responsibility 1—As team leaders and supervisors of paraeducators, teachers

- prepare work assignments for paraeducators based on program objectives and learner needs,
- monitor paraeducator performance,
- provide on-the-job training to prepare paraeducators to carry out team and learner goals, and
- share relevant information with principals or agency administrators and paraeducators about the strengths and training needs of the individual paraeducator.

Responsibility 2—As program and classroom managers, teachers create learner-centered environments, and as supervisors of paraeducators, they

- implement, with the assistance of paraeducators, district and agency procedures for protecting the safety, health, and well-being of learners and staff;
- involve parents or other caregivers in their child's education; and
- plan and involve paraeducators in learning activities that maintain supportive, inclusive, and safe learning environments that respect differences among children, youth, families, and staff.

Responsibility 3—As program planners, teachers align curriculum content with learning and performance standards developed by the state or local education agency. They

- develop lesson and behavioral plans to achieve learning and performance standards;
- modify plans, curriculum content, and instructional strategies to accommodate individual learner differences; and
- involve an appropriately prepared paraeducator in planning activities that increase individualized learning opportunities for children and youth based on each individual's qualifications.

Responsibility 4—As instructional facilitators, teachers engage children and youth in learning activities. They

- provide, with the assistance of paraeducators, learning experiences that take place in different environments (e.g., classrooms, libraries, study halls, worksites, and other community-based locations, and home- and center-based programs for young children and their families); and
- develop paraeducator assignments that include learning objectives for individual children and youth; instructional strategies,

(*continues*)

Table 2.1 *Continued.*

Responsibility 4 *Continued.*

materials, and equipment required to carry out the activities; and methods for documenting learner performance.

Responsibility 5—As diagnosticians of learner needs, teachers

- participate in assessment activities that involve families in establishing eligibility for special services programs;
- analyze, with the assistance of other licensed and credentialed professional personnel, results of standardized (formal) instruments for assessing learner achievement;
- develop and analyze the results of functional (informal) assessment tools to document learner strengths and needs;
- keep learner records required by federal laws, state regulations, and district or agency policies; and
- involve paraeducators in assessment and record-keeping activities for which they are prepared.

Responsibility 6—Teachers practice standards of professional and ethical conduct. They

- adhere to the ethical and professional standards related to the supervision of paraeducators established by the professional organization representing their discipline or field;
- model standards of professional conduct for paraeducators (i.e., maintaining confidentiality; demonstrating respect for the human, civil, and legal rights of learners and their families; and respecting diversity in learner abilities, heritages, and lifestyles); and
- participate in opportunities for professional development that improve supervisory and team building skills.

Note. Adapted from *Strengthening and Supporting Teacher/Provider–Paraeducator Teams: Guidelines for Paraeducator Roles, Supervision, and Preparation,* by A. L. Pickett, 1999, New York: National Resource Center for Paraprofessionals, Center for Advanced Study in Education, Graduate Center, City University of New York. Copyright 1999 by National Resource Center for Paraprofessionals. Adapted with permission.

other direct services to children and youth and their families (Pickett, 1989). These scopes of responsibilities provide guidance for identifying appropriate paraeducator roles and functions in inclusive general and special education, multilingual, Title I and other compensatory, and transition programs at the preschool and elementary, middle, and secondary school levels.

Like the scopes of responsibilities for teachers, those for paraeducators were finalized after a comparison of the survey results and paraeducator responsibilities identified by various agencies and programs, professional organizations, and researchers. Tasks and functions performed by paraeducators in different program areas were collapsed and assigned to the same six responsibility areas listed for teachers.

The comparisons revealed two important items of information about paraeducator roles and responsibilities. First, few if any of the tasks performed by paraeducators are solely their responsibility. Although teachers may share many tasks with paraeducators, the teachers also perform the tasks or are responsible for seeing that they are appropriately carried out. The second is linked to the wide range of tasks performed by paraeducators in different program areas. Although there is a great deal of similarity in the nature of the tasks performed by paraeducators that cross program lines, there are differences in the levels of skills and knowledge required to perform the various activities. Thus, a need for three tiers or levels of responsibilities and competencies for paraeducators is indicated.

- **Level 1** paraeducator responsibilities emphasize monitoring learners in nonacademic settings (playgrounds, lunchrooms, hallways), duplicating instructional materials, maintaining learning centers, and assisting teachers with providing supportive, safe, and healthy environments. Level 1 paraeducators do not act independently or participate in assessment activities. They may, however, reinforce skills introduced by teachers. In many learning environments they move from one classroom to another throughout the day, and therefore are supervised by more than one teacher. When this occurs, each individual teacher decides which tasks a paraeducator will carry out while in that teacher's classroom. A building administrator may also have responsibility for scheduling some paraeducator assignments (e.g., bus duty, monitoring playgrounds).

- **Level 2** paraeducator responsibilities include all of those performed by Level 1 paraeducators; however, greater emphasis is placed on the instructional nature of tasks performed by Level 2 paraeducators. Depending on program requirements, these paraeducators are likely to be supervised by one teacher. They help teachers organize classroom activities, but they do not usually participate in formal planning activities. The learning environments where they work include special education resource and self-contained classrooms, early childhood, and elementary rooms. The instructional tasks performed by Level 2 paraeducators are determined and planned by teachers and include, but are not limited to, reinforcing lessons with individuals and small groups of learners to help them master academic and other skills, assisting teachers with informal and functional assessment activities, and carrying out behavior management plans developed by teachers for individual learners. When required by learner needs, Level 2 paraeducators participate in learner IEP, ITP, and IFSP development meetings. Depending on LEA or other agency policy, they may have limited decision-making authority with regard to nonacademic education activities.

- **Level 3** paraeducators work in a cross-section of education programs and provider agencies, including inclusive general and special education, multilingual and multicultural programs, and Title I and other compensatory programs at the preschool through secondary levels. Although Level 3 paraeducator assignments are always planned, directed, and monitored by teachers, there are fewer restrictions on the tasks these paraeducators may perform in all phases of the learning process. They function at higher levels of independence than Level 2 paraeducators because they frequently provide learning experiences in homes, vocational or school-to-work settings, and other community-based learning environments. They are active participants in activities that assist teachers with the inclusion of learners with disabilities in general education classrooms, and they tutor learners who have diverse educational needs to help them master academic skills. When properly trained they may administer some standardized tests following SEA, LEA, or other agency policies and the protocol for conducting the tests. (Licensed and certified professionals are always responsible for interpreting the results and determining how they apply to learner programs and needs.) Level 3 paraeducators, in consultation with teachers, may assist with modifying materials, equipment, and instructional activities to meet the needs of individual learners with different abilities, learning preferences, or language backgrounds. In several programs (e.g., multilingual, preschool, transition services, Title I), under the supervision of a teacher they provide information and support to parents. Moreover, Level 3 paraeducators often assist teachers with documenting and maintaining records about learner achievement, behavior, and attendance. Level 3 paraeducators participate in IFSP, IEP, and ITP meetings with other staff and parents. Tables 2.2, 2.3, and 2.4 list the scopes of responsibilities for the three levels of paraeducators.

Similarities and Differences in Teacher and Paraeducator Knowledge and Skill Competencies

Analyses and comparison of the survey results with various SEA policies, guidelines established by professional organizations, and the work of independent researchers found that some compe-

Table 2.2
Level 1 Paraeducator Responsibilities

The scope of responsibilities for Level 1 Paraeducators includes the following:

- escorting learners to buses and different learning environments
- monitoring playgrounds, lunchrooms, hallways, and study halls
- preparing learning materials and maintaining learning centers
- assisting learners with personal and hygienic care
- assisting teachers in maintaining supportive learning environments that protect the safety, health, and well-being of learners and staff
- reinforcing learning experiences planned and introduced by teachers
- practicing standards of professional and ethical conduct that are within the scope of paraeducator responsibilities

Note. Adapted from *Strengthening and Supporting Teacher/Provider–Paraeducator Teams: Guidelines for Paraeducator Roles, Supervision, and Preparation,* by A. L. Pickett, 1999, New York: National Resource Center for Paraprofessionals, Center for Advanced Study in Education, Graduate Center, City University of New York. Copyright 1999 by National Resource Center for Paraprofessionals. Adapted with permission.

Table 2.3
Level 2 Paraeducator Responsibilities

The scope of responsibilities for Level 2 paraeducators includes all of the responsibilities of Level 1 paraeducators, plus the following:

- instructing individual or small groups of learners following lesson plans developed by the teacher
- assisting individual learners with supplementary or independent study projects as assigned by the teacher
- assisting teachers with documenting learner performance using functional (informal) assessment activities
- sharing with teachers information that facilitates the planning process
- implementing behavior management plans for individual learners developed by teachers
- preparing learning and instructional materials and maintaining adaptive equipment
- assisting teachers in providing supportive learning environments that facilitate inclusion of learners with diverse learning needs and in protecting the safety, health, and well-being of learners and staff
- participating in regularly scheduled teacher and paraeducator meetings that may also include other team members
- maintaining, as directed by an occupational or physical therapist, nurse, or speech–language pathologist, adaptive equipment required by learners with physical and sensory disabilities or health-related needs

Note. Adapted from *Strengthening and Supporting Teacher/Provider–Paraeducator Teams: Guidelines for Paraeducator Roles, Supervision, and Preparation,* by A. L. Pickett, 1999, New York: National Resource Center for Paraprofessionals, Center for Advanced Study in Education, Graduate Center, City University of New York. Copyright 1999 by National Resource Center for Paraprofessionals. Adapted with permission.

tencies—that is, demonstrating professional, ethical, and legal standards of conduct—are essential for all team members. (Professional and ethical codes of ethics for teachers and paraeducators are described more fully in Chapter 7.) Other shared competencies that are stressed in the various sources include understanding of distinctions in teacher and paraeducator roles and functions in all areas of the instructional process, and teaming,

Table 2.4
Level 3 Paraeducator Responsibilities

The scope of responsibilities for Level 3 paraeducators includes all of the responsibilities for Levels 1 and 2 paraeducators, plus the following:

- consulting with teachers during regularly scheduled meetings to share information that will facilitate the planning of learning experiences for individual or groups of students with disabilities, English language limitations, or other learning needs that may place learners at risk
- administering standardized assessment instruments, which are then scored and analyzed by teachers or other professional practitioners
- implementing lesson and other plans developed by teachers to increase academic skills and the development of social and communication skills, self-esteem, and self-reliance
- modifying curriculum and instructional activities for individual learners, under the direction of teachers
- assisting teachers to engage families in their children's learning experiences
- supervising students in community-based learning environments to prepare them to make the transition from school to work and to participate in the adult world (if required by learner or program needs)
- familiarizing employers and other members of the community with the needs of individual learners (if required by the program or learner needs)
- assisting occupational and physical therapists, speech–language pathologists, and nurses to provide related services (if required by learner or program needs)
- assisting teachers to maintain learner records required by the state, district, or agency
- participating in IEP, ITP, and IFSP planning team meetings as required by learner needs

Note. Adapted from *Strengthening and Supporting Teacher/Provider–Paraeducator Teams: Guidelines for Paraeducator Roles, Supervision, and Preparation,* by A. L. Pickett, 1999, New York: National Resource Center for Paraprofessionals, Center for Advanced Study in Education, Graduate Center, City University of New York. Copyright 1999 by National Resource Center for Paraprofessionals. Adapted with permission.

problem-solving, and communication skills (communication and teaming skills are discussed in Chapter 5).

The primary differences in teacher and paraeducator competencies in the various program areas are that teacher competencies are more broad-based and theoretical, whereas paraeducator competencies are more general and applied. For example, in all program areas teachers and paraeducators are required to have knowledge of instructional methods and principles of behavior management. The depth and breadth of knowledge and the ways in which the knowledge is applied vary significantly for the two groups. Teachers are expected to have a thorough knowledge of the theories of language acquisition and of cognitive, physical, social, and emotional development upon which they base diagnostic and programmatic decisions for a class or individuals. Paraeducators are required to have a general, practical knowledge of patterns of human development as they relate to the needs of learners they work with and to be able to effectively use age-appropriate instructional and behavior management strategies developed and introduced by the teacher.

Knowledge and Skills Required by Teachers Who Supervise Paraeducators

In the Level 2 analysis of teacher and paraeducator roles and competencies, the responses to the survey were compared and contrasted with the competencies developed by the various stakeholders. As we have noted throughout this chapter, very few SEAs, LEAs, or professional organizations have established standards for the preparation of teachers and paraeducators as members of education teams. However, several researchers (Drecktrah, 2000; French, 2001; French & Pickett, 1997; Miramontes, 1990; Pickett, 1999; Pickett et al., 1993; Wallace et al., 2001) have identified competencies for teachers who work primarily in special education environments. The results of the NRCP survey indicate that there is a great deal of similarity in the skill and knowledge required by teachers who work in multilingual, compensatory, and other instructional environments and who supervise paraeducators. A few states, most notably Iowa, Rhode Island, and Utah, have established standards for the supervision of paraeducators. Only Minnesota and Washington require as part of their licensure systems that special education teachers be trained to supervise paraeducators.

The quality of day-to-day supervision has a direct impact on the effectiveness of the team effort. The team will not effectively achieve instructional goals for the class or an individual unless assignments are prepared and communicated in advance to paraeducators; on-the-job coaching provides paraeducators with information about the needs of learners, the strategies that will be used to meet these needs, and the materials and equipment needed to carry out activities; and paraeducators' performance is systematically monitored and feedback provided. Table 2.5 contains knowledge and skill standards required by teachers to effectively supervise paraeducators. The six competency standards are aligned with the six teacher responsibilities listed in Table 2.1.

(*text continues on p. 72*)

Table 2.5

Standards for Teacher Supervisory Competencies

Standard 1: To supervise paraeducators, teachers demonstrate the following.

Knowledge Standards

K1	Understanding the value of a team approach in the delivery of services.
K2	Understanding of the distinctions in teacher and administrator roles in the employment, management, supervision, evaluation, and preparation of paraeducators.
K3	Understanding of distinctions in the roles and responsibilities of teachers and paraeducators.
K4	Awareness of the contributions that paraeducators make to increasing the availability of individualized learning experiences and services.
K5	Awareness of federal and state laws and regulations, as well as district or agency policies and practices, that influence the employment, roles and responsibilities, supervision, and preparation of paraeducators.
K6	Understanding of the responsibilities of teachers for supervising paraeducators in program implementation teams.
K7	Awareness of district or agency policies that may require paraeducators to participate on program planning teams.
K8	Awareness of interactive, problem-solving, and decision-making techniques that build and maintain effective teams.

(*continues*)

Table 2.5 *Continued.*

Standard 1 *Continued.*

Skill Standards

S1 Ability to plan work assignments for paraeducators based on program requirements and learning objectives for individuals and groups.

S2 Ability to appropriately delegate tasks to paraeducators based on their qualifications to carry out an assignment.

S3 Ability to share information with paraeducators about their roles as members of program planning teams as required by district or agency policies, as well as the roles of other team members, including families, in the development of learner goals.

S4 Ability to monitor the day-to-day performance of paraeducators and to provide principals or agency administrators with relevant information about the strengths and professional development needs of paraeducators.

S5 Ability to provide systematic on-the-job training and mentoring to paraeducators.

Standard 2: To ensure that paraeducators contribute to learner-centered, supportive environments, teachers demonstrate the following.

Knowledge Standards

K1 Understanding of the contributions that paraeducators make to serving children and youth in supportive, learner-centered environments.

K2 Awareness of district or agency and state and local governmental policies and procedures for reporting suspected physical, sexual, and psychological child abuse.

K3 Awareness of effective strategies for involving families in all aspects of their child's learning experiences.

K4 Awareness of distinctions in teacher and paraeducator responsibilities for sharing information with families about learner performance, and engaging families in their children's learning experiences.

Skill Standards

S1 Ability to share and reinforce information with paraeducators about federal, state, and local policies and procedures that ensure the safety, health, and well-being of learners and staff.

S2 Ability to appropriately involve paraeducators in activities that engage families in their children's learning experiences.

(continues)

Table 2.5 *Continued.*

Standard 2 *Continued.*

S3 Ability to model interactive skills that demonstrate respect for the views, rights, and contributions of children and youth, families, and school or agency personnel.

Standard 3: To appropriately involve paraeducators in assisting with planning and organizing learning experiences, teachers demonstrate the following.

Knowledge Standards

K1 Understanding of the distinctions in teacher and paraeducator roles in diagnosing learning needs, developing lesson plans, modifying learning activities for individuals, and identifying appropriate materials, equipment, and technology.

K2 Understanding of how the life experiences of paraeducators who come from diverse cultural, ethnic, and language heritages may contribute to planning and organizing learning experiences and environments.

K3 Understanding of how paraeducator familiarity with the needs and circumstances of families whose children have disabilities or other special needs may contribute to planning and organizing learning experiences and environments.

Skill Standards

S1 Ability to appropriately involve paraeducators in the planning of individualized learning experiences and organizing environments to promote learning.

Standard 4: To involve paraeducators in learning experiences, teachers demonstrate the following.

Knowledge Standards

K1 Understanding of differences and similarities in teacher and paraeducator roles and responsibilities in facilitating the learning process.

K2 Understanding of how different cultural heritages, ability and developmental levels, and other characteristics of children and youth impact their learning styles and preferences.

K3 Awareness of various learning strategies, materials, adaptive equipment, and assistive technologies that are required to meet the needs of individual children and youth.

Skill Standards

S1 Ability to share information with paraeducators about learning objectives for individual children and youth.

(continues)

Table 2.5 *Continued.*

Standard 4 *Continued.*

S2 Ability to provide on-the-job training to prepare paraeducators to follow learning plans developed by the teacher and to use methods, materials, adaptive equipment, and assistive technology selected or developed by the teacher.

Standard 5: To appropriately involve paraeducators in assessing the learning needs of children and youth, teachers demonstrate the following.

Knowledge Standards

K1 Awareness of the distinctions among teachers, other licensed district or agency professionals, and paraeducator roles and responsibilities in the assessment process.

K2 Understanding of the skills required by paraeducators to objectively gather information and report on the performance and achievement of individual children and youth.

Skill Standards

S1 Ability to provide on-the-job training to prepare Level 2 and 3 paraeducators to use functional (informal) assessment tools and to objectively share relevant information about learner strengths and needs.

S2 Ability to appropriately involve Level 3 paraeducators in administering standardized achievement tests based on state, district, and agency policies; the protocol for conducting a test; and the paraeducators' qualifications to carry out the task.

S3 Ability to prepare paraeducators to assist with record-keeping activities based on district or agency policies and procedures.

Standard 6: To ensure that professional and ethical standards connected with the supervision of paraeducators are met, teachers demonstrate the following.

Knowledge Standards

K1 Awareness of the human, civil, and legal rights of all children and youth and their families, and the responsibilities of all district or agency staff for respecting and protecting these rights.

K2 Understanding of the ethical and professional standards of conduct established by the discipline-appropriate professional organization, state, and district for the selection, supervision, assessment, and preparation of paraeducators.

K3 Understanding of appropriate roles and responsibilities of paraeducators in the learning process and delivery of other direct services to children, youth, and their families.

(continues)

Table 2.5 *Continued.*

Standard 6 *Continued.*

K4	Awareness of resources and opportunities for professional development to improve team leadership and supervisory skills of paraeducators.
Skill Standards	
S1	Ability to follow standards of professional and ethical conduct for the supervision, assessment, and preparation of paraeducators established by the discipline-appropriate professional organization, state, and district.
S2	Ability to model standards of professional and ethical conduct for paraeducators (i.e., maintaining confidentiality; respecting rights of children, youth, and families; demonstrating sensitivity to diversity in culture, ethnicity, family structure, learning styles, and abilities).

Note. Adapted from *Strengthening and Supporting Teacher/Provider–Paraeducator Teams: Guidelines for Paraeducator Roles, Supervision, and Preparation,* by A. L. Pickett, 1999, New York: National Resource Center for Paraprofessionals, Center for Advanced Study in Education, Graduate Center, City University of New York. Copyright 1999 by National Resource Center for Paraprofessionals. Adapted with permission.

The paraeducator knowledge and skill competencies in Table 2.6 are aligned with the three levels of paraeducator positions contained in the paraeducator scopes of responsibilities presented in Tables 2.2, 2.3, and 2.4. Tables 2.5 and 2.6 reflect the differences between teacher and paraeducator competencies required by the functional capacities of their positions.

The final step in the process was to develop a core curriculum for paraeducators (see Table 2.7). The training domains in the curriculum are designed to ensure that paraeducators have access to an articulated system of inservice or academic preparation that will enable them to advance through the various levels of paraeducator positions based on personal career goals and program needs. This curriculum can serve as a model that SEAs, LEAs, and other education provider agencies can use as a basis for developing job-embedded coaching and standardized, systematic inservice training for paraeducators. Although the training topics remain the same for the three position levels, course content is developed to meet the needs of paraeducators who work at higher levels of independence and require more complex

(*text continues on p. 80*)

Table 2.6

Standards for Paraeducator Knowledge and Skill Competencies[a]

Standard 1: To serve as members of program implementation teams, paraeducators demonstrate the following.

Knowledge Standards

LEVEL 1 PARAEDUCATORS

K1 Understanding of the value of a team approach to the delivery of education and related services for learners and their families.

K2 Understanding of the distinctions in teacher and administrator roles in the employment, supervision, management, evaluation, and preparation of paraeducators.

K3 Awareness of federal, state, and district or agency policies, regulations, and practices connected with paraeducator employment, roles, supervision, and preparation.

K4 Awareness of interactive techniques that contribute to effective participation in program implementation teams.

LEVEL 2 PARAEDUCATORS

All of Level 1 standards, plus the following:

K5 Understanding of the distinctions in the roles and responsibilities of teachers, families, paraeducators, and other team members in identifying learner needs, developing plans to meet learner needs, and implementing programs to achieve learner goals.

LEVEL 3 PARAEDUCATORS

All of Level 1 and 2 standards, plus the following:

K6 Awareness of problem-solving and decision-making strategies that strengthen program planning teams and program implementation teams.

Skill Standards

LEVEL 1 PARAEDUCATORS

S1 Ability to follow teacher instructions and carry out team decisions.

S2 Ability to interact constructively with and demonstrate respect for learners, families, and other school or agency personnel.

LEVEL 2 PARAEDUCATORS

All of Level 1 standards, plus the following:

S3 Ability to contribute relevant objective information to teachers to facilitate planning, problem solving, and decision making.

(continues)

Table 2.6 *Continued.*

Standard 1 *Continued.*

LEVEL 3 PARAEDUCATORS

All of Level 1 and 2 standards, plus the following:

S4 Ability to participate in program planning team meetings, when required by program, district, or agency policies and procedures; and to prepare IEPs and ITPs for school-age students who have disabilities or IFSPs for young children and their parents.

Standard 2: To assist in maintaining learner-centered, supportive environments, paraeducators demonstrate the following.

Knowledge Standards

LEVEL 1 AND 2 PARAEDUCATORS

K1 Understanding of the value of serving all children and youth in supportive, inclusive learning environments.

K2 Understanding of the distinctions and similarities in teacher and paraeducator roles and responsibilities for creating and maintaining supportive and inclusive learning environments.

K3 Awareness of district or agency procedures for protecting the safety, health, and well-being of learners and staff.

K4 Awareness of district or agency policies and procedures for disciplining all children and youth.

K5 Awareness of district policies, procedures, and methods for managing learner behaviors that are disruptive or aggressive.

LEVEL 3 PARAEDUCATORS

All of Level 1 and 2 standards, plus the following:

K6 Awareness of distinctions in teacher and paraeducator roles in involving families in their children's learning experiences.

K7 Understanding of strategies that support families and strengthen their ability to assist their children with learning activities, and encourage their participation in the learning process.

Skill Standards

LEVEL 1 AND 2 PARAEDUCATORS

S1 Ability to implement proactive, teacher-developed behavior and learning strategies that maintain supportive and inclusive learning environments.

(continues)

Table 2.6 *Continued.*

Standard 2 *Continued.*

S2 Ability to follow and use prescribed district or agency policies and procedures to ensure the safety, health, and well-being of learners and staff.

S3 Ability to use universal health precautions for preventing illnesses and infections and proper body mechanics for lifting learners and heavy objects.

S4 Ability to perform emergency first aid and CPR (cardiopulmonary resuscitation) procedures.

LEVEL 3 PARAEDUCATORS

All of Level 1 and 2 standards, plus the following:

S5 Ability to carry out teacher plans to enhance family interactions with infants and young children that facilitate physical, social, language, and cognitive development, and to share information about community support services and resources.

S6 Ability to carry out teacher plans to support and share information with families about community services and resources available to students making the transition to the workforce, postsecondary education, and the adult world.

S7 Ability to provide translation services for families with limited English proficiency and follow teacher plans to support and encourage family participation in their children's learning environment.

Standard 3: To assist with planning and organizing activities, paraeducators demonstrate the following.

Knowledge Standards

LEVEL 1 PARAEDUCATORS

K1 Understanding of the value of organized environments that facilitate and promote learning.

K2 Awareness of resources and equipment for duplicating and preparing learning materials developed by teachers.

LEVEL 2 PARAEDUCATORS

All of Level 1 standards, plus the following:

K3 Understanding of the distinctions in teacher and paraeducator roles in developing curriculum content, learning strategies, and modifying learning programs to meet the needs of individual and groups of children and youth.

(continues)

Table 2.6 *Continued.*

Standard 3 *Continued.*

LEVEL 3 PARAEDUCATORS

All of Level 1 and 2 standards, plus the following:

K4 Understanding of district, agency, or school procedures for maintaining accurate records.

Skill Standards

LEVEL 1 PARAEDUCATORS

S1 Ability to use copy machines, computers, and other assistive technology that facilitates learning.

LEVEL 2 PARAEDUCATORS

All of Level 1 standards, plus the following:

S2 Ability to assist physical therapists, occupational therapists, speech–language pathologists, and nurses to maintain adaptive equipment for learners with disabilities.

S3 Ability to objectively gather and report relevant information about learners to assist the planning process.

LEVEL 3 PARAEDUCATORS

All of Level 1 and 2 standards, plus the following:

S4 Ability to assist teachers with modifying learning materials and activities to meet the needs of individuals with different ability levels, learning styles, or language backgrounds.

S5 Ability to assist teachers with maintaining accurate records.

Standard 4: To assist children and youth in learning experiences, paraeducators demonstrate the following.

Knowledge Standards

LEVEL 1 PARAEDUCATORS

K1 Understanding of the rationale, mission, philosophy, and goals of the program to which the paraeducator is assigned.

K2 Awareness of the distinctions in teacher and paraeducator roles in engaging children and youth in learning experiences.

K3 Understanding of the distinctions in the roles and responsibilities of teachers and paraeducators in the development and implementation of behavior intervention plans.

K4 Awareness of different methods used by teachers to accommodate an individual's learning needs.

(*continues*)

Table 2.6 *Continued.*

Standard 4 *Continued.*

K5	Awareness of developmentally and age-appropriate reinforcement techniques that facilitate the learning of children and youth with different needs.
K6	Understanding of state and district rules and procedural safeguards regarding the management of behaviors of individual learners.
K7	Understanding of basic principles of proactive behavior management strategies that increase learner independence, motivation, and self-esteem.
K8	Understanding of effective strategies for dealing with verbal aggression and other forms of resistance.
K9	Understanding of how the purposeful utilization of technology can promote learning.
LEVEL 2 PARAEDUCATORS	
All of Level 1 standards, plus the following:	
K10	Understanding of different strategies used by teachers to support learners who come from different ethnic, cultural, and language backgrounds.
K11	Understanding of how various assistive and adaptive devices and materials facilitate learning and inclusion for children and youth with developmental, physical, and sensory disabilities and those who are medically fragile.
K12	Awareness of patterns of cognitive, physical, social, emotional, and language development typically achieved at different ages and factors that prohibit or impede typical development.
K13	Awareness of the impact of different learning styles or preferences on the performance of individual children and youth.
LEVEL 3 PARAEDUCATORS	
All of Level 1 and 2 standards, plus the following:	
K14	Understanding of the purpose and need for learning and performance standards.
K15	Understanding of validated practices for working with individuals with severe and challenging behaviors.
Skill Standards	
LEVEL 1 PARAEDUCATORS	
S1	Proficiency in basic reading, math, and writing.
S2	Proficiency in English and, if required by program or learner needs, other languages.
S3	Ability to develop and maintain effective interactions with all learners.

(*continues*)

Table 2.6 *Continued.*

Standard 4 *Continued.*

S4 Ability to carry out teacher-developed proactive behavioral strategies.

S5 Ability to use developmentally and age-appropriate reinforcement and other learning activities developed by teachers.

S6 Ability to use teacher-developed positive behavioral strategies and procedures that facilitate the learning of children.

S7 Ability to monitor and assist children and youth in other learning environments (e.g., libraries, computer labs, lunchrooms, playgrounds, buses).

LEVEL 2 PARAEDUCATORS

All of Level 1 and 2 standards, plus the following:

S8 Ability to carry out teacher-developed behavioral strategies that increase learner independence, motivation, and self-esteem.

S9 Ability to use teacher-developed behavioral strategies and procedures that facilitate the learning of children and youth with challenging behaviors.

S10 Ability to follow and carry out teacher plans for strengthening academic skills for school-age learners.

S11 Ability to carry out teacher plans for developmentally appropriate learning activities for infants and children.

S12 Ability to preview lessons in native languages to ensure that English language learners understand instructions and concepts.

S13 Ability to use teacher-developed learning strategies for English language learners.

S14 Ability (based on state and local policies) to assist nurses with administering medications, tube feedings, and other procedures required by learners who have special health care needs.

LEVEL 3 PARAEDUCATORS

All of Level 1 and 2 standards, plus the following:

S15 Ability to assist teacher in implementing advanced behavioral strategies to facilitate learning of children and youth with challenging behaviors and promote an orderly and safe learning environment for all.

S16 Ability to carry out teacher-developed plans in community-based vocational and transitional programs for students entering the workforce.

S17 Ability to carry out teacher plans in home- and center-based environments that support families of infants and toddlers

(*continues*)

Table 2.6 *Continued.*

Standard 4 *Continued.*	
	with disabilities and increase their ability to interact with their children.
S18	Ability to assist physical and occupational therapists and speech–language pathologists with the delivery of related services based on the qualifications of the paraeducators to carry out their assigned tasks.

[a] This list includes standards for only the first four of six responsibility areas discussed in the text.

Note. Adapted from *Strengthening and Supporting Teacher/Provider–Paraeducator Teams: Guidelines for Paraeducator Roles, Supervision, and Preparation,* by A. L. Pickett, 1999, New York: National Resource Center for Paraprofessionals, Center for Advanced Study in Education, Graduate Center, City University of New York. Copyright 1999 by National Resource Center for Paraprofessionals. Adapted with permission.

Table 2.7

A Core Curriculum for Paraeducators

1. Strengthening the instructional team
   - Distinctions in roles and duties of teachers or service providers and paraeducators
   - Interactive and problem-solving techniques
2. Legal and human rights of learners and their families or caregivers
3. Human growth and development
4. The learning process
   - Learning and lesson plans
   - IEPs, IFSPs, ITPs
   - Documenting learner performance and other assessment activities
   - Maintaining learner-centered environments
   - Behavior management strategies
   - Instructional methods for learners with diverse needs
5. Appreciating diversity
6. Working with families
7. Emergency, health, and safety procedures

Note. Adapted from *Strengthening and Supporting Teacher/Provider–Paraeducator Teams: Guidelines for Paraeducator Roles, Supervision, and Preparation,* by A. L. Pickett, 1999, New York: National Resource Center for Paraprofessionals, Center for Advanced Study in Education, Graduate Center, City University of New York. Copyright 1999 by National Resource Center for Paraprofessionals. Adapted with permission.

knowledge and skills. The core curriculum is flexible enough to serve as a framework for developing community college certificate or associate's degree programs for paraeducators. Additional information on professional development and training models is contained in Chapter 6.

In the text that follows, several models of competency-based personnel development for teachers and paraeducators are highlighted. They include a model developed by the National Association for the Education of Young Children (NAEYC), two models aimed at improving the preparation of transition services providers, and a competency-based model developed by the National Joint Committee on Learning Disabilities (NJCLD, 1999) with guidelines for teacher and paraeducator roles as team members in programs for learners with special needs.

An Early Childhood Model

A conceptual framework developed by the NAEYC (1994) provides a model designed to promote "a coordinated, articulated system of high-quality early childhood professional preparation and development" (p. 77). This position statement identified key assumptions, guiding principles, and a body of knowledge and skill competencies to be used in personnel preparation at levels ranging from entry-level paraeducator to doctoral-level professional. The NAEYC identified the common core elements required for all early childhood personnel, and established guidelines for expanding and adding depth to the core competencies for all early childhood personnel to include areas of specialization such as administration, parent education, and human development. The core competencies, listed in Table 2.8, are used as a foundation upon which to build personnel development programs at various levels. Personnel at the *entry level,* with a Child Development Associate (CDA) credential, demonstrate "competency to meet the specific needs of children and to work with parents and other adults to nurture children's physical, social, emotional and intellectual growth" (NAEYC, 1994, p. 72); personnel at the *associate level* are able to work independently with groups of children; those at the *baccalaureate level* can apply and analyze the knowledge to plan and develop curriculum and instructional activities; and those at the *doctoral level* conduct research contributing to best practices in an emerging body of knowledge.

Table 2.8
Core Competency Domains for Early Childhood Professionals

1. Demonstrating an understanding of child development and applying this knowledge in practice
2. Observing and assessing of child behavior
3. Establishing and maintaining safe and healthy environments for children
4. Planning and implementing developmentally appropriate curriculum
5. Establishing supportive relationships with children
6. Implementing developmentally appropriate guidance and group management techniques
7. Establishing and maintaining positive and productive relationships with families
8. Supporting the development and learning of individual children in the context of family, culture, and society
9. Demonstrating an understanding of the early childhood profession and making a commitment to professionalism

Note. From "NAEYC Position Statement: A Conceptual Framework for Early Childhood Professional Development," by National Association for the Education of Young Children, 1994, *Young Children, 49*(3), pp. 68–77. Copyright 1994 by the National Association for the Education of Young Children. Adapted with permission.

The NAEYC model also includes a continuum of personnel development that has six levels of early childhood professional preparation programs for which standards have been established nationally. Levels I through III are comparable to paraeducator models developed by other professions and occupations that recognize formal education levels below a baccalaureate degree. (The three levels are also similar to the three paraeducator levels described in this chapter.) The entry level requires supervision or enrollment in a supervised practicum, Level II requires the successful completion of a 1-year early childhood certificate program, and Level III requires the successful completion of an associate's degree program that conforms to the NAEYC guidelines.

Transition Services Models

Transition services, aimed at preparing and supporting students for moving from school to work and independent adult life, is an area within education that reflects significant changes in the traditional role of educator or human service provider (deFur & Taymans, 1995). With an emphasis on coordination, facilitation, and an interdisciplinary approach, this discipline requires competence in domains that have not been widely recognized for teacher effectiveness. Because transition services are by definition cross-disciplinary, the need for role clarification is particularly important. The use of consultative collaboration is a useful model for integrating the work of licensed and certified transition specialists and paraeducators. Gajar, Goodman, and McAffee (1993) described the process as "an interactive process which enables people with diverse expertise to generate creative solutions to mutually defined problems. The outcome is enhanced, altered, and produces solutions that are different from those that the individual team members would produce independently" (p. 61). The model relies on the systematic coordination of services, stressing an individualized, holistic approach to services and instruction, and personnel are not limited to prescribed functions.

DeFur and Taymans (1995) identified competency domains for transition services professionals, which are listed in Table 2.9. When individual competencies were ranked, those relating to coordination, communication, and collaboration were among the highest required by professional personnel. The direct services competencies, such as those involving instruction, curriculum, and learning theory, were ranked lowest. The authors suggested, "Perhaps these areas constitute specialty areas where a school working knowledge of these skills is needed by the transition services practitioner, but the direct application of these important skills is performed by someone else" (p. 46). This statement indicates a team approach to staff differentiation, involving the licensed transition service specialist as a facilitator with paraeducators within and outside the LEA contributing in various capacities.

Safarik et al. (1991), in a similar study, identified competencies for paraeducator transition service providers who were at various stages of training and career development. Their work

Table 2.9
Core Competencies for Transition Services Personnel

1. Knowledge of systems change
2. Development and management of Individualized Transition Plans
3. Working with others in the transition process
4. Vocational assessment and job development
5. Professionalism, advocacy, and legal issues
6. Job training and support
7. Assessment (general)

Note. Adapted from "Competencies Needed for Transition Specialists in Vocational Rehabilitation, Vocational Education and Special Education," by S. H. deFur and J. M. Taymans, 1995, *Exceptional Children, 62*(1), pp. 38–51. Copyright 1995 by the Council for Exce-ptional Children. Adapted with permission.

was based on prior research (Morehouse & Albright, 1991) that identified competencies for transition services paraeducators as reported by 95 paraeducators and 45 administrators in schools and agencies serving Southern California youth and adults with disabilities. Safarik et al. used a three-phase competency validation process. A national panel of 18 experts who represented secondary and 2- and 4-year IHEs that provided training for transition services personnel reviewed the original set of competencies developed by the research team. A sample of 21 practitioners (paraeducators enrolled in a university training program) was surveyed to identify (a) criticality, (b) relative time spent using the competencies, and (c) perceived need for training in each of the competencies. The study yielded 54 competencies that were organized into eight categories (the categories are listed in Table 2.10).

The purpose of Safarik et al.'s (1991) study was to develop a comprehensive curriculum for paraeducators at three training levels: secondary, community college, and university. (Training at the secondary level included vocational training and inservice education typically provided by regional occupation programs and centers that serve both high school students and adults in California.) Reviewers were asked to identify competencies as *essential, important, somewhat important,* or *not important* for each

Table 2.10
Competency Categories for All Transition Services Personnel

1. Foundations of transition services
2. Assessing transition program needs
3. Assessing learner needs
4. Planning transition programs for special needs learners
5. Implementing training and instructional components
6. Job development and placement
7. Job site training and instruction
8. Developing professional skills

Note. Adapted from *A Career Ladder Program for Transition Services Personnel: A Collaborative Curriculum Development Approach,* by L. Safarik et al., 1991, Long Beach: California State University at Long Beach. Adapted with permission.

level. The three training levels corresponded roughly to three levels of personnel: entry-level paraeducators were trained at the secondary level for positions such as job coach; mid-level training occurred at the community college level; and professional-level training was conducted at the university for roles such as transition coordinator or specialist.

Paraeducators training to become certified transition services specialists at the professional level complete a bachelor's degree program encompassing the entire range of competencies. Articulated programs at the entry and mid-levels emphasize applied competencies. The curriculum for training transition services paraeducators uses the competency differentiation framework shown in Table 2.11.

Certain competencies (developing management skills; program evaluation skills; participating in local, state, and national professional organization activities) are essential at only the professional level. In competency areas such as implementing training or instructional activities, the collaborative role is emphasized at all levels. Assessment and program planning functions are *essential* training areas for professionals but are *important* or *somewhat important* at entry and mid-levels. In other categories, such as job development and placement and on-site and community training, training in the implementation

Table 2.11
Transition Services Competencies for Entry-Level and Mid-Level Paraprofessionals and Professionals

Transition services foundations	Entry level	Mid-level	Professional level
1. Demonstrate knowledge of the unique transition service of individuals with disabilities.	E	E	E
2. Demonstrate knowledge of the professional, ethical, and legal standards of conduct in relationships with students, parents, school personnel, adult service providers, clients, employers, and coworkers.	E	E	E
3. Compare and contrast the theoretical models and current practices for providing transition services to youth and adults with disabilities.	I	I	E
4. Identify, describe, and differentiate between various systems, agencies, businesses, communities, their use of terms, and the roles of personnel that participate in the transition process.	I	I	E
5. Demonstrate communication, conflict resolution, and negotiation skills that facilitate inter- and intraagency collaboration.	I	I	I
6. Demonstrate knowledge of the legislative history and current mandates that address the provision of transitional services and the rights and entitlement of students or clients with disabilities and their families.	S	S	E

E = essential, I = important, S = somewhat important.

Note. Adapted from *A Career Ladder Program for Transition Services Personnel: A Collaborative Curriculum Development Approach,* by L. Safarik et al., 1991, Long Beach: California State University at Long Beach. Adapted with permission.

of behavior management, data collection, instruction, and task analysis is essential at the mid-level (community college) for paraeducators. Conceptually this approach assumes that the professional must be competent in all areas but, as a facilitator, is likely to be less involved in instruction and delivery of other direct services. However, paraeducators who provide transition services must be competent in providing instruction and other direct services at work sites and other community learning environments.

A Model for Preparing Paraeducators To Work with School-Age Learners with Special Needs

In 1999, the NJCLD, with a membership of 10 professional organizations representing a cross-section of education and related services disciplines, issued guidelines for the supervision of paraprofessionals and competency recommendations for two levels of paraprofessional positions. The agreed upon supervisory roles and competencies for teachers and other practitioners are listed in Table 2.12. The recommended core competencies for paraprofessionals employed in different education and related services programs are found in Table 2.13.

The NJCLD identified appropriate responsibilities for paraprofessionals in two position levels. The entry level is for paraprofessionals who have a high school diploma or GED, or equivalent training and experience, and who may do the following: (a) assist with informal documentation, prepare materials, and assist with other clerical duties as directed by the supervising teacher; (b) prepare charts, records, or graphs, or otherwise display data; (c) perform checks and maintenance of equipment; and (d) implement instructional assistance activities under the direction of a qualified supervising teacher. Paraprofessionals who have a community college associate's degree may perform the following higher level activities that supplement the work of teachers and licensed related services professionals: (a) conducting screenings (but not interpreting results) following specified screening protocols; (b) assisting in providing supplementary work or reinforcing learning in small groups or with individuals; (c) recording student progress toward meeting established objectives as stated in the IEP and reporting the information to the supervising teacher; (d) providing direct supplemental instruction or intervention services as identified and directed by the su-

Table 2.12
Responsibilities of the Qualified Teacher or Service Provider with Regard to Paraprofessional Supervision

For effective use of a paraprofessional, the supervising teacher or service provider should

1. Participate in supervision training prior to using a paraprofessional and upgrade supervision knowledge and skills on a regular basis.
2. Participate significantly in the hiring of the paraprofessional for whom he or she will be responsible.
3. Inform the family and student about the level (professional vs. paraprofessional), frequency, and duration of services, as well as the extent of supervision.
4. Review each individual plan with the paraprofessional at least weekly.
5. Delegate specific tasks to the paraprofessional while retaining legal and ethical responsibility for all services provided or omitted.
6. Sign all formal documents (e.g., individual plans, reports).
7. Review and sign all informal progress notes prepared by the paraprofessional.
8. Provide ongoing on-the-job training for the paraprofessional.
9. Provide and document appropriate supervision of the paraprofessional.
10. Ensure that the paraprofessional performs only tasks within the scope of the paraprofessional's responsibility.
11. Participate in the performance appraisal of the paraprofessional for whom he or she is responsible.

Note. Adapted from "Learning Disabilities: Use of Paraprofessionals," by National Joint Committee on Learning Disabilities, 1999 (Winter), *Learning Disability Quarterly, 22,* pp. 23–28. Copyright 1999 by the Council for Learning Disabilities. Adapted with permission.

pervising teacher; and (e) using positive behavior supports consistent with those used by the supervising teacher.

In addition to these models, the Association for Education and Rehabilitation for the Blind and Visually Impaired (Wiener et al., 1990) has established guidelines for the supervision of orientation and mobility assistants. The AERBVI also recognizes roles and responsibilities for assistants that are similar to the entry-level

Table 2.13

Recommended Competencies for Paraprofessionals

Following are basic competencies needed by paraprofessionals employed in programs serving individuals with learning disabilities.

I. Interpersonal Skills
   A. Deals effectively with attitudes and behaviors of the individual with learning disabilities.
      1. Maintains appropriate relationships.
      2. Is sensitive to the cultural values of the student and family.
      3. Takes into proper consideration the individual's strengths and needs.
      4. Demonstrates an appropriate level of self-confidence when performing assigned tasks.
      5. Demonstrates insight into attitudes and behaviors.
      6. Directs the individual, family, and professionals to supervisor for information regarding testing, services, and referral.
   B. Uses appropriate language (written and oral) in dealing with the individual with learning disabilities and others.
      1. Uses language appropriate for the individual's and others' age and educational levels.
      2. Is courteous and respectful at all times.
      3. Maintains appropriate social interaction.
   C. Deals effectively with supervisor.
      1. Is receptive to constructive criticism.
      2. Requests assistance from supervisor as needed.
      3. Actively participates in interaction with supervisor.

II. Personal Qualities
   A. Manages time effectively.
      1. Arrives punctually and prepared for appointments.
      2. Arrives punctually for work-related meetings (e.g., meetings with supervisor, staff, etc.).
      3. Turns in all documentation on time.
   B. Demonstrates appropriate conduct.
      1. Respects and maintains confidentiality of the individual and family.
      2. Maintains personal appearance appropriate for the work setting.
      3. Uses appropriate language for the work setting.
      4. Evaluates own performance.
      5. Recognizes own professional limitations and performs within boundaries of training and job responsibilities.

(continues)

Table 2.13 *Continued.*

III. Technical Skills
A. Maintains a facilitating environment for assigned tasks.
1. Adjusts lighting and controls noise level.
2. Organizes work space.
B. Uses time effectively.
1. Performs assigned tasks with no unnecessary distractions.
2. Completes assigned tasks within designated time.
C. Prepares and presents materials effectively.
1. Selects materials ahead of time.
2. Uses appropriate materials based on the individual plan.

Note. Adapted from "Learning Disabilities: Use of Paraprofessionals," by National Joint Committee on Learning Disabilities, 1999 (Winter), *Learning Disability Quarterly, 22,* pp. 23–28. Copyright 1999 by the Council for Learning Disabilities. Adapted with permission.

guidelines for paraeducators established by the NJCLD. The Council for Exceptional Children (2000) and several researchers (Killoran et al., 2001; Miramontes, 1990; Office of Education Research and Improvement, 1990; Pickett, 1999; Pickett, Faison, & Formanek, 1999; Pickett, Faison, Formanek, & Semrau, 1999; Pickett et al., 1998; Snodgrass, 1991; Wallace et al., 2001) also have developed guidelines for roles and responsibilities and supervision of paraeducators who work in multilingual and multicultural learning environments, Title I and other compensatory programs, and early childhood education.

Summary

Working together, paraeducators, teachers, and other licensed professionals can be a powerful team. When roles and responsibilities are not clearly defined, however, the best efforts of the team are compromised and result in a poor quality of services that do not meet the needs of children and youth. The benefits of establishing scopes of responsibilities for teachers and paraeducators and defining the competencies they require are quality programs and improved opportunities for career development. A cross-disciplinary approach to the training and professional development of paraeducators is a natural outgrowth of the movement toward integrated education services that characterizes recent education reform efforts. Finding a common ground for paraeducator competencies forms the basis for designing comprehensive systems of on-the-job training and formal inservice and postsecondary personnel development programs in education, human services, and related services career areas. As the supervisory competencies for teachers and paraeducator competencies as team members are refined and existing training models are improved, policymakers, program administrators, and personnel developers will be better equipped to ensure the availability of a highly skilled education workforce.

Discussion Questions

1. What are the program and administrative functions typically performed by teachers and other professional practitioners in education, transitional, and early childhood services?
2. What are the teacher responsibilities that may not be delegated to paraeducators?
3. What are the teacher responsibilities that may be shared with paraeducators?
4. Are there any responsibilities that are the sole responsibility of paraeducators?
5. Do any programs in your SEA, LEA, or other agency have an identifiable hierarchy of knowledge and skill competencies for paraeducators?
6. Is there a core curriculum in your state for paraeducators? Is it linked to a comprehensive system of career development for paraeducators that includes standardized, competency-based training linked to career advancement for paraeducators?
7. Does your state's licensure or credentialing system recognize the need to prepare teachers to plan for, direct, and monitor paraeducators? If not, does the state have standards or written policies that are part of its administrative guidelines?

EXERCISES

1. Divide participants into groups of five or six. Using Worksheet 2.1, the Teacher and Paraeducator Role Perception Activity, discuss the various tasks with your group to determine whether a specific task is performed exclusively by a teacher or is a shared responsibility. Be prepared to share the results of this activity with the entire class.

2. Working as a group, brainstorm a list of education provider agencies in your community or state that offer programs to learners of different ages and diverse needs.

3. Arrange for individual members of your group to visit early childhood, elementary, middle, and secondary programs serving children and youth to observe and interview teacher–paraeducator teams about their roles and responsibilities, their training needs, and the personnel practices in the district, building, or agency that supports their work as instructional teams.

4. Working as a group, obtain examples of job descriptions for paraeducators from early childhood provider agencies, one or more local school districts, and vocational or school-to-work programs or agencies. Review the job descriptions to determine whether the supervisory responsibility has been established and whether duties that are solely the responsibilities of the supervisors are established. Compare and contrast the similarities and differences in the tasks assigned to paraeducators in the different program areas. Use the three levels of paraeducator positions described in this chapter to determine to which level the tasks contained in the job descriptions should be assigned. Identify the skill and knowledge competencies required by paraeducators working in the different programs.

WORKSHEET 2.1

Teacher and Paraeducator Role Perception Activity

Directions: Discuss the following tasks with the members of your group. When the group reaches consensus about whether a task should be performed exclusively by teachers or shared with paraeducators, place an X in the appropriate box.

Task	Teacher	Shared
1. Recording and charting data about learner performance	☐	☐
2. Administering standardized tests	☐	☐
3. Scoring standardized tests	☐	☐
4. Grading tests and papers	☐	☐
5. Analyzing and interpreting results of various assessment activities	☐	☐
6. Setting goals and objectives for class and individual learners	☐	☐
7. Planning lessons	☐	☐
8. Introducing new skills or concepts	☐	☐
9. Modifying or adapting instructional plans for individual learners	☐	☐
10. Carrying out lesson plans	☐	☐
11. Instructing individual or small groups of learners	☐	☐
12. Developing behavior management plans	☐	☐
13. Implementing behavior management programs	☐	☐
14. Disciplining students	☐	☐
15. Developing instructional materials	☐	☐
16. Preparing instructional materials	☐	☐
17. Evaluating learner performance and progress	☐	☐

(*continues*)

WORKSHEET 2.1 *Continued.*

Task	Teacher	Shared
18. Conducting training in community learning sites	☐	☐
19. Recording attendance and maintaining other records	☐	☐
20. Setting up and maintaining learning centers and adaptive equipment	☐	☐
21. Inventorying and ordering supplies	☐	☐
22. Participating in individualized program planning and other school-based meetings	☐	☐
23. Meeting and conferring with parents	☐	☐
24. Consulting with professional staff about a learner's program and behaviors	☐	☐
25. Maintaining a clean, safe learning environment	☐	☐

Note. Based on activities contained in *Handbook for Special Education Paraprofessionals*, by A. L. Pickett and J. Formanek, 1982, New York: New York City Public Schools, and in *Issues and Responsibilities in Utilizing, Training, and Managing Paraprofessionals*, by S. F. Vasa and A. L. Steckelberg, 1991, Lincoln: University of Nebraska.

References

American Occupational Therapy Association. (1999). *Guidelines for the use of aides in occupational therapy practice.* Bethesda, MD: Author.

American Physical Therapy Association. (2000). *Providing physical therapy services under parts B and C of the Individuals with Disabilities Education Act (IDEA).* Alexandria, VA: Author.

American Speech-Language-Hearing Association Information Services. (2000). *Speech–language pathology assistants.* Rockville, MD: Author.

Americans with Disabilities Act of 1990, 42 U.S.C. § 12101 *et seq.*

Carl D. Perkins Vocational and Applied Technology Education Act of 1990.

Council for Exceptional Children. (2000). *What every special educator must know: The international standards for the preparation and licensure of special educators.* Reston, VA: Author.

deFur, S. H., & Taymans, J. M. (1995). Competencies needed for transition specialists in vocational rehabilitation, vocational education and special education. *Exceptional Children, 62*(1), 38–51.

Downing, J. E., Ryndak, D. L., & Clark, D. (2000). Paraeducators in inclusive classrooms: Their own perspectives. *Remedial and Special Education, 21,* 171–181.

Drecktrah, M. E. (2000). Pre-service teacher preparation to work with paraeducators. *Teacher Education and Special Education, 23,* 157–164.

Education for All Handicapped Children Act of 1975, 20 U.S.C. § 1400 *et seq.*

Education of the Handicapped Act Amendments of 1986, 20 U.S.C. § 1400 *et seq.*

Elementary and Secondary Education Act of 1965, 79 Stat. 27.

French, N. K. (1998). Working together: Resource teachers and paraeducators. *Remedial and Special Education, 19,* 357–368.

French, N. K. (2001). Supervising paraprofessionals: A survey of teacher practices. *Journal of Special Education, 35,* 41–53.

French, N. K., & Pickett, A. L. (1997). The utilization of paraprofessionals in special education: Issues for teacher educators. *Teacher Education and Special Education, 20*(1), 61–73.

Gajar, A., Goodman, L., & McAffee, J. (1993). *Secondary schools and beyond: Transition of individuals with mild disabilities.* New York: Macmillan.

Giangreco, M. F., Edelman, S. W., Luiselli, T. E., & McFarland, S. Z. C. (1997). Helping or hovering? Effects of instructional assistant proximity on students with disabilities. *Exceptional Children, 64,* 7–18.

Individuals with Disabilities Education Act of 1990, 20 U.S.C. § 1400 *et seq.*

Individuals with Disabilities Education Act Amendments of 1997, 20 U.S.C. § 1400 *et seq.*

International Reading Association. (1998). *Standards for reading professionals.* Newark, DE: Author.

Job Training Partnership Act of 1982, P.L. 97-300.

Job Training Reform Amendments of 1992, 106 Stat. 1021.

Killoran, J., Templeman, T. P., Peters, J., & Udell, T. (2001). Identifying paraprofessional competencies for early intervention and early childhood special education. *Teaching Exceptional Children, 34*(1), 68–73.

Marks, S. U., Schrader, C., & Levine, M. (1999). Paraeducator experiences in inclusive settings: Helping, hovering or holding their own? *Exceptional Children, 65,* 315–328.

Miramontes, O. B. (1990). Organizing for effective paraprofessional services in special education: A multilingual/multiethnic instructional service team model. *Remedial and Special Education, 12,* 29–36.

Morehouse, J., & Albright, L. (1991). Training trends and needs of paraprofessionals in transition services delivery agencies. *Teacher Education and Special Education, 14,* 248–256.

Moshoyannis, T., Pickett, A. L., & Granick, L. (1999). *The evolving roles and education/training needs of paraprofessionals and teachers in the New York City public schools: Results of survey research and focus groups.* New York: City University of New York, Paraprofessional Academy, Center for Advanced Study in Education.

National Association for the Education of Young Children. (1994). NAEYC position statement: A conceptual framework for early childhood professional development. *Young Children, 49*(3), 68–77.

National Joint Committee on Learning Disabilities. (1999, Winter). Learning disabilities: Use of paraprofessionals. *Learning Disability Quarterly, 22,* 23–28.

No Child Left Behind Act of 2001, P.L. 107-110.

Office of Education Research and Improvement, U.S. Department of Education. (1990). *Paraprofessional training manual* (Rep. No. TAC-B-140). Portland, OR: Chapter 1, Rural Technical Assistance Center, Regions 6 and 7; Northwest Regional Educational Laboratory. (ERIC Document Reproduction Service No. ED 334151)

Passaro, P., Pickett, A. L., Latham, G., & HongBo, W. (1994). The training and support needs of paraprofessionals in rural special education settings. *Rural Special Education Quarterly, 13*(4), 3–9.

Pickett, A. L. (1989). *Restructuring the schools: The role of paraprofessionals.* Washington, DC: Center for Policy Research, National Governors' Association.

Pickett, A. L. (1999). *Strengthening and supporting teacher/provider–paraeducator teams: Guidelines for paraeducator roles, supervision, and preparation.* New York: National Resource Center for Paraprofessionals, Center for Advanced Study in Education, Graduate Center, City University of New York.

Pickett, A. L., Faison, K., & Formanek, J. (1999). *A core curriculum and training program to prepare paraeducators to work in inclusive classrooms serving school-age students with disabilities* (2nd ed.). New York: National Resource Center for Paraprofessionals, Center for Advanced Study in Education, Graduate Center, City University of New York.

Pickett, A. L., Faison, K., Formanek, J., & Semrau, B. (1999). *A core curriculum and training program to prepare paraeducators to work in center and home based programs for young children with disabilities from birth to age five* (2nd ed.). New York: National Resource Center for Paraprofessionals, Center for Advanced Study in Education, Graduate Center, City University of New York.

Pickett, A. L., & Formanek, J. (1982). *Handbook for special education paraprofessionals.* New York: New York City Public Schools.

Pickett, A. L., Likins, M., & Wallace, T. (2002). *A state of the art report on paraeducators in education and related services.* Logan, UT: National Resource Center for Paraprofessionals in Education, Utah State University and the University of Minnesota.

Pickett, A. L., Safarik, L., & Echiverria, J. (1998). *A core curriculum to prepare paraeducators to work with children and youth who are English language learners.* New

York: National Resource Center for Paraprofessionals, Center for Advanced Study in Education, Graduate Center, City University of New York.

Pickett, A. L., Vasa, S. F., & Steckelberg, A. L. (1993). *Using paraeducators effectively in the classroom* [Fastback No. 358]. Bloomington, IN: Phi Delta Kappa Educational Foundation.

Riggs, C. G., & Mueller, P. H. (2001). Employment and utilization of paraeducators in inclusive settings. *Journal of Special Education, 35,* 54–62.

Rogan, P. M., & Held, M. (1999). Paraprofessionals in job coach roles. *Journal of the Association for Persons with Severe Handicaps, 24,* 273–280.

Rueda, R. S., & Monzo, L. D. (2000). *Apprentices for teaching: Professional development issues surrounding the collaborative relationship between teachers and paraeducators.* Washington, DC: Center for Research on Education, Diversity, and Excellence.

Safarik, L. (1999). *Lives in transition.* Retrieved from the National Resource Center for Paraprofessionals Web site: http://www.nrcpara.org

Safarik, L., Prather, M., Hanson, G., Guzman, G., Ryan, C., & Schwan, D. (1991). *A career ladder program for transition services personnel: A collaborative curriculum development approach.* Long Beach: California State University at Long Beach.

School-to-Work Opportunities Act of 1994, 20 U.S.C. § 6101 *et seq.*

Snodgrass, A. S. (1991). *Actual and preferred practices of employment, placement, supervision, and evaluation of teacher aides in Idaho school districts.* Unpublished doctoral dissertation, University of Idaho, Moscow.

Wallace, T., Jongho, S., Bartholomay, T., & Stahl, B. J. (2001). Knowledge and skills for teachers supervising the work of paraprofessionals. *Exceptional Children, 67,* 520–533.

Wiener, W. R., Deaver, K., DiCorpo, D., Hayes, J., Hill, E., Manzer, D., Newcomer, J., Pogrund, R., Rosen, S., & Usland, M. (1990). The orientation and mobility assistant. *RE:View, 22,* 69–77.

3 Management of Paraeducators

Nancy K. French

OVERVIEW

Classrooms and other education environments are complex and dynamic workplaces that require management by skilled professionals who perform certain well-documented executive functions (Berliner, 1983a, 1983b). Teachers and related services professionals are not commonly thought of as executives, yet the dual metaphors of the classroom as a workplace and the school professional as an executive make particular sense in exploring the role of the school professional with regard to paraeducator or paratherapist supervision.[1]

This chapter first explores the issue of which professional or professionals take on the management role and how the executive functions may be shared among the professional team members. It then examines the first six executive functions of paraeducator or paratherapist supervision listed in Table 3.1: orientation, delegation, schedule management, planning, on-the-job training, and evaluation. The seventh, managing the work environment (team building and communication), requires such extensive attention that an entire chapter of this text is devoted to that function (see Chapter 5).

[1] In this chapter, both words, *paraeducator* and *paratherapist*, have been used to convey the concept that the management functions apply to those employees who work alongside professional educators as well as professional therapists in schools. To avoid wordiness throughout the chapter, sometimes only one of the titles is used.

Table 3.1

Executive Functions Associated with Paraeducator Supervision

1. Orientation
    - Introduce people, policies, procedures, roles, and responsibilities
    - Analyze styles and skills
    - Create personalized job assignment
2. Delegation
    - Analyze tasks
    - Determine what to delegate
    - Create work plans
    - Select the right person
    - Direct tasks
    - Monitor performance
3. Managing Schedules
    - Identify task importance and urgency
    - Identify locations, persons, and tasks
4. Planning
    - Set goals
    - Describe activities, methods
    - Set expectations for outcomes
5. On-the-Job Training
    - Assess current skills
    - Teach or coach new skills
    - Give feedback on skill performance
6. Evaluation
    - Track performance of duties
    - Provide summative information about job performance
7. Managing the Work Environment
    - Provide team leadership
    - Maintain effective communications
    - Set goals for the team
    - Manage conflicts
    - Solve problems

Instructional Objectives

After studying this chapter and completing the discussion questions and exercises, the learner will be able to do the following:

1. Identify and define the seven executive functions of supervisory paraeducators.
2. Explain how to distribute the executive functions of paraeducator supervision among team members.
3. Discuss the tests of effective plans and planning formats; identify the components of a schedule and differentiate a schedule from a plan.
4. Define *delegation;* explain why professionals should delegate and why they sometimes fail to delegate; and define the steps for delegation.
5. Identify and define the components of paraeducator orientation.
6. Describe the purposes of a personalized job assignment for paraeducators.
7. Discuss ways of providing training to the paraeducator.
8. Describe the role of the professional in the evaluation process.
9. Describe the importance of holding effective meetings with paraeducators.

Who Supervises?

Individual Supervision

A single professional is often responsible for performing all the functions associated with paraeducator or paratherapist supervision. The executive functions of paraeducator or paratherapist supervision are often performed by individual teachers, therapists, school nurses, or school psychologists. This is most often the case when the paraeducator or paratherapist is assigned directly to a single classroom or specifically to an individual professional.

For example, one professional typically supervises in a traditional self-contained special education program for children with severe or profound needs where a single special education teacher and several paraeducators work with a group of children who remain in that room for a significant portion of the day. Another situation, often found in early childhood education programs, is where a single licensed or certified professional runs a program in which all the group instruction, supervision of learners, personal assistance, and individual help is provided by paraeducator personnel.

Shared Supervision

Sometimes a paraeducator is employed to support the work of a program that also employs a variety of professionals. In this case, the team is composed of both paraprofessional and professional members. In teams with a designated leader, that person is most likely to perform the functions of paraeducator supervision. However, many school teams are leaderless in the sense that they do their fundamental work without a designated leader and they share the functions of team leadership. The functions of paraeducator supervision also may be shared by several professional team members. The lines of authority and communication that are so readily apparent in one-on-one supervisor–supervisee relationships become less obvious when teams share supervisory responsibilities. When this is the case, teams must clarify who will perform the executive functions of paraeducator supervision. The following are three examples of teams with shared responsibility for paraeducator supervision.

▶ Example 1: General Education Teams

An instructional team includes three fifth-grade teachers who share supervision of a single paraeducator. Initially, they provided orientation to the paraeducator at a team meeting, developed a personalized job assignment, and clarified areas where they would provide on-the-job training. The team teachers work together to plan, determine the paraeducator's schedule, delegate tasks, and monitor the work of the paraeducator. They meet with the paraeducator regularly to share information and to provide feedback on performance of the assigned tasks.

▶ Example 2: Special Education–General Education Teams

A special education team includes various professionals—school psychologist, physical therapist, occupational therapist, speech–language pathologist, school nurse, and special education teacher—all of whom share assessment and planning responsibilities for students with significant needs even though those students receive most of their education in a general education classroom. The critical feature in this case is that all the team members except the special education and general education teachers are itinerant. That is, many team members are present in the building only once or twice a week. Thus, the day-to-day scheduling, direction, and monitoring of the paraeducator's work is shared by the general education teacher and the special education teacher. Even though the two teachers assume the daily functions of supervision, the itinerant professionals provide plans, direction, on-the-job training, and monitoring of the paraeducator's performance.

▶ Example 3: Paraeducator Supports Students

A paraeducator is assigned to support learners with disabilities or learners who speak English as a second language (ESL) who spend most of their time in general education classes. In this case, the classroom teacher assumes responsibility for planning instruction for the whole class. The special education or ESL teacher assumes responsibility for consulting with the general education teacher, planning the types of modifications and adaptations necessary, providing any specialized curriculum or instruction necessary, providing on-the-job training to the paraeducator, and monitoring the learner outcomes.

Each of the three examples demands a unique response to the distribution of supervisory functions. Teams may use the following questions to help decide which supervisory functions will be performed by each professional team member.

1. *Who holds ultimate responsibility for the outcome of the instruction?*

This person (or persons) may or may not be physically present; however, this person has the greatest responsibility and is accountable for outcomes. This person also has responsibility for ensuring that the individualized health plan, behavior plan, or language acquisition plan is met. This person may have been designated as the case manager or may have signed the individualized plan. This person must, at the very least, provide plans, schedules, on-the-job training, and monitoring of the paraeducator's performance.

2. *Who will be in the best position, logistically speaking, to direct the performance of the tasks?*

This is the person who is physically present with the paraeducator. In cases where no single professional is physically present at all times, teams may want to identify the professionals who have proximity at various times during the paraeducator's scheduled day. This professional should, at the least, be involved in giving directions for a specific task, monitoring performance, and providing feedback to the paraeducator.

3. *Who is in the best position to provide training for the assigned tasks?*

This person may or may not be physically present on a daily basis, but must provide the training because of his or her licensing requirements or specific training or skills. Examples include school nurses who delegate the tasks of giving medications or providing other health-related services to students. By law, the nurse must provide training and monitoring of these tasks. Also included are occupational and physical therapists and speech–language pathologists who determine the necessary interventions, but who are not physically present to carry out those interventions on a daily basis.

4. *Who is in the best position to observe and document performance?*

This may be the person who is present daily or another professional team member who creates opportunities to conduct firsthand observations. In the cases of licensed therapists and nurses, regulations guiding their professions require regularly scheduled observations and documentation of paraeducator task performance (this is described in Chapter 5).

Executive Functions

Seven executive functions are associated with paraeducator supervision. Whether supervision is performed by an individual or by a team, the executive functions remain the same: orientation, delegating tasks, scheduling, planning for the paraeducator, on-the-job training, performance evaluation, and managing the work environment. When paraeducators are assigned to teams, licensed team members must clarify roles with regard to paraeducator supervision and respond in unique ways to variations in paraeducator assignments.

Orientation

When people accept employment, they typically experience an initial orientation to the workplace and the specific job duties, as well as introductions to their fellow employees. Such an orientation has not always been the case, however, with paraeducators. For example, Gretchen accepted a position at an elementary school near her home to work 3 hours a day as a paraeducator. The school year had already begun and she was told to report at 8:00 A.M. the following Monday. Gretchen arrived half an hour early. The supervising teacher, Monica, greeted her and took her to the small adjoining room. Monica told Gretchen that she should look at the materials in the top drawer and select some to use with third graders and some others for fourth graders. Gretchen was told that a group of students would arrive at her doorstep about 8:15 and that she would have them for 30 minutes before a new set of students would rotate in, and so on for the entire 3 hours. Gretchen was shocked. She had worked as a high school English teacher before her children were born, but she had no idea how to teach math to third and fourth graders. She spent her entire first day on the job with little adult contact, and no information about the layout of the school building, school rules, emergency procedures, other faculty, or appropriate materials or instruction for children this age.

What kind of orientation should Gretchen have received? There are five components of paraeducator orientation: introductions, written information review, getting acquainted interview, work style preferences analysis, and needs versus skills analysis.

First, common courtesy demands that newly employed paraeducators should be introduced to the other people who work in the school. Second, the paraeducator should be provided with any and all written policies and procedures used in the building. At a minimum, such written information should include emergency and safety procedures; school rules, routines, and standard procedures; the school calendar; the building-level schedule; phone numbers and addresses of fellow employees; and protocols for reporting absences, requesting substitutes, and getting information about emergency school closures. Many schools have developed a handbook that contains vital information about safety issues such as fire drills, emergency warning systems, playground or assembly rules, and so forth. It may not be necessary to create a separate handbook or packet for paraeducators if a schoolwide handbook already exists. In fact, it makes sense to provide the same written information to paraeducators and professionals. Information about the privacy rights of students, confidentiality of information, and ethical standards should be provided at the same time. Ideally, a building administrator will meet with newly employed paraeducators to ensure that all the basic information is reviewed and understood.

New paraeducators should have a structured opportunity to get to know the individual or team members who will supervise them. One way for school professionals and newly employed paraeducators to get to know one another is to interview one another. Emery (1991) and Alexander (1987) each listed questions that may be used and recommended that the pair (or the entire team) engage in a systematic interview and that the interviews be documented. Some possible interview questions selected from their lists and offered by others are contained in Table 3.2. Professionals may create other questions that will help them know the new person well enough to establish a strong working relationship. This orientation interview is not meant to replace

Table 3.2
Getting Acquainted: Paraeducator Orientation Interview Questions

1. Where did you grow up?
2. What are your leisure time activities?
3. What was your best memory of school?
4. What teachers had a positive impact on you?
5. What is your understanding of this position?
6. Why are you interested in this kind of work?
7. What skills do you have that will help children in the classroom?
8. What are your unique talents and skills?

a hiring interview. Rather, it is meant to occur at the beginning of employment to help newly employed paraeducators gain knowledge of the building and their fellow workers and to help all the team members get to know one another.

The third component of orientation includes an introduction to the role of the paraeducator, the schedule, and the specific job duties. This introduction should not be unidirectional. Because paraeducator roles are somewhat negotiable (within certain legal and ethical limits) and because of the possible overlapping of responsibilities, it is most appropriate to gain some additional information about the paraeducator at this stage. Throughout the orientation stage, encourage the paraeducator to ask questions or share concerns about his or her position or assigned duties.

The fourth component of orientation is the work style preferences analysis. It is important to discuss and analyze both the paraeducator's and the professional's preferred work styles. The professional reflects on his or her own preferences in order to communicate them to the newly employed paraeducator. The paraeducator then clarifies his or her own preferences in order to communicate them. For example, the professional may be a morning person who prefers to come in early, prepare for the day, and meet with colleagues. If the paraeducator is also a morning person, the two may effectively share information during that early morning time. If not, the paraeducator may not be as responsive to ideas and directions in the morning. This exercise is intended to be a vehicle for communication about how the two (or the team) will work together. Knowing one another's preferences enables the team to start off on the right foot. Worksheets 3.1 through 3.3 at the end of this chapter may be used for analyzing work styles. The professional completes Worksheet 3.1, the paraeducator completes Worksheet 3.2, and the scores from those sheets are transferred to Worksheet 3.3 to determine how the two can work best together.

Professionals must recognize that style preferences are not inherently good or bad, but simply that they exist. The lack of initial recognition of differences often creates a breeding ground for interpersonal problems between paraeducators and professionals. Tolerance and management of differences begin with the recognition of work style preferences. Problems can result when no discussion about work style preferences occurs at the beginning of the relationship. Gabriella, a paraeducator, after being closely monitored by the supervising special education teacher, Michelle, filed a grievance with the school principal. When the two sat down with the principal to discuss their differences, Gabriella complained that Michelle did not trust her and watched over her shoulder too much. Michelle responded that she had no lack of trust for Gabriella and that she thought she was doing her job responsibly. Neither was right or wrong. Their error was that they had not held the conversation about their stylistic preferences and differences until their irritation with one another became apparent.

The fifth component of orientation is for the supervisor to analyze program and learner needs and then compare these needs to the paraeducator's skills. Although forms are not necessary to do the analysis and comparison, a systematic format, once created, saves time in the future and assures team members that they have addressed all relevant issues. It may be useful to create an inventory of all the tasks that need to be done within the scope of the program, considering the needs of every student currently in the program or classroom, the teacher's work style and preferences, and the school's expectations. For example, paraeducators in a preschool program might help the children get dressed to go outdoors or read to them. In a classroom with students who are not yet proficient in English, a teacher might need a bilingual paraeducator to translate notes that go home to families, or to hold a discussion in the child's native language about key science concepts taught by the teacher in English. A speech–language pathologist might ask a paraeducator to work on articulation skills with children. A special education teacher might need someone to assist students in using the restroom. A professional in a vocational preparation program might need the paraeducator to help students apply basic computational skills on the job. The wide variety of programs, as well as differences in learner ages and needs, precludes the possibility of creating a single list that is useful in all situations. Worksheet 3.4, included at the end of the chapter, is an example of a Professional, Program, and Student Needs Inventory.

After the needs inventory is completed, a needs versus preferences analysis occurs. To do so, the needs inventory may be used as the basis for a skills and confidence inventory to be given to the paraeducator so that the paraeducator can identify his or her own preparation and comfort levels regarding each needed task. A rating scale is added to the Professional, Program, and Student Needs Inventory to make it easier for the paraeducator to rate each item. Worksheet 3.5 is an example of a Paraeducator Skills and Confidence Inventory that matches the Professional, Program, and Student Needs Inventory shown in Worksheet 3.4.

Personalized Job Assignments

The need for job descriptions for paraeducators is well documented (Pickett, Vasa, & Steckelberg, 1993). A section titled Personalized Job Assignments serves as an addendum to the general job description that school districts use when hiring paraeducators and, for legal reasons, should never exceed the limits of the district's formal job description. A personalized job assignment delineates the specific duties for which a particular paraeducator will be held responsible, and it clarifies the training and coaching necessary to prepare the paraeducator to perform all of the tasks needed by the supervisor, the program, or the team on behalf of the learners.

Personalized job assignments may be created from the Professional, Program, and Student Needs Inventory and the Paraeducator Skills and Confidence Inventory by simply changing the title, keeping on the list those tasks that will actually be assigned to the individual paraeducator, and removing those that will be performed by someone else. Tasks that need to be done, for which the paraeducator is prepared and comfortable performing, become parts of a personalized job assignment. Tasks for which training is needed may be listed with a note that the paraeducator needs training before being expected to perform those tasks.

Providing a personalized job assignment for a paraeducator who has held the position for a long time may help clarify the differences in roles and responsibilities among team members. For newly employed paraeducators, the development of a personalized job assignment creates a common basis of understanding about the nature of the job and about the circumstances that exist in the particular workplace. It allows the newly employed paraeducator a glimpse into the future. It also opens the door for the person who is not well suited to the position to make a move quickly. As difficult as it may seem, it is better for everyone to recognize a poor fit early.

For example, Madison, a newly employed speech–language therapy aide, accepted employment after responding to a newspaper advertisement. She had taken some college courses toward a degree in speech communication and thought the position sounded interesting. She interviewed well and appeared to have a good understanding of the position. Tracy, the speech–language pathologist, provided Madison with orientation information and they completed the companion needs and skills inventories the second day on the job. Madison realized right away that this job was not what she thought it would be. She found herself in the awkward position of having accepted a position that she did not really want. Madison tried to be honest with Tracy, but Tracy begged Madison to stay and give it a try. Four months later, Madison resigned. Only then did Tracy realize that she had expended tremendous effort training and coaching a person who was not well suited to the position in the first place. She regretted that she had not heeded Madison's initial concerns (French, 1996).

A personalized job assignment provides the professional a glimpse into the paraeducator's immediate and long-range training needs. Training plans can be created and the training process can begin soon after employment. Meanwhile, delegated tasks can be selected or modified to match the paraeducator's present skill level.

Summary

Paraeducators should receive an initial orientation to the workplace and their job duties, as well as an introduction to other staff and faculty. Once paraeducators have had the opportunity to become acquainted with their supervising professional or team, they should receive written information regarding the policies, procedures, rules, and regulations that govern the district or agency. During the orientation phase, the work style preferences of paraeducator and supervising professional or team members should be compared. Then a needs versus skills analysis should be conducted to determine the match between the needs of the program or professional and the paraeducator's current skill level.

Personalized job assignments may be created from the information accumulated in the preferred work style inventories and the needs versus skills analysis. When developed during the orientation phase of employment, personalized job descriptions may serve as an introduction to the roles and responsibilities of the position and may have the side effect of ending the employment of a person who is not well suited to the position.

Delegating and Directing

What Is Delegation?

According to Drawbaugh (1984), delegation is the process of getting things done through others who have been trained to handle them. It is the act of entrusting enough authority to another to get the task done without giving up responsibility. As classroom managers, school professionals delegate tasks to paraeducators who are prepared to do the tasks and then the professionals monitor the completion of the task because they retain ultimate responsibility and accountability for the outcomes of instruction. Delegation is an executive function that is fundamentally important to the supervision of paraeducators.

Why Delegate?

There are numerous reasons why school professionals, as managers, delegate tasks to paraeducators. First, delegation frees the teacher to do work that cannot be delegated, such as assessment, planning, and scheduling. Second, it increases the professional's productivity. By delegating judiciously, a professional doubles the amount of work that is accomplished. Third, judicious delegation emphasizes the management of various aspects of instruction. Fourth, it provides opportunities for others to develop new skills and initiative. Therefore, not only is delegation a way to achieve increased amounts of attention to students, it is also a way to help paraeducators grow and develop their skills.

How To Delegate

One management expert compared delegation to a legal contract. In a legal contract, the parties reach a meeting of the minds as to the content and meaning of the contract's provisions (McConkey, 1974). So it is with delegation. The delegatory contract between a paraeducator and a school professional includes agreement on (a) the scope of the task, (b) the specific goals or objectives to be reached, (c) the time frame, (d) the authority needed to carry out the task, and (e) the means by which the paraeducator's performance will be monitored and judged.

Sullivan (1980) wrote that effective delegation requires that the professional "focus on results, not the methods, and allow for mistakes" (p. 6). Thus, delegation provides guidance without being overbearing. It must specify the outcomes, the time frame, and the level of authority, but should not demand that the paraeducator perform in exactly the same manner as the professional and should not demand perfection.

Time Management

Effective delegation requires effective time management. Effective time management requires the examination of tasks in terms of two factors: the degree to which it is pressing and the consequences (or outcomes) of doing or not doing the task. A task is pressing if someone is urged or pushed to attend to it or to complete it immediately. The pressing nature of a task may be determined by assessing the consequences of not doing the task immediately, by the absence or presence of a demanding person, or by organizational expectations. For example, the teachers at West Side Middle School generally do not meet with parents during class time, but when an upset parent is standing in the principal's office and demanding to speak to the teacher immediately, that task becomes pressing. The second factor, consequences of the task, is relative to the contribution it makes to the overall purpose or professional goal of the individual. Tasks fall somewhere on a continuum between major contributions and minor contributions. Each professional then judges the consequences of each task according to the contribution that the task makes to his or her program goals.

Employing those two factors, school tasks may be placed into one of four quadrants (see Figure 3.1). The tasks located in the upper right quadrant, for the most part, are tasks for which the professional should remember the key word "Do." Tasks in the "Do" quadrant are not appropriately delegated to a paraeducator. For some professionals, such tasks are difficult to get to because they are not very pressing, yet each of these tasks makes a major contribution to the professional's goals. Doing these tasks gains major positive consequences for the professional. Deferring and delegating these tasks are both bad choices for the professional who aims to use time well. Although school professionals may also choose to do the tasks that fall into the upper left (the "Delegate or Do") quadrant themselves, many of the tasks are appropriate for delegation to a paraeducator. School professionals who delegate tasks appropriately take these factors into account along with the skills, preferences, programmatic needs, and job description of the paraeducator.

The lower left ("Delegate or Defer") quadrant contains tasks that are appropriately delegated to a paraeducator, but may be deferred until more pressing issues are completed. For example, Ruby always kept two baskets on her desk from which Antoine, the paraeducator assigned to her classroom, drew his assignments. They were labeled "Deadlines" and "No Deadlines." Antoine would go first to the "Deadlines" basket to get information about his assigned tasks, but when he had an odd moment or unexpected downtime, he would go to the "No Deadlines" basket to draw a task that also needed to be done eventually.

The lower right ("Defer or Discard") quadrant contains tasks that are not particularly pressing and do not result in consequences of major significance. Those tasks may be delegated to a paraeducator, but for the most part they are tasks that should simply be discarded and not done by anyone.

	Pressing	Not Pressing
Major	**Key "D" Words: Delegate or Do** • Sudden student behavior crises • Parent conferences or meetings re: crises • Student health crises • Monitoring students in non–classroom settings • Providing or adapting instruction • Creating adapted instructional materials • Certain documentation or paperwork • Grading some papers (tests) • Taking attendance or lunch counts • Implementing behavior plans, health plans, or curricular modifications and adaptations	**Key "D" Word: Do** • Designing individual behavior plans, health plans, curricular modifications, or adaptations • Assessment of students' progress • Assessment of students for program eligibility • Long-range planning of instruction • Curriculum development or revision • Building relationships among professionals and paraeducators • Coplanning of behavioral interventions or instruction • Meeting to provide supervision to paraeducators
Minor	**Key "D" Words: Delegate or Defer** • General office announcements • Some mail or flyers • Some meetings • Interruptions by students or other professionals • Some parent visits • Grading some daily student work	**Key "D" Words: Defer or Discard** • Some copy work or filing • Some mail • Some phone calls • Some teachers' lounge conversations • Some classroom decorating activities • Grading some papers • Some record keeping, filing, and cleaning up

Figure 3.1. Delegation decision matrix for school professionals with key "D" words.

Professionals Fail To Delegate

Many school professionals fail to delegate except in limited ways (Drawbaugh, 1984). Table 3.3 lists many of the reasons school professionals fail to delegate. One of the main reasons, although school professionals do not necessarily articulate this reason clearly, is that when they entered their profession they were unprepared to supervise other adults (Vasa, Steckelberg, & Ulrich-Ronning, 1982). Their university programs may not have prepared them to think of themselves as managers who fulfilled executive functions. They likely began their careers under the erroneous assumption that they, and they alone, would have

Table 3.3
Some Reasons School Professionals Fail To Delegate

Professionals

- Believe they can do the job faster and are unwilling to wait.
- Recognize that it takes time to train the paraeducator.
- Lack confidence in the paraeducator's work.
- Cannot tolerate less than perfect results.
- Fear being disliked by someone who may expect them to do the task themselves, or by the person to whom they delegate an unpleasant task.
- Fear that they will lose control.
- Think it is easier to do it themselves than to tell others how to do it.
- Are convinced that delegation burdens more than benefits the other person.
- Lack the skill to delegate well.
- Lack the skills to communicate well with adults.
- Fear that delegation reveals incompetence.
- Feel insecure when depending on others.
- Want to account only for themselves and not for others.
- Believe that "teaching is for teachers" and are unwilling to give the necessary authority.

Note. Adapted from *Time and Its Use: A Self-Management Guide for Teachers* (pp. 76–77), by C. C. Drawbaugh, 1984, New York: Teachers College Press. Copyright 1984 by Teachers College Press. Adapted with permission.

to do everything needed to provide instruction for their students. For years, school professionals have protested that they have little time to plan, collaborate with others, coteach, and do long-range planning. In spite of the presence of paraeducators in the schools since the 1950s and substantial increases in the numbers of paraeducators since 1973 (Gartner, 1971; Pickett, 1986, 1994), school professionals have continued to believe that they alone must respond to all the urgent tasks of schools.

Steps for Delegation to Paraeducators

Delegation is a process that consists of a series of steps, which can be learned by school professionals even if they entered the profession not believing that paraeducator supervision was part of their job. Once the professional recognizes that paraeducator supervision is, indeed, an important part of the professional's role, the steps are straightforward. Table 3.4 provides a list of steps for delegation to paraeducators that are much like the steps identified by Douglass (1979) who worked with corporate executives on similar issues.

The first step, analyzing the task, consists of three substeps. The first substep relates to time management considerations in that the professional must first assess the task in terms of importance and urgency. Next, the professional decides whether the task could be done by someone else, based on legal and ethical standards. Third, the professional breaks the task apart and identifies the components or subtasks; this process is completed by considering the skills of the person who will perform the task. Thus, the analysis may be more or less detailed depending on the paraeducator's competencies.

Deciding what to delegate should be based on three factors: the student and program needs, the styles and preferences of the people involved, and the skills and confidence of the paraeducator. Creating the work plan is the next step and has been discussed at length in the previous section. The tasks of assessing work styles and preferences, skill levels, and student and program needs and the task of creating a systematic training or coaching plan will be discussed in a later section. The quality of a paraeducator's performance is affected significantly by the professional's choice of tasks to delegate.

Table 3.4
Steps for Delegation to Paraeducators

1. Analyze the task.
   a. Assess the task in terms of urgency and importance.
   b. Decide whether someone else could do the task.
   c. Identify component parts of the larger task.
2. Decide what to delegate.
   a. Consider programmatic and learner needs, preferences of professionals and paraeducators, and paraeducator skills.
   b. Decide what training or coaching the paraeducator needs to perform the tasks.
3. Create the plan.
   a. Review components of the task.
   b. Clarify limits of authority.
   c. Establish performance standards.
   d. Determine how to direct and monitor the paraeducator.
   e. Determine when and how to train or coach the paraeducator.
4. Select the right person.
   a. Consider interests, preferences, and abilities.
   b. Consider the degree of challenge the task presents.
   c. Balance and rotate unpleasant tasks.
5. Direct the task.
   a. Clarify objectives and purposes.
   b. Clarify degree of authority.
   c. Clarify the importance or urgency of the task.
   d. Communicate effectively.
6. Monitor performance.
   a. Create system for ongoing and timely feedback.
   b. Provide prompt and appropriate feedback.
   c. Insist on achievement of objectives, but not perfection.
   d. Encourage independence.
   e. Tolerate or manage style differences.
   f. Do not short-circuit paraeducator effort by taking tasks back prematurely.
   g. Document and reward good performance.

Selecting the right person is a consideration if multiple paraeducators work in a program or if other human resources are available (e.g., volunteers, peer tutors, peer coaches). For example, at Rampart High School, a schoolwide peer support program prepares typical students to assist special education students. Sometimes the typical peer takes notes for another student, redirects a student who has difficulty attending to tasks, or helps a student regain composure during a stressful moment. In this school, the special education teacher on the team makes a decision regarding whether to delegate a particular task to a student's peer or to a paraeducator. A situation that developed in music class exemplifies this type of decision. Laura, a special education student, became infatuated with one of her classmates and insisted on standing next to him in the choir. Ms. Myers, the vocal music teacher, had her hands full with the 105 choir students and requested help from the special education team. Mr. Wright, one of the special education teachers, came to the choir room to assess the situation. After determining the nature of the problem, he decided that he should assign a paraeducator to the situation on a temporary basis rather than trying to assign a peer to maintain the situation (French & Chopra, 2000).

The corollary to selecting the right person is selecting the right task for the person. If a paraeducator is especially skillful in a particular area, it may make sense to delegate those tasks to the person regularly. For example, Ivory, an experienced paraeducator, is a particularly gifted storyteller. The school professionals with whom she works all recognize and value her accomplishments in storytelling. They frequently find opportunities to take advantage of this unique contribution that Ivory makes to their school.

On the other hand, paraeducators grow and develop as they are assigned challenging work that they learn to do. Edee was reluctant at first to use the computer in the special education program, but when the team urged her to gradually take on some computer-based record keeping, she found that her fear of the technology dissipated as her skills grew.

Another important consideration in selecting the right person is that some tasks are more unpleasant than others. Even if a person is very good at accomplishing an unpleasant duty, that duty should be rotated and shared by others. For example, in special education and early childhood programs, diaper changing is sometimes necessary. Although no one really likes to do, it is important and sometimes urgent. It also has a tremendous impact on the student. The student's privacy is encroached upon and his or her dignity is at risk during such an intimate procedure. Thus, it is crucial that the personnel who do the task maintain the student's dignity and privacy. Effective managers consider student privacy and dignity while ensuring a fair distribution of unpleasant tasks among all the professionals and paraeducators. Diane, a third-grade teacher at Cherrydale Elementary School, works with Laura, a paraeducator assigned to her classroom. Laura is assigned to the classroom on behalf of Melinda, a child with significant support needs. Melinda needs "freshening" (as they call it) every few hours. Sometimes Diane takes Melinda to the "private learning corner" to do the freshening while Laura continues working with a small group of students on math skills. At other times, Laura takes Melinda while Diane continues with the class. Neither prefers diaper changing but they share the task equally.

When school professionals provide good direction, they make the objectives and purposes of the task or lesson clear and they let the paraeducator know how much authority he or she has to make decisions associated with the task. Explicit information about the extent of authority associated with the task helps paraeducators know how to handle difficult situations. For example, Barbara was given a lesson plan that tells her to work with Javier to reinforce the two-digit multiplication algorithm he learned the day before. Barbara finds that Javier remembers exactly how to perform the function and is able to complete all the assigned problems in a few minutes. Her supervisor is not immediately available and Javier looks to her for direction. What Barbara needs to know is the level of authority she has to determine whether to proceed with a more advanced skill, or to make him continue to practice the same skill, or to stop and reward him with a pleasant but unrelated activity.

When professionals clarify the importance and urgency of a task, they help paraeducators know how to make on-the-spot decisions about whether to pursue a task or end it when the student seems uncooperative or when something else interferes with the activity. It also helps when the paraeducator understands how a task fits into the broader goal and how the objective contributes to the end-goal or outcome for the student. For example, Eric, a student with severe and multiple disabilities, has been learning to raise and lower his left arm. If Maize, the paraeducator who works with him, understands that Eric is destined for an augmentative communication device that depends on this skill, she will be sure that he practices many times a day and that he practices correctly.

Additionally, the need to communicate the plan effectively and clearly is paramount. Unless the plan is communicated in a format that both the professional and the paraeducator understand in the same way, little will happen to assure the outcomes that students deserve. In creating lesson plans, the professional should consider ease of use and user friendliness. Addressing these two criteria while creating a planning form or format helps the professional communicate well, but it takes one more communicative action to ensure that the paraeducator has actually received and understood the plan in the way it was intended. Merely asking, "What questions do you have?" is one way to open the opportunity for clarification. Another way might be to ask a specific question that requires the paraprofessional to summarize what he or she just heard. For example, a teacher might ask, "What directions will you give after Seth completes the alphabetizing task?"

The professional who delegates to a paraeducator must also monitor the performance of the assigned tasks. Of course, the amount and intensity of monitoring depend on the history of the working relationship. Longer histories and high skill levels require less direct monitoring, whereas shorter histories or fewer skills require more intensive, direct observation. According to the demands of the situation, the professional must create a system for ongoing monitoring and timely feedback to paraeducators about their work. Professionals also need to act promptly and appropriately on feedback they receive from paraeducators about the nature of the task or the outcomes. The general rule of thumb is to focus on the objectives rather than the perfect execution of prescribed actions. However, there are times when precise execution of a technique is necessary. Identifying such times is easier when precision and perfection are not constant demands. Paraeducators are generally quite able to work independently. Although monitoring is necessary for ethical practice, it is not necessary to hover over the paraeducator during instructional episodes. In fact, many paraeducators become uncomfortable and find their self-confidence diminished if the professional monitors too closely. Professionals should encourage paraeducators' independence and initiative in accomplishing the goals and can do so by emphasizing the outcomes rather than the procedures. Communication style and work style differences sometimes result in tasks being performed differently than the planner had envisioned. The professional who delegates tasks should clearly differentiate between idiosyncrasies of style and incorrect task performance.

Sometimes professionals who are concerned with perfection err by withdrawing a task from a paraeducator too soon. It is a mistake to short-circuit or diminish paraeducator effort before the paraeducator has a chance to improve his or her skills or understanding of the task. If the delegation was made correctly, the professional stated the time frame and the expected quality of the performance. Professionals should remind themselves to be patient enough to allow the paraeducator to reach the performance standard. The effective manager provides coaching and feedback on a difficult task rather than removing the task from the paraeducator. Finally, highly effective managers document and reward good performance. Everyone enjoys a bit of praise now and then, but the issue of documenting and rewarding good performance goes beyond the level of "niceness." Documentation of performance should be specific to the objectives of the task and the specifications of the plan. Even when paraeducator performance is not yet perfect, recognition of the good aspects of the performance provides the motivation to continue to grow and improve.

Summary

Delegation is an executive function that is fundamentally important to the supervision of paraeducators. School professionals delegate tasks to paraeducators because, by doing so, they free themselves to do work that cannot be delegated, and thus increase their productivity. They double the amount of work that is accomplished and free themselves from the restriction of having to do it all themselves. Through delegation, professionals also provide opportunities for paraeducators to develop new skills and initiative. Professionals who manage their time well consider every school task in light of its urgency and its importance. They distinguish among tasks that they must do themselves and those that may be accomplished by someone else. Teachers and other school professionals sometimes fail to delegate appropriately because of time management problems, errors in their thinking, or lack of organization and planning.

Schedule Management

Schedules indicate when tasks should be completed, who should do them, and where people are during the day or week. They are often developed simultaneously with lesson or work plans, and provide a graphic display that accompanies the specific information contained in the lesson or work plan. While the plan answers the question "What does the paraeducator do?" the schedule answers the questions "When?" and "Where?"

It is most useful to have schedules that include information about all team members, whether the team consists of two members (e.g., teacher and paraeducator) or more. It is also useful to display schedules publicly so that the information is readily available to others. Like plans, schedules can and should reflect the unique needs of the team and the circumstances. The unvarying features include times, locations, and activities of all team members.

Figure 3.2 is an example of a schedule form used at a middle school. In this case, the whereabouts of the teacher and the paraeducator are publicly available and a notation telling what each is doing during each time block is included. The schedule does not tell the nature of the activity, the goals, or the materials used in lessons or classes. That information is contained in related plans.

Planning

When asked, "Who plans for the paraeducator?" special education teachers, general education teachers, school psychologists, speech–language pathologists, occupational therapists, and physical therapists may all find themselves pointing the finger at one another, or at no one at all. Often they say, "I don't need to plan; he just knows what to do." Or they say, "She doesn't need a written plan. I just tell her what to do on the fly" (French, 1998). Or the paraeducator may speak up in response, saying, "I make my own plans" or "No one plans; I just follow along trying to do what I'm supposed to" (French, 1998). Although these responses may reflect the current state of affairs, none of them exemplifies a legal or ethical position.

DAILY SCHEDULE

for week of ____________

Time	Paraeducator Activity / Location	Teacher Activity / Location
8:00 to 8:40	Support Jason, Michele, Taneesha / Room 29	Plan with social studies teachers / SS office
8:40 to 8:50	Accompany Eric to PE / from Room 38 to gym	" "
8:50 to 9:20	Support Jason, Michele, Tanya, Roy / Room 44	Coteach with Smith / Room 29
9:20 to 10:05	7th-grade lang arts group / Resource room	" "
10:05 to 10:30	Plan time / SPED office	Plan time / SPED office
10:30 to 10:50	Accompany Eric to health room for respiration treatment and medication; Take Eric to music	Coteach with Jones / Room 44
10:50 to 11:25	Lunch	Coteach with Jones / Room 44
11:25 to 11:50	Computer lab	Plan with lang arts teachers / LA office
11:55 to 12:25	Support Ana, Carol, David, Kayla, Jim / Room 44	Testing / Consultation / IEP meetings

Figure 3.2. Sample daily schedule.

Designing instructional environments and making decisions about the goals, objectives, activities, and evaluations of instructional episodes are tasks that are well outside the paraeducator's scope of responsibility. As discussed in Chapter 2, it is clearly the responsibility of the teacher or other school professional to provide plans, which the paraeducator then follows. Legally and ethically speaking, paraeducators should not make their own plans or operate without written plans. Specifically, it is not legal or ethical for a special education paraeducator to create or plan modifications or adaptations of lessons that have been designed by general educators. It is the duty of the school professional to plan the lessons, the modifications, and the adaptations, with consultation from other appropriate professionals and based on any existing individualized plans for the student. A general modification plan may be created by a special educator to cover several types of lesson activities and tasks that classroom teachers typically employ. The paraeducator may then apply the general modification plan to the specific instructional activity or task on a day-to-day basis.

Planning Forms and Formats

Plans do not necessarily adhere to a predetermined format. Many professionals and teams use their creative talents to design forms and formats that respond to the unique characteristics of their own situations. Professionals have sufficient latitude to create a planning form or format that pleases them and addresses the combined needs of the team. The contents of the written plan, the amount of detail, and the specificity of directions are all negotiable. The factors that should be considered include the skills and preferences of the individuals involved, as well as the needs of the program and the student.

Although a paper-based planning form is not necessary and plans may be written on any type of surface (chalkboards, dry-mark boards) or electronic platform (handheld electronic planner, or centrally located computer), school professionals still tend to rely on paper. The use of blank paper means that the plan writer will have to write certain pieces of information or structural aspects of the plan over and over again. Forms eliminate the duplication of effort and streamline the planning process.

Paper-based planning forms, like other planning formats, must meet the dual tests of ease of use and user friendliness. Ease of use means that the plan form or format should be readily available and comprehensive enough to cover all the important topics, yet simple enough that it is easily comprehensible. For example, a template form created and kept on a word processor may be readily available for use by the professional with a computer, whereas multiple copies of the printed form kept in a nearby file folder may be easier for another professional. Form length is also important. Too many topics and subtopics make it difficult to know what to write in each space. Including too few topics may result in the transmission of too little information or of information that is too general to be useful.

User friendliness of the form or format is best judged by the paraeducator. However, user friendliness often means that there is pleasant use of white space or graphics on the page and that the length is sufficient but not overwhelming. A paraeducator, faced with two- to three-page plans, will be less likely to read the plan carefully than if given a single page that is neatly written or typed with plenty of white space. The use of terminology and reading level that is consistent with the paraeducator's knowledge and literacy level is also an important factor in user friendliness. In designing planning forms, professionals should use the following considerations:

1. Contents should reflect the skills of the paraeducator; the needs of the program, student, or professional; and the preferences of both the professional and the paraeducator.
2. The form should be easy to use, readily available, and of appropriate length.
3. The form should be user friendly; it should be easy to read at a glance, use a reading level that all users enjoy, and use the fewest words possible to convey the information.

Newly created forms should be pilot tested for a period to work out the "kinks" and correct omissions.

Examples of Planning Forms

The examples contained in Figures 3.3 through 3.5 have been created by individual teachers and teams of professionals to fit their own circumstances. Each meets the two requirements of ease of use and user friendliness. Although the content is unique to particular situations, there are common elements. The objective or purpose of the activity, lesson, or adaptation is clearly specified. In each case, the goal or purpose of the activity, the specific modifications listed, and the behavioral interventions reflect the decisions made about the needs of students. In early childhood special education programs, plans may be based on Individualized Family Service Plans (IFSPs). In special education programs, plans are guided by Individualized Education Plans (IEPs), Individualized Health Plans (IHPs), or Individualized Behavior Plans (IBPs). In Title I programs, plans are guided by literacy assessment information and, in the case of students with limited English proficiency, language assessment information. Students with needs that require modifications, but who do not qualify for special education, may have a Section 504 plan.

Because many variations in programs and service delivery approaches are used in schools today, it is impossible to create even a few standard forms that would work for everyone. The supervising professional may want to create a form or a format that works for the particular professional and paraeducators involved. The examples in this chapter may serve as planning guides.

Figure 3.3 shows a lesson plan form for a situation where the paraeducator is assigned to a series of general education classrooms because students who need curricular and instructional modifications and adaptations are placed in those classrooms. This type of plan could have been developed by an individual or a team. In this instance, the classroom teacher has prepared a unit for an entire class and has created curricular and instructional modifications and adaptations in collaboration with a special education professional. The paraeducator is assigned to provide support for the modifications or adaptations made for the individual students, as well as general instructional support for the class. Therefore, in addition to Jason's lesson plan, shown in the example, the paraeducator would be carrying plans for each student served in that classroom on a clipboard.

As you examine the contents of this plan, you may notice that there are abbreviations with which you may not be familiar. For example, the term QAR is not familiar to many people.[2] The important factor is that the paraeducator who works from this plan *does* know what QAR is, how to instruct students in the use of QAR, and how to cue students to remember to use QAR. This means that the person who made this plan either taught the

---

[2] QAR stands for Question–Answer Relationship. It is a way for students to recognize that certain kinds of questions demand certain kinds of answers. The use of QAR helps students know how to formulate answers differently according to the demand of the question and the type of source material they are using to find the answer.

Lesson Plan for Application of Modifications and Adaptations

Student: Jason **Date of Plan:** ________ **Duration of Plan:** 3 weeks

1. IEP Objectives
   I. J. will attend to tasks for 20 minutes.
   II. J. will employ self-monitoring strategies to redirect his own attention to assigned tasks.
   III. J. will use knowledge of QARs to find answers in texts and lecture notes.
2. Tasks for General Class Topic: Post-Soviet Eastern Europe
   - Listening to lectures, video, guest speakers
   - Reading from text, periodicals
   - Discussing answers to questions in small groups
   - Writing answers to questions on individual papers
3. Expectations for Jason
   - ☐ Attend to lectures, take notes for 20 minutes, take break, return.
   - ☐ Use QARs to find answers.
   - ☐ Participate in group discussions by finding and contributing answers to group.
   - ☐ Write answers to every other question (either even or odd numbered items, not both).
4. Paraeducator Tasks
   - ☐ Cue Jason with tap on shoulder when he needs to redirect his attention to task during lectures (note taking), reading, and writing tasks.
   - ☐ Provide QAR cue cards for J. to use while looking for answers in text and notes.
   - ☐ Remind J. which questions to answer; assist him in QAR.
   - ☐ Assist all students in use of QAR as they write answers.

Figure 3.3. Sample lesson plan.

paraeducator how to teach QAR or knew that the paraeducator already possessed that skill. Finally, it is important that the responsible professional periodically monitors to see that the paraeducator is using the cueing systems and QAR appropriately.

Figure 3.4 is a lesson plan form for a paraeducator assigned to work with a single student either in an inclusionary situation

Eric's Plan
Week of: ________

Eric's Goal for the Week: To understand that he can choose among activities, but that once he makes a choice he has to stick with it for a period of time.

Sequence of Activity:

1. Eric makes a choice from the choice book.
2. He selects the materials he needs for that choice from the shelf.
3. He sticks with the choice he made for 10 minutes.
4. He stops the activity when the timer rings.

Time Period(s): Frequently throughout every day, whenever an opportune moment arises.

Location: Vary location daily between Room 17, library, computer lab, and fifth-grade classroom.

Activity Choices:

1. Nested boxes
2. Sticker book
3. Alphabet cards
4. Name game
5. Other choices that other fifth-grade students make

Friends' Goals:

1. Observe how to cue Eric to make choices, get materials
2. Know how to redirect Eric when he gets off task
3. Know how to cue Eric to stop when bell rings

Figure 3.4. Sample lesson plan.

or in a pull-out situation or resource room. This plan is for a student with severe cognitive needs and limited social functioning. Eric is included in a fifth-grade classroom for much of the day, but is pulled out to the resource room for frequent, short periods to work on various communication and academic skills. In this case, the team varies the location of the activity because they want Eric to learn that he can make choices in lots of places throughout the day. This plan is good for a week, but the team will vary the plan just a little in subsequent weeks and thus reuse large portions of this week's plan. For example, the goal statement and the activity sequence will be the same next week but the activity choices will change. The team finds that using a planning form makes them very efficient. They do not have to rewrite everything every week. This is especially important because it is not the only plan they make for Eric every week. There are also plans for how he will work and what he will do for every period of the day. The section in the plan that specifies the objectives for Eric's friends is a unique feature of this team's planning format. In this situation, the team is trying to educate students to provide some of the support for Eric so that the adults do not serve to isolate him from his peers. The professionals on the special education team negotiated with the fifth-grade teacher to release several designated students to work with Eric as part of a circle of friends.

The team added the Friends' Goals feature to the planning form when they noticed that the fifth graders were overprotective and tended to do too much for Eric. They realized that to achieve his social goals, they had to teach the other students how to work with him. Thus, whenever Eric is pulled out during these periods of the day, certain of his friends are assigned to accompany him and the paraeducator has clear direction on what they are to learn from the experience.

The form in Figure 3.5 was designed by a special education teacher for a paraeducator working in small groups with students practicing specific skills associated with a particular class. This type of lesson plan format is appropriate for paraeducators who work in resource rooms or in general education classrooms. As in all plans, the paraeducator must understand how to complete all aspects of the lesson. This lesson happens to be about basic vocabulary recognition in ninth-grade biological science for students who have difficulty remembering words and definitions. The teacher who wrote the plan includes a memory device called Keyword.[3] It is not important for the paraeducator to know or understand the theoretical basis for this technique or the instructional method for teaching Keyword to the students, as the teacher does, but it is necessary for the paraeducator to know how to explain it to students and to give good examples. Thus, the paraeducator must be trained and coached to deliver this lesson.

---

[3] *Keyword* is a method where the learner links a word with a definition by constructing a mental image or drawing of a scene that includes the word itself and illustrates the meaning of the word. Like any other skill, students must be taught to understand and use the Keyword method.

Vocabulary Drill and Practice Plan

Objective: Students will read and define vocabulary words with 100% accuracy using a Keyword device.

Activity:

1. Students sit together at round table.
2. Show one card at a time.
3. Say, "What is this word?" and "What does it mean?"
4. If student gives incorrect response or can't respond, say, "This is _____. It means _____." Then help student generate a Keyword memory device to recognize and define the word.

Materials: Prepare 3×5-inch file cards with the following words on one side and definitions on the other: Kingdom, Phyla, Class, Family, Genus, Species. (Use definitions from Chapter 1 of Bio. Sci. Text.)

Student Performance: Record performance:
R = reads it correctly / date *D* = defines it correctly/date

	Kingdom	Phyla	Class	Family	Genus	Species
Ana						
Carol						
David						
Kayla						
Tim						

Figure 3.5. Sample lesson plan.

Modifications and Adaptations to General Education Curriculum and Instruction

The Individuals with Disabilities Education Act (IDEA) amendments of 1997 require that students with special education needs have an individualized plan that includes goals and objectives that enable the student to participate in the general curriculum. In addition, the law specifies that schools must plan for program modifications or supports that permit the student to be involved in the general education curriculum (Sands, Kozleski, & French, 2000). Thus, special education students must have access to the same general education curriculum that their peers receive. IDEA has shifted the emphasis of inclusion of students with disabilities in general education classrooms from a social purpose to an academic purpose. Moreover, it has elevated the importance of careful planning for modifications and adaptations to classroom curriculum and instruction. Now there is legal accountability for the planning of modifications, and school professionals assume the responsibility for providing such plans to paraeducators.

Many people report that paraeducators make decisions about the modifications and adaptations to classroom instruction for individual students when they are assigned one to one (French & Chopra, 1999). This practice has always been ethically questionable, but now IDEA makes it legally dangerous. School professionals hold the responsibility for designing the types of modifications and adaptations that are appropriate and acceptable for students with individualized plans, and for providing written guidance to paraeducators regarding appropriate modifications and adaptations to make on the spot.

What, then, is the role of the paraeducator in modifying and adapting curriculum? The paraeducator holds the ethical responsibility to follow written plans and oral directions provided by any or all of the school professionals assigned to the student with disabilities. The written plans need not be complex or unduly time consuming, however. A simple list of goals and the related modifications and adaptations, covering the range of classroom instructional situations, meets the legal requirements if it is shared with the paraeducator as well as general education teachers. Table 3.5 shows a list of goals with related modifications and adaptations that have been determined to be appropriate for Nick, a 6-year-old who sustained a traumatic head injury.

Table 3.5 makes it clear that any adult working with Nick has the permission to modify or adapt curriculum, materials, and instruction, and to support his achievement of the goals. This list is wordier than other formats, and may not meet the user-friendly criteria for plans, but it does provide a thorough listing of the kinds of adaptations that should be made by the paraeducator. In time, a paraeducator working with Nick will memorize the types of modifications appropriate in various classroom situations.

Table 3.5

Goals and Related Modifications and Adaptations for Nick

Goals for Nick

1. Acquire independence in tasks of daily living.
2. Participate in general education curriculum.
3. Improve eye–hand coordination.
4. Strengthen left side

Modifications and Adaptations Appropriate for Nick (taken from his IEP)

1. Handouts used for coloring are outlined with ¼-inch marker. Cutting papers are also outlined before he cuts. Nick receives hand-over-hand guidance while starting to cut, but such guidance should be gradually diminished as he acquires proficiency.
2. Materials are presented to Nick to the right of his visual field (because of a left-field deficit approximately 45 degrees from midline).
3. Whenever manipulative objects are used in class, Nick should be directed and given hand-over-hand guidance in grasping the objects to strengthen his thumb and index finger grasping. As his proficiency increases, guidance should be reduced.
4. Bead stringing is an activity that may be used when Nick has completed assigned tasks, or during class times when he is unable to participate in typical instructional activities. The purpose of bead stringing is to practice patterning and to improve his visual–motor activities. To help him do this independently, use a plastic straw supported with clay on the table. Guide him to use self-talk about the patterns (as directed).
5. Because Nick's ability to write is limited, while the rest of his class writes sight words, he uses letter stamps to stamp the words on the writing paper.
6. Computer adaptations: Use enlarged numbers and letters on keyboard and screen.
7. During writing time, while other students are writing, Nick dictates his ideas to the paraeducator, or uses a tape recorder to record his story. As his keyboarding skill increases, he will increasingly be expected to key his thoughts rather than dictate them.
8. Provide physical prompts paired with verbal prompts initially. Then fade the physical prompts and use only verbal prompts when Nick uses the bathroom, to encourage his independence in removing and replacing his elastic-waist clothing.

(continues)

Table 3.5 *Continued.*

Modifications and Adaptations Appropriate for Nick *Continued.*

9. Provide verbal prompts to remind Nick to keep his left hand on the tabletop or to use both hands when carrying objects. Remind him to self-monitor and use self-talk.
10. Whenever other students are working on activities on the floor, put Nick in a prone position on hands and knees and ask him to pick up or manipulate objects with his right hand. This encourages him to put weight on his left side and build strength on that side. Make a game of it and include other children in the activity.

Summary

It is legally and ethically correct for professionals who hold responsibility and accountability for the outcomes of an educational program to provide written plans for paraeducators. It is outside the paraeducator's realm of responsibility to create lessons or make modifications to lessons. When children are served by a team, or when a paraeducator is assigned to a team, a decision must be made as to who creates the plans. Teams may choose to plan together or to assign a professional team member to plan for a particular segment. When the school professional plans for the paraeducator, numerous decisions about the goals and objectives, the environment, the behavior management, the activities, and the materials are made and then communicated in written form. Planning forms and formats may vary in content and style according to the unique needs of the team members, but should always contain the goal or purpose of the activity and should meet the dual tests of ease of use and user friendliness. Examples of planning forms show how unique circumstances may be addressed through the use of individually created forms and formats.

Paraeducator Growth and Development: On-the-Job Training

Planning

There are two key reasons for creating a paraeducator growth and development plan and two corresponding plan components.

When a gap exists between the programmatic and professional needs and the paraeducator's skills or levels of confidence, the first reason is readily apparent: Training is needed. Due to the many constraints inherent in bureaucratic systems such as schools, however, training is unlikely to occur incidentally. It must be conscientiously planned if it is to occur at all.

The second reason, while less obvious, is just as important: Paraeducators, like everyone else in schools, are lifelong learners. They need to continually strive for renewal and refinement of their skills and to maintain current knowledge. Areas in which skill refinements are needed are often noted during observations and monitoring of task completion by professionals. In addition, schoolwide initiatives, as well as the paraeducator's personal interests, often provide the substance of other growth and development areas. For example, Ophelia, a paraeducator in a Title I reading program, had a growth and development plan that included training in the district's new balanced literacy curriculum. She participated in the training with many Title I teachers who were also becoming acquainted with the new curricular format and objectives.

Professionals who supervise paraeducators should lead the work of creating a growth and development plan that specifies (a) the training that is needed or desired, (b) the person responsible for securing or arranging the training, (c) the date by which it will be accomplished, and (d) the accountability measures that will assure application of the training to the job duties. An individual growth and development plan should include training areas identified through the needs versus skills analysis, as well as training needs identified through on-the-job monitoring, personal interest, or schoolwide initiative.

Providing Training

Training activities may be provided in numerous ways. Some training may occur on the job, incidentally throughout the day or week, or during team meetings. Other knowledge and skills demand a more formal setting, perhaps a workshop, course, or seminar held either outside of the school day or away from the school setting. To be most effective, training should include theory, demonstration, practice, feedback, and coaching for application (Joyce & Showers, 1980). Theory means that the skill, strategy, or concept is clearly explained or described. Demonstration describes or shows how the skill, strategy, or concept is applied in realistic situations. Practice means that the paraeducator actually tries out the skill or applies the concept in carefully controlled and safe circumstances, either through role play, small group discussion, or actual student interaction.

Feedback then is provided to the paraeducator regarding his or her performance so that, in this safe situation, the paraeducator can continue to practice until the skill is developed well enough to use on the job. Feedback is a communication that gives a person information about how he or she performs. It should help paraeducators consider and alter their performances and thus better achieve the goal. According to Pfeiffer and Jones (1987), feedback is most effective when it is

- descriptive rather than judgmental,
- specific rather than general,
- considerate of the needs of the paraeducator,
- directed toward performance rather than personal characteristics,
- well timed, and
- an accurate transmission of the message (check with the paraeducator).

Finally, coaching occurs on the job while the paraeducator works with students. Coaching is the most significant of all training practices because it allows for fine tuning of newly acquired skills until they become solidly cemented into the paraeducator's repertoire. Without coaching, newly acquired skills also become habitual but may not be correct. When supervisors take on the coaching role, they must take care to separate the coaching functions from the evaluative aspect of their jobs. Paraeducators do not thrive in situations where the supervisor's coaching actions make them feel as through they are being "called on the carpet." Just as coaching of Olympic athletes consists of giving and getting feedback about athletic performance, the coaching of paraeducators consists of giving and getting feedback about performance of essential instructional and other job duties. Coaching may be perceived as threatening to the paraeducator, but a supervisor who takes care to adhere to the feedback criteria listed in the previous paragraph diminishes the threat.

Documenting Training

Documenting paraeducators' training episodes and skill acquisition helps to establish the importance of the training in the culture of the team. It also provides a safeguard in two situations: (a) working with a paraeducator who does not meet the employment standards and (b) protecting the safety and welfare of students.

In the first situation, where a paraeducator is unable or unwilling to do the work, it is important that the professional provide the paraeducator every opportunity to improve the knowledge, skills, or dispositions necessary to do the job. The opportunities should be documented, along with the resulting performances. If performance remains substandard after training, feedback, and coaching have been provided, then, and only then, should dismissal proceedings be enacted.

The second consideration, protecting students' safety and welfare, is especially relevant in programs that include students with health needs. Some health needs are so significant that the lack of proper attention to the task could result in serious injury or health risk to a student. Documentation of specific training regarding health care functions helps the professional remember who is qualified to perform certain tasks and who is not. It also helps the professional remember to provide the same training for paraeducators who are hired midyear that they provided for those hired at the beginning of the year.

For example, Alice, a teacher of students with significant cognitive and physical needs, participated in selecting three paraeducators when her program moved to a new school building. The school nurse, who held ultimate responsibility for the IHPs for these students, trained everyone to perform all necessary health care tasks during the first week of school. Alice showed the new paraeducators some of the video clips she had filmed of herself working with the students during the previous school year. The paraeducators could see exactly how these students needed to be positioned and transferred and how Alice protected her back while lifting or moving the students. Alice worked with the group to demonstrate several instructional methods that were useful with the students. In spite of all the effort Alice spent on appropriate training, within the month one paraeducator left because she decided this job was not right for her. Only 3 weeks later another paraeducator left her position to take a higher paying clerical position in the district's administration building. The third paraeducator left just before Thanksgiving when her husband lost his job and the family had to move. Alice found herself once again engaged in the selecting process, and each time a new paraeducator was chosen Alice had to remember the list of skills on which to provide training and gather the resources to do the training. She knew better than to try to hold all this information in memory. She kept copies of each paraeducator's growth and development plan inside her lesson plan book for handy reference. As she taught each skill to each person, she noted the date and time of day on the plan. Thus, she did not forget any of the procedures and the physical well-being of her students was assured.

Summary

Planning for paraeducator training is important because it is unlikely to occur incidentally and because paraeducators should be lifelong learners. Training should include theory, demonstration, practice, feedback, and coaching for application. Feedback is most effective when it is descriptive, specific, considerate, directed toward performance, well timed, and checked with the recipient. Coaching involves giving feedback to the paraeducator to improve skill performance. Documentation of training activities is necessary to protect the safety of students, as well as the welfare of paraeducators and programs.

Evaluating

Frequently, school professionals play a substantial role in the evaluation of paraeducator performance. Even when their professional contracts preclude direct evaluative responsibility, school professionals often are asked to contribute information that will assist in summative evaluation processes required by the district or agency. The professional's interest in evaluation should go beyond the district's or agency's formal evaluation procedure, however, to promote the paraeducator's growth and development (Pickett et al., 1993). Evaluating the paraeducator's performance may highlight the need for additional training or coaching or may identify high-quality work. Summative performance evaluations may occur at designated times, such as the end of a semester or year, but should reflect multiple reviews of performance rather than the review of a single episode.

Evaluation requires judgment. Fair evaluation is based on a comparison of performance to a standard, on facts rather than opinions, and on first-hand knowledge rather than hearsay. There are four characteristics of fair evaluation: frequency, specificity, honesty, and consistency.

- **Frequency.** Frequent performance ratings yield fairer overall ratings because they document multiple performances of the same or similar tasks and conditions. From the paraeducator's point of view, multiple ratings also help reduce the amount of anxiety or nervousness associated with being evaluated. When Josh was observed for the first time by his supervising school professional, he was extremely nervous and noticed that his hands were shaking. Now, he is more at ease with the process because it has occurred so often.

- **Specificity.** Specificity means that the information contained in the performance rating describes, in behavioral terms, exactly what behavior the paraeducator does or does not display and the judgment regarding that behavior. When a paraeducator receives specific information about poor performance, he or she knows exactly what behavior to avoid in the future. Specificity also means that good performance is recognized and named. For example, after Peggy, a special education teacher, observed Elodia assisting James to eat his lunch, she commented, "Elodia, I noticed that James showed greater interest in eating when you gave him the choice of which food to eat first. That is a good thing to do because it helps him understand that he can make choices."

- **Honesty.** Honesty in evaluation is crucial. Supervisors who simply tell the paraeducator that he or she is doing fine, or who say nothing at all, often find that they have deluded themselves into believing that things will be okay. Eventually, poor performance of tasks or unsatisfactory knowledge, skills, or attitudes will hurt the quality of services to students or may damage the work of the entire team. Honesty means that the supervisor must know and be able to articulate the expected performance as well as the discrepancy that exists. On the other hand, some supervisors make the mistake of believing that the paraeducator already knows that he or she is doing well and, thus, fail to honestly appraise good performance. Honestly identifying and recognizing good performance is as important as honestly confronting poor performance.

- **Consistency.** To be consistent in evaluations, multiple professional team members should either work together to provide performance evaluation information or they should designate a single team member to do so. Because judgment is idiosyncratic, different evaluators are likely to describe the same performance in different ways unless they discuss and come to consensus on the descriptors that apply.

Performance Standards

The establishment of performance standards is one basis for fair evaluation. Performance standards that foster growth and development emerge from the personalized job assignments that were discussed earlier in the orientation section. Once a personalized job assignment is created, a rating scale may then be attached to it and used to document the performance of each duty. The following rating scale reflects the developmental nature of learning how to teach and participate as a team member:

- **Independent**—The paraeducator is able to perform the task, as taught, without guidance.
- **Developing**—The paraeducator can perform the task, as taught, but relies on cues or prompts as guidance for portions of the performance.
- **Emerging**—The paraeducator performs parts of the task or tries to perform but requires substantial guidance or assistance to complete all aspects.

- **Unable to perform**—The paraeducator does not know how to perform the task.

No one learns to perform job duties instantly, and no one is born knowing how to teach well. It takes time and practice to acquire sophisticated levels of skill. Skill level markers such as those listed recognize teaching as a developmental sequence of skills that improve with time and practice.

Ratings of this type may be used to determine the need for further training and coaching or a change of assigned responsibilities. Judgments about whether a paraeducator can reasonably be expected to perform at a given level should be specified in advance. For example, when Audrey, a newly employed paraeducator, started to work, her supervisor, Ed, specified that she would be expected to teach groups of students to use QAR and the Keyword method. Ed expected that, prior to training, Audrey would be unable to perform the task but that, immediately following training, Audrey would perform at an "Emerging" level of performance. He specified that by the end of the first quarter Audrey should be able to provide instruction in both of these learning strategies at an "Independent" level.

Observations

The supervisory function of monitoring performance is best accomplished through firsthand observations of task performance. The most fruitful observations involve written data (Goldhammer, Anderson, & Krajewski, 1980). The data that may be collected during observations vary with the type of observation. The following is a list of several types of data that are useful in unfocused observations, that is, observations that have no particular skill or task as the central feature (French, Kozleski, & Sands, 1992):

- **Audio, video recording**—Observer tapes all events within auditory or visual range.
- **Scripting**—Observer writes down everything he or she hears.
- **Notes on significant instructional events**—Observer writes down instructional events he or she interprets as related to the target skill or behavior.

- **Notes on significant interpersonal events**—Observer writes down interpersonal events he or she interprets as related to the target skill or behavior.

The decision to conduct a focused or an unfocused observation depends on the anticipated outcome. If the goal is to gather general performance information, then an unfocused observation may be appropriate (French et al., 1992). The following are some potential applications of unfocused observation methods:

- personal style components
- voice, gestures, delivery
- content of lesson
- interactions with students or adults
- organization of lesson or materials
- time use
- overall behavior or group management

For example, Martha, a special educator at Blue Ridge High School, wants to monitor the work of the paraeducator, Jose, in general education classes. They meet to plan the observations and Jose indicates that he just wants general feedback on how he moves in and out of classes, how he relates to students, and how he fits in with the flow of the classroom teacher. This calls for data collected by video camera, audio recorder, or scripting. Later, after the observation, Martha and Jose can meet to analyze the data and make evaluative judgments about Jose's performance based on those data.

On the other hand, the supervisor may need specific information about a certain skill or the performance of a particular duty. Or the paraeducator may be working on a certain skill and requesting feedback in that area. A focused observation is in order in these and other cases. The following is a list of some focused observational methods:

- **Checklist**—Identifies or tallies the presence, absence, or frequency of specific behaviors
- **Selective verbatim**—Captures word for word certain preselected events

- **Timeline coding**—Tracks the behaviors of either the paraeducator or the students at frequent intervals during an observation period
- **Seating chart observation records**—Identifies or tallies the specified behaviors of individual students during instruction

The following are some specific target behaviors for which focused methods are best:

- rephrasing or restating questions
- touching, courtesy, listening
- frequency of questions
- types of questions (open vs. closed, factual vs. higher order thinking)
- amount or type of "teacher" talk (giving directions, pertinent examples, talking about tangential topics)
- number of directions
- student at-task behavior
- student or paraeducator movement through the room

The specific target behavior, skill, or task dictates the types of data to be collected. For instance, when Audrey learned the skill of teaching students to use the Keyword method discussed previously, she was concerned that she had difficulty guiding students to use it properly. She asked Ed to observe and take data. They decided that the most useful information would result from the selective verbatim method. Selective verbatim is a technique where the observer writes down all instances of a certain type of interaction or communication (Acheson & Gall, 1980). In this case, Audrey wanted to know if her directions to students about how to use the Keyword method were clear and sequential. Ed observed and recorded all the directions that Audrey gave to her group of students. Later, they examined the written record together. Together, they analyzed the directions for clarity and sequence. Audrey was able to see what she needed to do by studying the data from her own instructional episode. This type of monitoring of job performance honors the dignity of the paraeducator and promotes continual growth and development.

Documenting Performance Ratings

Earlier, the documentation of training episodes was discussed. Documenting training episodes is important because it protects the professional, the student, and the program from various risks, and helps ensure that the training actually takes place. Likewise, documenting performance ratings protects all parties against risk and reminds team members about the need for training. Documentation is most easily and readily accomplished when a paraeducator performance rating form is used to write the date on which oral feedback regarding performance of duties was given and to indicate the skill marker that applies on that date.

Summary

Evaluation of paraeducator performance is also included in the list of executive functions for supervisors of paraeducators. Paraeducator skill development in instructional methods is a developmental process. Different levels of development are expected at different stages of paraeducator employment. Evaluation of paraeducator job performance requires judgment and should be based on fair performance standards, firsthand observations, written data, and appropriate documentation of performance.

Conducting Meetings

Supervisor–paraeducator meetings are fundamental to ethical supervisory behavior. Many of the executive functions of paraeducator supervision can be accomplished only during meetings. Giving directions, providing on-the-job training, providing feedback on performance, solving problems, managing conflicts, communicating about goals, and evaluating are functions that are accomplished primarily when sitting face to face. In one study, however, about 25% of the special education teachers who supervised paraeducators admitted that they never held formalized, sit-down meetings; another 25% said that such meetings were rare (French, 2000). Meetings must be frequent enough to ensure legal and ethical completion of educational tasks and to ensure smooth operation of the team. Meetings must also include the right people and be of significant enough duration to get the agenda accomplished. Whether the team consists of two people—teacher and paraeducator—or of a multidisciplinary group of people, the considerations are the same: establishing when to meet, establishing group norms, establishing a functional meeting location, using an agenda, facilitating discussion, documenting the group's decisions, and reviewing meeting effectiveness.

When To Meet

One of the most frequent laments of teachers is, "There's no time to meet with the paraeducator!" Finding time to meet is important even when it is not urgent. Like many other tasks, professional–paraeducator meetings are among the major but not pressing activities on the matrix presented in Figure 3.1, earlier in the chapter. This group of activities tends to be among the most important of any profession, yet they are the most difficult to attend to because they lack the adrenaline-producing characteristic of urgency. When professionals begin to recognize that paraeducator supervision is indeed an important part of their jobs, then they can begin solving the problem of when to meet. Finding a consistent meeting time may require some creativity. Some teams have requested and received permission to pay paraeducators for meeting time outside of student contact time. In other schools and agencies, that solution is not possible. Some teams have relied on a flexible schedule, where some paraeducators come early or stay late 1 day of the week but leave earlier or later on another day to compensate.

One team in the Ames Elementary special education program for children with severe cognitive, affective, language, and physical needs used a flex schedule to address the dilemma. The program team consisted of a special education teacher, a speech–

language pathologist, four paraeducators, a school nurse 1 morning a week, and a physical therapist 1 morning a week. They also worked with an occupational therapist who consulted with them on a periodic basis. Establishing team meetings where all the members could be present was no small task. After much consideration, Nancy, the team leader, set Thursday mornings at 7:15 as the team meeting time. The usual start time for the paraeducators was 8:15, students arrived at 8:25, and the paraeducators had to greet the buses. This gave the team 1 hour and 10 minutes a week of uninterrupted time to meet, but required the paraeducators to arrive an hour earlier than their usual start time. In trade, each of the four paraeducators selected 1 day of the week to leave 1 hour early. It worked for them because it gave them a predictable extra hour 1 afternoon a week to do errands or make special appointments. When the team took their plan to Mr. Colin, the principal, he wanted to know how they had planned to cover the duties of each paraeducator for that hour. Nancy's job as team leader and schedule-maker was to create a schedule that assured the ongoing education of all the students while the team operated short handed. The Ames Elementary solution may not be the right one for all situations, but the use of flex time makes sense for many types of programs.

Other possible solutions include the creation of a master schedule that permits all team members to have a common planning time during the school week. After school, lunchtime, or school time meetings are possible in some cases and places. No solution, however, is likely to happen without negotiation and careful planning.

Establishing Meeting Norms

Meeting times, once established, are preciously short. Short meetings generally suit most people, but getting the job done is paramount. To maintain short meetings that get the job done requires several organizational conditions. The first is to establish meeting norms and discuss them early in the team's relationship. Norms may be reviewed or changed when needed. Some teams set norms that include punctuality and considerations such as how decisions get made, what problem-solving process to use when a tough challenge presents itself, who will record meeting notes, who will facilitate the conversation, and whether there will be snacks and who will bring them. Teams that have established norms spend less time arguing or rehashing old subjects and get more work done in shorter amounts of time. Teams that fail to establish norms often find themselves wrestling with the same difficult problems repeatedly. For example, one team's members used to drift into the meeting one at a time so that no quorum existed for the first half of the meeting. Those who were punctual sat and discussed the issues but were unable to make final decisions without all the players. By the time the quorum was established, the team had only half the time to do the complete agenda. Items were delayed until the next meeting and the cycle continued. What did they do? One displeased team member took it upon herself to lead a discussion about the way their team functioned. They spent what was left of one meeting talking about their lack of effectiveness and how it was caused by the lack of a norm about punctuality. They made a decision to correct the situation and to self-review at the end of each meeting to decide how they had done. The stress was alleviated and the team's functioning improved.

Meeting Location, Setup, and Atmosphere

Another meeting consideration includes setting a consistent place, away from distractions, and establishing a norm that no one leaves the meeting or accepts outside interruptions. Seating arrangements should also be considered. Teams that get work done at short meetings sit face to face at a table where everyone can see the materials. Some teams have food at meetings, either to establish a pleasant atmosphere or because the meeting occurs during lunchtime. Food, however, can become a distraction. If food causes distraction from the business at hand, it should either be eliminated or a team norm should be established to preserve the businesslike atmosphere.

Agendas

The use of an agenda characterizes effective task-oriented meetings. Agendas may be created in advance by a team leader or by members of the group. Some teams post the blank agenda form in a common location so that all team members can post items that need to be discussed. This system has the advantage of alerting everyone to the topics in advance so that individuals can prepare for the discussion or bring relevant materials. Another approach is to begin each meeting with a statement of the anticipated agenda and allow participants to add items. If the number or complexity of topics promises to exceed the time limit, the group must then prioritize the topics to determine those that must be discussed immediately and those that can be delayed.

Facilitating the Discussion

In smoothly functioning meetings, one person is designated as the meeting facilitator. A facilitator makes sure that each person has a chance to talk and that the conversation is not monopolized by a few members. Facilitators also ensure that each topic is discussed to closure and that the topic is either tabled or terminated. The role of facilitator may be assigned to one team member or rotated among team members.

Sometimes it is difficult for the facilitator to keep track of time. In that case, another person in the meeting may be designated as timekeeper and given the authority to remind meeting participants when time is up on a particular topic. Or the timekeeper may ask the group whether they want to continue the discussion, and therefore extend the length of the meeting.

Documenting Decisions

The decisions made or actions taken at a meeting are irrelevant if no one can remember what they were 2 months later. Documentation is essential to help individuals remember decisions and actions and to establish a written record of plans, training topics, coaching episodes, schedule changes, and decisions about behavioral and instructional interventions for students. An easy way to document meetings is to have a recorder write directly on the agenda form, then make copies for participants. Another way is to have a "Meeting Memo" format that includes topics such as discussions, decisions, and next steps. The sample agenda shown in Figure 3.6 is a combination meeting agenda and record form that can be adapted to fit many specific needs.

AGENDA		
Date:	In attendance:	
TOPIC	**ACTION NEEDED**	**TIME ALLOTMENT**
1.		
2.		
3.		
4.		
MEETING RECORD		
Action / Decision	Person Responsible	Target Date

Figure 3.6. Sample meeting agenda and record form.

Assessing Meeting Effectiveness

Periodically, teams must invest time to self-reflect and review the value and effectiveness of their meetings. Through periodic self-assessment, teams may minimize wasted meeting time, distinguish the tasks they must do together from those that could be done apart, and evaluate the quality of their interactions. It is most useful to monitor meeting components that frequently cause problems, such as participant notification, perceived importance of the meeting, expectations of participants, agenda, punctuality of participants, time flow, time management, listening, problem management, and overall satisfaction with the outcomes.

Summary

Meetings are important because many of the executive functions of paraeducator supervision are accomplished during meetings. Finding a place in the schedule, appropriate locations, and sufficient time challenges the supervising professional. Precious meeting time should be managed by establishing meeting norms, using agendas, facilitating the discussion, and documenting the work of the meeting. Finally, maximum meeting effectiveness is maintained by periodic review of problem areas.

Discussion Questions

1. Discuss how the job of the school professional is like that of an executive or a manager in a corporation or business.
2. Think about a school situation (where you work or where you have observed). Briefly describe the way paraeducators are deployed in the school. Where are they located throughout the day? Who is with them? What impact or effect does that placement have on the supervision provided to them? Who supervises them?
3. Think about jobs you have held. What steps has the employer or the supervisor taken to make sure that you were oriented to the job? Now discuss what you could do to orient new paraeducators to their jobs.
4. Think about the best and the worst working relationships you have had with other people. To what extent were the working relationships affected by similarities and differences in your work styles and preferences?
5. Think about the major tasks required of you (or someone else) each week or month. How do you decide what you do and what the other people do?
6. Think about the types of tasks you might assign to a paraeducator. For each task, decide what skills the paraeducator would need to possess. How can a person learn those skills?
7. Think about times that you have failed to delegate a task to another person. Tell why. Reread the section on why teachers

sometimes fail to delegate when they could. Then talk about your reasons and how they compare to those listed.

EXERCISES

1. Complete a Professional's Work Style form (Worksheet 3.1) for yourself. Consider your own style in terms of how you like to work.
2. Ask someone else to respond to the same questions you have asked yourself. Compare your answers. Then discuss how you would manage the similarities and the differences if you were working in close proximity as teacher and paraeducator.
3. Use Worksheet 3.4 to help you personalize or create a Professional, Program, and Student Needs Inventory that addresses the everyday needs of your classroom or program (or a program that you have observed). Consider which tasks could be performed by a paraeducator and which tasks must remain within the control of the professional.
4. Create a Paraeducator Skills and Confidence Inventory (similar to Worksheet 3.5) to match the Professional, Program, and Student Needs Inventory that you designed in Exercise 3. Ask the paraeducator you supervise to complete the inventory; then work together to create a personalized job description for the paraeducator.
5. Using the instruments you created in Exercises 3 and 4, consider where there is a good match between what needs to be done by the paraeducator and the paraeducator's skills or confidence. Now think about the places in which a gap exists between the two. Are there places where some kind of training would help? If so, create a list of these items so you will remember to find training opportunities that meet the needs.
6. Examine and modify the meeting agenda and record form (Figure 3.6) to suit your own needs and preferences. Create a form that you can copy to reuse. Share it to get feedback from others in the group before finalizing your form.
7. In a small group, discuss the situation Alice experienced in the section titled "Documenting Training," and compare how you

currently keep track of the training a paraeducator receives. Create a way of keeping track of the training you provide to paraeducators who work for you.

8. Think about the components of fair performance ratings or evaluations. If you were being evaluated on your work performance, which of these practices would you want to apply to your situation? What basis should your supervisor use to judge your work?
9. Describe your experiences with meetings of various types. Are there differences in the ways that you participate in and feel about different meetings? What makes a meeting effective? What makes a meeting ineffective?
10. Read the following case study. Then meet with others to discuss the discussion questions that follow the case.

CASE STUDY: SUPERVISION ISSUES

Chris is a special education paraeducator assigned to Diane's fifth-grade classroom because there are three special education students who need additional behavioral and academic supports to be able to succeed in her class. Diane asked Chris to lead a small group reading activity with those students and two others while she observed unobtrusively from a nearby table. She noticed that Chris was slipping into some biased interactions with the students: He was calling on the boys more often than girls; giving boys additional probes and delving more deeply into their thinking to help them answer correctly, while giving girls only one chance before moving on; and avoiding calling on the poorer readers at the table. During the lunch break, she spent a few moments talking about the lesson with Chris. When she began to point out the mistakes, he became defensive, turned away, and muttered loudly enough for her to just barely hear, "You didn't see much of the lesson. You were busy catching up on your paperwork."

Case Study Discussion Questions

a. What executive functions of supervision does Diane need to consider in this case?

b. Whose responsibility is it to provide supervision to Chris?
c. What is the problem? Could it have been avoided?
d. Could Diane have foreseen that this problem was coming?
e. Should Chris have received prior training on how to distribute response opportunities equitably? Who is responsible for such training?
f. Should Diane confront Chris or let it go?
g. Was Diane correct to assign Chris such a task?
h. What do you think about the circumstances under which Diane began to discuss the lesson with Chris?

WORKSHEET 3.1

Professional's Work Style

Directions: Circle the number that indicates your level of agreement or disagreement with each statement.

Item	Disagree				Agree
1. I like to supervise	1	2	3	4	5
2. I like a flexible work schedule	1	2	3	4	5
3. I like to let team members know exactly what is expected	1	2	3	4	5
4. I like to provide (or at least determine) all the materials that will be used	1	2	3	4	5
5. I like to have a written work schedule	1	2	3	4	5
6. I need time to think ahead to the next task	1	2	3	4	5
7. I like to determine the instructional methods that will be used	1	2	3	4	5
8. I like the paraeducator to try new activities independently	1	2	3	4	5
9. I like to give explicit directions for each task	1	2	3	4	5
10. I like to do several things at one time	1	2	3	4	5
11. I like a team that takes on challenges and new situations	1	2	3	4	5
12. I like taking care of details	1	2	3	4	5
13. I like to be very punctual	1	2	3	4	5
14. I like to get frequent feedback on how I can improve as a supervisor	1	2	3	4	5
15. I like to bring problems out in the open	1	2	3	4	5
16. I like to give frequent performance feedback to the paraeducator	1	2	3	4	5
17. I like to discuss when activities do not go well	1	2	3	4	5

(continues)

WORKSHEET 3.1 *Continued.*

Item	Disagree				Agree
18. I like working with other adults	1	2	3	4	5
19. I like to encourage others to think for themselves	1	2	3	4	5
20. I am a morning person	1	2	3	4	5
21. I like to speak slowly and softly	1	2	3	4	5
22. I like to work alone with little immediate interaction	1	2	3	4	5
23. I need a quiet place to work without distractions	1	2	3	4	5
24. I prefer that no one else touches my things	1	2	3	4	5
25. I prefer to work from a written plan	1	2	3	4	5

WORKSHEET 3.2

Paraeducator's Work Style

Directions: Circle the number that indicates your level of agreement or disagreement with each statement.

Item	Disagree				Agree
1. I like to be supervised	1	2	3	4	5
2. I like a flexible work schedule	1	2	3	4	5
3. I like to know exactly what is expected	1	2	3	4	5
4. I like to be told which materials to use	1	2	3	4	5
5. I like to have a written work schedule	1	2	3	4	5
6. I need time to think ahead on the next task	1	2	3	4	5
7. I like to be told the instructional methods I use	1	2	3	4	5
8. I like to try new activities independently	1	2	3	4	5
9. I like to be told how to do each task	1	2	3	4	5
10. I like to do several things at one time	1	2	3	4	5
11. I like to take on challenges and new situations	1	2	3	4	5
12. I like taking care of details	1	2	3	4	5
13. I like to be very punctual	1	2	3	4	5
14. I like to give frequent feedback on how I prefer to be supervised	1	2	3	4	5
15. I like to bring problems out in the open	1	2	3	4	5
16. I like to get frequent feedback on my performance	1	2	3	4	5
17. I like to discuss when activities do not go well	1	2	3	4	5
18. I like working with other adults	1	2	3	4	5
19. I like to think things through for myself	1	2	3	4	5
20. I am a morning person	1	2	3	4	5

(continues)

WORKSHEET 3.2 *Continued.*

Item	Disagree				Agree
21. I like to speak slowly and softly	1	2	3	4	5
22. I like to work alone with little immediate interaction	1	2	3	4	5
23. I need a quiet place to work without distractions	1	2	3	4	5
24. I prefer that no one else touches my things	1	2	3	4	5
25. I prefer to work from a written plan	1	2	3	4	5

WORKSHEET 3.3

Work Style Score Sheet

Directions: Transfer scores from Worksheets 3.1 and 3.2 to this form. Examine areas of agreement and disagreement. Your combined profile is unique. There are no "correct" scores or combinations. Decide whether or not your combinations are okay. Have a conversation in which you strive to determine how you will proceed to work together in light of your areas of agreement and disagreement.

Professional Disagree Agree	General content of item	Paraeducator Disagree Agree
1 2 3 4 5	1. Supervision	1 2 3 4 5
1 2 3 4 5	2. Flexibility of work schedule	1 2 3 4 5
1 2 3 4 5	3. Preciseness of expectations	1 2 3 4 5
1 2 3 4 5	4. Decisions on which materials to use	1 2 3 4 5
1 2 3 4 5	5. Written work schedule	1 2 3 4 5
1 2 3 4 5	6. Time to think ahead to the next task	1 2 3 4 5
1 2 3 4 5	7. Decisions about instructional methods	1 2 3 4 5
1 2 3 4 5	8. Trying new activities independently	1 2 3 4 5
1 2 3 4 5	9. Specifying how to do each task	1 2 3 4 5
1 2 3 4 5	10. Doing several things at one time	1 2 3 4 5
1 2 3 4 5	11. Taking on challenges	1 2 3 4 5
1 2 3 4 5	12. Taking care of details	1 2 3 4 5
1 2 3 4 5	13. Punctuality	1 2 3 4 5
1 2 3 4 5	14. Feedback on supervision	1 2 3 4 5
1 2 3 4 5	15. Dealing with problems out in the open	1 2 3 4 5

(continues)

WORKSHEET 3.3 *Continued.*

Professional Disagree Agree		General content of item	Paraeducator Disagree Agree
1 2 3 4 5	16.	Frequent performance feedback	1 2 3 4 5
1 2 3 4 5	17.	Discussing activities that do not go well	1 2 3 4 5
1 2 3 4 5	18.	Working with other adults	1 2 3 4 5
1 2 3 4 5	19.	Thinking things through for myself	1 2 3 4 5
1 2 3 4 5	20.	Being a morning person	1 2 3 4 5
1 2 3 4 5	21.	Speaking slowly and softly	1 2 3 4 5
1 2 3 4 5	22.	Working alone with little interaction	1 2 3 4 5
1 2 3 4 5	23.	Quiet place to work without distractions	1 2 3 4 5
1 2 3 4 5	24.	Touching others' things	1 2 3 4 5
1 2 3 4 5	25.	Working from a written plan	1 2 3 4 5

WORKSHEET 3.4

Professional, Program, and Student Needs Inventory

Directions: Consider the needs of the team, program, and students as a whole. Decide whether each task or duty could be completed by a paraeducator. Teams may individualize this inventory by changing items that are not applicable as stated, or by replacing items with more appropriate tasks or duties. Specify details as needed for clarity.

Task or duty	Paraeducator can do: Yes	Paraeducator can do: No
Delivery of Instruction		
1. Observe and record student progress in academic areas	☐	☐
2. Help students in drill and practice lessons (e.g., vocabulary, math facts)	☐	☐
3. Read or repeat tests or directions to students	☐	☐
4. Listen to students read orally	☐	☐
5. Help students with workbooks or other written assignments	☐	☐
6. Assist students to compose original work (e.g., stories, essays, reports)	☐	☐
7. Tape-record stories, lessons, or assignments	☐	☐
8. Modify instructional materials according to directions (e.g., lesson plans, IEPs)	☐	☐
9. Read to students (e.g., texts, stories)	☐	☐
10. Help students work on individual projects	☐	☐
11. Facilitate students' active participation in cooperative groups	☐	☐
12. Help students select library books or reference materials	☐	☐
13. Help students use computers (specify purpose _______)	☐	☐
14. Translate instruction or student responses (e.g., sign or other language)	☐	☐
15. Translate teacher-made materials or text materials into another language	☐	☐

(continues)

WORKSHEET 3.4 *Continued.*

Task or duty	**Paraeducator can do** Yes	No
Delivery of Instruction *Continued.*		
16. Explain or reteach concepts to students in other language (e.g., sign, Spanish)	☐	☐
17. Carry out lessons on field trips as directed	☐	☐
18. Monitor student performance as directed	☐	☐
19. Reteach or reinforce instructional concepts introduced by the classroom teachers	☐	☐
Activity Preparation and Follow-up		
20. Find or arrange materials or equipment (e.g., mix paints, set up lab materials)	☐	☐
21. Modify or adapt materials or equipment for particular student	☐	☐
22. Construct learning materials	☐	☐
23. Prepare classroom displays	☐	☐
24. Order materials and supplies	☐	☐
25. Organize classroom supplies or materials	☐	☐
26. Operate equipment (e.g., tape recorders, VCRs, overhead projectors)	☐	☐
27. Make audio or visual aids (e.g., transparencies, written notes, voice notes)	☐	☐
28. Schedule guest speakers or visitors as directed	☐	☐
29. Help prepare and clean up snacks	☐	☐
30. Help students clean up after activities	☐	☐
31. Distribute supplies, materials, or books to students	☐	☐
32. Collect completed work from students	☐	☐
33. Participate in planning of learning experiences for students with teacher	☐	☐

(continues)

WORKSHEET 3.4 *Continued.*

Task or duty	Paraeducator can do: Yes	Paraeducator can do: No
Supervision of Groups of Students		
34. Assist students on arrival or departure	☐	☐
35. Supervise groups of students during lunch	☐	☐
36. Supervise groups of students during recess	☐	☐
37. Supervise groups of students loading or unloading buses	☐	☐
38. Monitor students during hall-passing periods	☐	☐
39. Escort groups of students to bathroom, library, gym, etc.	☐	☐
40. Accompany students to therapy sessions, individual appointments	☐	☐
Behavior Management		
41. Participate in classroom behavior system as directed	☐	☐
42. Observe and chart individual student behavior	☐	☐
43. Give positive reinforcement and support as directed by IEPs or Individualized Behavior Plans	☐	☐
44. Mediate interpersonal conflicts between students	☐	☐
45. Provide instruction to students on how to mediate their own conflicts	☐	☐
46. Provide cues or prompts to students who are mediating conflicts	☐	☐
47. Provide physical proximity for students with behavior problems	☐	☐
48. Circulate in classroom to provide behavioral supports where needed	☐	☐
49. Enforce class and school rules	☐	☐
50. Assist students who are self-managing behavior (e.g., provide cues, prompts)	☐	☐
51. Help students develop or self-monitor organizational skills	☐	☐
52. Provide cues or prompts to students to use impulse or anger control strategies	☐	☐

(continues)

WORKSHEET 3.4 *Continued.*

Task or duty	**Paraeducator can do** Yes	No
Behavior Management *Continued.*		
53. Provide cues or prompts to students to employ specific prosocial skills	☐	☐
54. Teach prosocial skill lessons	☐	☐
55. Facilitate appropriate social interactions among students	☐	☐
56. Assist other students in coping with the behaviors of specific students	☐	☐
Ethics		
57. Maintain confidentiality of all information regarding students	☐	☐
58. Respect the dignity and rights of every child at all times	☐	☐
59. Report suspected child abuse according to the law, local policies, and procedures	☐	☐
60. Abide by school district policies, school rules, and team standards in all areas	☐	☐
61. Communicate with parents and families as directed by the teacher	☐	☐
62. Provide accurate information about the student to those who have the right to know (e.g., team members)	☐	☐
63. Carry out all assigned duties responsibly, in a timely manner	☐	☐
64. Protect the welfare and safety of students at all times	☐	☐
65. Maintain composure and emotional control while working with students	☐	☐
66. Demonstrate punctuality and good attendance; report absences as directed	☐	☐
67. Maintain acceptable hygiene and appearance	☐	☐

(continues)

WORKSHEET 3.4 *Continued.*

Task or duty	Paraeducator can do: Yes	Paraeducator can do: No
Team Participation and Membership		
68. Meet with team as scheduled or directed	☐	☐
69. Participate in team meetings by contributing information, ideas, and assistance	☐	☐
70. Participate in team meetings by listening carefully to the ideas of others	☐	☐
71. Engage in appropriate problem-solving steps to resolve problems	☐	☐
72. Engage in mature, conflict management steps and processes	☐	☐
73. Use appropriate communicative actions in adult–adult interactions	☐	☐
74. Respect the privacy and dignity of other adults	☐	☐
75. Participate in learning activities as specified in growth and development plan	☐	☐
76. Participate in schoolwide growth and development activities as specified	☐	☐
Clerical Work		
77. Take attendance	☐	☐
78. Type reports, tests, seatwork, IEPs, assessment reports	☐	☐
79. Make copies	☐	☐
80. Sort and file student papers	☐	☐
81. Record grades	☐	☐
82. Collect fees (e.g., lab, book, milk, activity)	☐	☐
83. Correct assigned student lessons and homework	☐	☐
84. Grade objective tests	☐	☐
85. Help with paperwork to facilitate parent–teacher appointments	☐	☐

(continues)

WORKSHEET 3.4 *Continued.*

Task or duty	Paraeducator can do: Yes	Paraeducator can do: No
Clerical Work *Continued.*		
86. Inventory materials and fill out routine forms	☐	☐
87. Make arrangements for field trips	☐	☐
88. Maintain files for IEPs, assessment reports, other program reports	☐	☐
89. Maintain databases of student information	☐	☐
Other		
90. Attend IEP meetings with classroom teacher	☐	☐
91. Attend parent–teacher conferences with classroom teacher	☐	☐
92. Communicate with families (specify ______)	☐	☐
93. Contribute unique skills and talents (specify ______)	☐	☐
94. Attend after-school activities (specify ______)	☐	☐

WORKSHEET 3.5

Paraeducator Skills and Confidence Inventory

Directions: Complete this form by considering your own skills and confidence to perform each task. Decide how well prepared and confident you feel on each task or duty. Scores may range from 1 to 5. Circle 1 if you are unprepared to do the task and want or need training in order to begin. Circle 2 to indicate that you may begin doing the task, but need further instruction on how to do it well. Circle 3 or 4 to indicate that you are confident enough to do the task but want to improve your skills. Circle 5 if you feel well prepared and highly skilled to perform that task.

	Paraeducator preparation				
Task or duty	**Unprepared**				**Highly skilled**
Delivery of Instruction					
1. Observe and record student progress in academic areas	1	2	3	4	5
2. Help students in drill and practice lessons (e.g., vocabulary, math facts)	1	2	3	4	5
3. Read or repeat tests or directions to students	1	2	3	4	5
4. Listen to students read orally	1	2	3	4	5
5. Help students with workbooks or other written assignments	1	2	3	4	5
6. Assist students to compose original work (e.g., stories, essays, reports)	1	2	3	4	5
7. Tape-record stories, lessons, or assignments	1	2	3	4	5
8. Modify instructional materials according to directions (lesson plans, IEPs)	1	2	3	4	5
9. Read to students (e.g., texts, stories)	1	2	3	4	5
10. Help students work on individual projects	1	2	3	4	5
11. Facilitate students' active participation in cooperative groups	1	2	3	4	5

(continues)

WORKSHEET 3.5 *Continued.*

Task or duty	**Paraeducator preparation** Unprepared				Highly skilled
Delivery of Instruction *Continued.*					
12. Help students select library books or reference materials	1	2	3	4	5
13. Help students use computers (specify purpose _______)	1	2	3	4	5
14. Translate instruction or student responses (e.g., sign or other language)	1	2	3	4	5
15. Translate teacher-made materials or text materials into another language	1	2	3	4	5
16. Explain or reteach concepts to students in other language (e.g., sign, Spanish)	1	2	3	4	5
17. Carry out lessons on field trips as directed	1	2	3	4	5
18. Monitor student performance as directed	1	2	3	4	5
19. Reteach or reinforce instructional concepts introduced by the classroom teachers	1	2	3	4	5
Activity Preparation and Follow-Up					
20. Find or arrange materials or equipment (e.g., mix paints, lab materials)	1	2	3	4	5
21. Modify or adapt materials or equipment for particular student	1	2	3	4	5
22. Construct learning materials	1	2	3	4	5
23. Prepare classroom displays	1	2	3	4	5
24. Order materials and supplies	1	2	3	4	5
25. Organize classroom supplies or materials	1	2	3	4	5
26. Operate equipment (e.g., tape recorders, VCRs, overhead projectors)	1	2	3	4	5

(continues)

WORKSHEET 3.5 *Continued.*

Task or duty	Paraeducator preparation: Unprepared				Highly skilled
Activity Preparation and Follow-Up *Continued.*					
27. Make audio or visual aids (e.g., written transparencies, notes, voice notes)	1	2	3	4	5
28. Schedule guest speakers or visitors as directed	1	2	3	4	5
29. Help prepare and clean up snacks	1	2	3	4	5
30. Help students clean up after activities	1	2	3	4	5
31. Distribute supplies, materials, or books to students	1	2	3	4	5
32. Collect completed work from students	1	2	3	4	5
33. Participate in planning learning experiences for students with teacher	1	2	3	4	5
Supervision of Groups of Students					
34. Assist students on arrival or departure	1	2	3	4	5
35. Supervise groups of students during lunch	1	2	3	4	5
36. Supervise groups of students during recess	1	2	3	4	5
37. Supervise groups of students loading or unloading buses	1	2	3	4	5
38. Monitor students during hall-passing periods	1	2	3	4	5
39. Escort groups of students to bathroom, library, gym, etc.	1	2	3	4	5
40. Accompany students to therapy sessions, individual appointments	1	2	3	4	5
Behavior Management					
41. Participate in classroom behavior system as directed	1	2	3	4	5

(continues)

WORKSHEET 3.5 *Continued.*

Task or duty	Paraeducator preparation: Unprepared				Highly skilled
Behavior Management *Continued.*					
42. Observe and chart individual student behavior	1	2	3	4	5
43. Give positive reinforcement and support as directed by IEPs or Individualized Behavior Plans	1	2	3	4	5
44. Mediate interpersonal conflicts between students	1	2	3	4	5
45. Provide instruction to students on how to mediate their own conflicts	1	2	3	4	5
46. Provide cues or prompts to students who are mediating conflicts	1	2	3	4	5
47. Provide physical proximity for students with behavior problems	1	2	3	4	5
48. Circulate in classroom to provide behavioral supports where needed	1	2	3	4	5
49. Enforce class and school rules	1	2	3	4	5
50. Assist students who are self-managing behavior (e.g., provide cues, prompts)	1	2	3	4	5
51. Help students develop or self-monitor organizational skills	1	2	3	4	5
52. Provide cues or prompts to students to use impulse or anger control strategies	1	2	3	4	5
53. Provide cues or prompts to students to employ specific prosocial skills	1	2	3	4	5
54. Teach prosocial skill lessons	1	2	3	4	5
55. Facilitate appropriate social interactions among students	1	2	3	4	5
56. Assist other students in coping with the behaviors of specific students	1	2	3	4	5

(continues)

WORKSHEET 3.5 *Continued.*

Task or duty	Paraeducator preparation: Unprepared				Highly skilled
Ethics					
57. Maintain confidentiality of all information regarding students	1	2	3	4	5
58. Protect the privacy of students during personal care	1	2	3	4	5
59. Respect the dignity and rights of every child at all times	1	2	3	4	5
60. Report suspected child abuse according to law, policies, and procedures	1	2	3	4	5
61. Abide by school district policies, school rules, and team standards in all areas	1	2	3	4	5
62. Communicate with parents and families as indicated by the teacher	1	2	3	4	5
63. Provide accurate information about the student to those who have the right to know (e.g., team members)	1	2	3	4	5
64. Carry out all assigned duties responsibly, in a timely manner	1	2	3	4	5
65. Protect the welfare and safety of students at all times	1	2	3	4	5
66. Maintain composure and emotional control while working with students	1	2	3	4	5
67. Demonstrate punctuality and good attendance; report absenses as directed	1	2	3	4	5
68. Maintain acceptable hygiene and appearance	1	2	3	4	5
Team Participation and Membership					
69. Meet with team as scheduled or directed	1	2	3	4	5

(*continues*)

WORKSHEET 3.5 *Continued.*

Task or duty	**Paraeducator preparation** Unprepared				Highly skilled
Team Participation and Membership *Continued.*					
70. Participate in team meetings by contributing appropriate information, ideas, and assistance	1	2	3	4	5
71. Participate in team meetings by listening carefully to the ideas of others	1	2	3	4	5
72. Engage in appropriate problem-solving steps to resolve problems	1	2	3	4	5
73. Engage in mature conflict management steps and processes	1	2	3	4	5
74. Use appropriate communicative actions in adult–adult interactions	1	2	3	4	5
75. Respect the privacy and dignity of other adults	1	2	3	4	5
76. Participate in learning activities as specified in growth and development plan	1	2	3	4	5
77. Participate in schoolwide growth and development activities as specified	1	2	3	4	5
Clerical Work					
78. Take attendance	1	2	3	4	5
79. Type reports, tests, seat work, IEPs, assessment reports	1	2	3	4	5
80. Make copies	1	2	3	4	5
81. Sort and file student papers	1	2	3	4	5
82. Record grades	1	2	3	4	5
83. Collect fees (e.g., lab, book, milk, activity)	1	2	3	4	5
84. Correct assigned student lessons and homework	1	2	3	4	5

(continues)

WORKSHEET 3.5 *Continued.*

Task or duty	Paraeducator preparation				
	Unprepared				Highly skilled
Clerical Work *Continued.*					
85. Grade objective tests	1	2	3	4	5
86. Help with paperwork to facilitate parent–teacher appointments	1	2	3	4	5
87. Inventory materials and fill out routine forms	1	2	3	4	5
88. Make arrangements for field trips	1	2	3	4	5
89. Maintain files for IEPs, assessment reports, other program reports	1	2	3	4	5
90. Maintain databases of student information	1	2	3	4	5
Other					
91. Attend IEP meetings with classroom teacher	1	2	3	4	5
92. Attend parent–teacher conferences with classroom teacher	1	2	3	4	5
93. Communicate with families (specify ____________)	1	2	3	4	5
94. Contribute unique skills and talents (specify ____________)	1	2	3	4	5
95. Attend after-school activities (specify ____________)	1	2	3	4	5

References

Acheson, K. A., & Gall, M. D. (1980). *Techniques in the clinical supervision of teachers: Preservice and inservice applications*. New York: Longman.

Alexander, H. L. (1987). *Developing a working relationship with teachers and paraeducators.* Topeka: Kansas State Department of Education.

Berliner, D. (1983a). The executive functions of teaching. *Instructor, 93*(2), 28–33, 36, 38, 40.

Berliner, D. C. (1983b). *If teachers were thought of as executives: Implications for teacher preparation and certification* (EDRS Document No. 245357). Paper prepared for the National Institute of Education Conference on State and Local Policy Implications of Effective School Research.

Douglass, M. E. (1979). *The time management workbook.* Grandville, MI: Time Management Center.

Drawbaugh, C. C. (1984). *Time and its use: A self-management guide for teachers.* New York: Teachers College Press.

Emery, M. J. (1991). *Building team pride: Teachers and paraeducators working together.* Columbus: University of Missouri.

French, N. K. (1996). A case study of a speech–language pathologist's supervision of assistants in a school setting: Tracy's story. *Journal for Children's Communication Development, 18*(1), 103–110.

French, N. K. (1998). Working together: Resource teachers and paraeducators. *Remedial and Special Education, 19*, 357–368.

French, N. K. (2000). *A survey of special education teachers who supervise paraprofessionals.* Unpublished manuscript, University of Colorado at Denver.

French, N. K., & Chopra, R. V. (1999). Parent perspectives on the roles of paraprofessionals. *JTASH, 24*(4), 259–272.

French, N. K., & Chopra, R. V. (2000). *Paraprofessional roles in inclusion: Problems and promising practices.* Unpublished manuscript, University of Colorado at Denver.

French, N. K., Kozleski, E. B., & Sands, D. S. (1992, December). *Practicum experiences for special education teachers: A handbook for teachers who supervise special education practicum students.* Resources in Education (EDRS Document No. 334 778).

Gartner, A. (1971). *Paraeducators and their performance: A survey of education, health and social services programs.* New York: Praeger.

Goldhammer, R., Anderson, R. H., & Krajewski, R. J. (1980). *Clinical supervision: Special methods for the supervision of teachers* (2nd ed.). New York: Holt, Rinehart and Winston.

Individuals with Disabilities Education Act Amendments of 1997, 20 U.S.C. § 1400 *et seq.*

Joyce, B., & Showers, B. (1980). Improving inservice training: The messages of research. *Educational Leadership, 37,* 379–385.

McConkey, D. D. (1974). *No-nonsense delegation.* New York: AMACOM.

Pfeiffer, J. W., & Jones, J. E. (1987). *A handbook of structured experiences for human relations training* (Vol. 3). San Diego, CA: University Associates.

Pickett, A. L. (1986). Certified partners: Four good reasons for certification of paraprofessionals. *American Educator, 10*(3), 31–34, 47.

Pickett, A. L. (1994). *Paraprofessionals in the education workforce.* Washington, DC: National Education Association.

Pickett, A. L., Vasa, S. F., & Steckelberg, A. L. (1993). *Using paraeducators effectively in the classroom* [Fastback No. 358]. Bloomington, IN: Phi Delta Kappa Educational Foundation.

Sands, D. J., Kozleski, E. B., & French, N. K. (2000). *Inclusive education for the 21st century: A new introduction to special education.* Belmont, CA: Wadsworth.

Sullivan, M. (1980). *Managing your time and money . . . Strategies for success.* New York: American Express.

Vasa, S. F., Steckelberg, A. L., & Ulrich-Ronning, L. (1982). *A state of the art assessment of paraprofessional use in special education in the state of Nebraska.* Lincoln: University of Nebraska–Lincoln, Department of Special Education and Communication Disorders.

4 Team Roles in Therapy Services

Thomas M Longhurst

OVERVIEW

The focus of this chapter is on employees who serve in partnership with or alongside professional-level therapists as aides or assistants in schools and other educational settings. These multidisciplinary, multilevel service providers are often referred to as support personnel because they support therapists, teachers, and parents. For ease of collective reference in this chapter, the aides and assistants in related services are designated *paratherapists*. These paratherapists are increasingly recognized by state licensure regulations and in the Individuals with Disabilities Education Act (IDEA) regulations. The chapter includes discussions of occupational therapy, physical therapy, and speech–language pathology services; distinctions in the roles and duties of therapists, aides, and assistants; preservice and inservice training for paratherapists including paratherapist career pathways; and a discussion of appropriate standards of paratherapists' roles. The chapter concludes with a discussion of therapist supervision of aides and assistants. Because there is considerable specialized terminology in this chapter that may be new to teachers, administrators, and paraeducators, a glossary of key terms is provided at the end of the chapter.

Instructional Objectives

After studying this chapter and participating in discussions and exercises, the reader will be able to do the following:

1. Describe changes in education and early intervention programs that have increased the need for therapy aides and assistants in these settings.
2. Describe the practice of speech–language pathology and physical and occupational therapy in the schools.
3. Describe the differences between aides' and assistants' roles in therapy services.
4. Identify responsibilities of the therapy team that are reserved for the therapists.
5. Describe standards for paratherapist employment and training across the three disciplines.
6. Compare and contrast different forms of credentials in use for paratherapists.
7. Describe career pathways for paratherapists.
8. Describe therapist responsibilities in the supervision and management of paratherapists.
9. Interpret common acronyms used in therapy services.

The Need for Paratherapists in Education and Early Intervention

Two major factors in the last two decades have significantly increased the need for paratherapists. First, the number of children and youth with disabilities attending schools has increased over this time period. Education systems are serving more children with more severe, multiple disabilities than ever before. Our school systems are also serving much younger children. The advent of expanded services to infants, toddlers, preschoolers, and their families has increased the need for therapists and the paratherapists who work alongside them. This increased need for more and improved services has occurred at the same time that state governments and schools are being faced with cuts in education funding and generally decreased resources.

As the therapy professions have developed and because their practice consists both of technical, routine tasks and executive, diagnostic or decision-making tasks, the technical or routine tasks are increasingly assigned or delegated to paratherapists. Because of increased diversity of therapy sites, frequency of services, and daily follow-through, a therapist can serve more students and serve them better with the appropriate use of paratherapists.

The administrative aspects of therapy services must be a concern of all therapists as well as school administrators. The quality of therapy services and their relevance to the educational goals of students, families, and administrators must be paramount. With increasing costs for therapists working either as school employees or on contract, the cost-effectiveness and clinical efficacy of therapy services take on increasing importance. Utilizing paratherapists appropriately can decrease costs and thereby increase clinical efficiency. The frequency of therapy can be increased, which often increases effectiveness.

A philosophy of appropriate paratherapist utilization in the schools should be that well-trained, appropriately assigned or delegated, and well-supervised paratherapists can be an effective and efficient adjunct to therapist services. Appropriate paratherapist utilization can stabilize increasing costs or even decrease costs while maintaining high-quality services.

The School Therapy Team

Professional School Therapists

The professionals who provide therapy in the schools are known as (a) speech–language pathologists or SLPs, (b) physical therapists or PTs, and (c) occupational therapists or OTs. Sometimes SLPs are called speech therapists, speech–language clinicians, communication disorders specialists, as well as other titles, but the generally accepted title is speech–language pathologist. Often therapists will list their related degrees after their names and designate their credential(s), as in Carrie L. Mori, MS, OTR/L, which means that Carrie has a master of science degree, is registered by the American Occupational Therapy Association (AOTA), and is licensed by the state. Speech–language pathologists often list their degrees and then designate CCC-SLP after their degree to indicate they hold a certificate of clinical competence in speech–language pathology from the

American Speech-Language-Hearing Association (ASHA) and state licensure. The AOTA offers an Advanced Practitioner (AP) credential in school services for both OTs and occupational therapy assistants (OTAs). Physical therapist Gordon E. Rosenberg, MPT, FAPTA, for example, has a master's degree in physical therapy and is a Fellow of the American Physical Therapy Association (APTA). The APTA provides board certification in pediatrics as a specialty recognition.

SLPs have a long history of service in the schools and are the therapists with whom teachers, administrators, students, and their families are most likely to be familiar. Although SLPs work in a variety of settings with all age groups, the greatest proportion work in the schools. Changes in education delivery systems, increasing numbers of children who need services for communication disorders, and technological advances have resulted in an expanding scope of practice for SLPs in the schools. SLPs are integral to the rehabilitation of students with traumatic brain injury (TBI), students developing communication skills through augmentative and alternative communication (AAC) systems, and students with feeding and swallowing problems.

SLPs work with many students with hearing disabilities, learning disabilities, and language impairment. Students with speech articulation and phonological, or sound production, problems are a major segment in most public school caseloads. Although SLPs traditionally worked mostly with younger children (Grades K through 3), more recently they have moved into secondary education where they have experienced great success in developing better communication skills in adolescents and facilitating these students' transitions to work or postsecondary training or education. SLPs also play a major role in communication skill development of infants, toddlers, and preschool children.

Physical therapists often contract their services to schools or other provider agencies and occasionally may be employees. The minimum practice requirements for professional entry is a master's degree in physical therapy. PTs are specialists in the use of assistive and supportive devices that improve mobility, in positioning students, in performing therapeutic modalities, and in using exercises with and without equipment that improve strength of muscles and range of motion of joints. They teach use of safety harnesses, walkers, and other adaptive equipment. They teach the skills of safely lifting and transferring students. Their work is designed to develop strength and range of motion that can then be used in walking, sitting, feeding, writing, using a keyboard, and performing other activities of daily life.

Occupational therapists are often employed by the schools or may have contracts for service with the schools. They are skilled at using the muscle strength and range of joint movement developed by physical therapists to adapt and teach activities of daily living (ADLs). They determine effective adaptive equipment needs and classroom modifications for individual students. Some school employees or families may question the need for OTs in the schools because they assume OTs are trained to focus on adults who are undergoing vocational rehabilitation to reenter the workforce after an accident or other physical trauma. Occupational therapists, however, are sometimes employed to work with adolescent students who have traumatic brain injury and especially with infants, toddlers, preschool, and early elementary children, and their families in teaching ADLs that most educators take for granted in more typical students. It tends to improve understanding of the role of OTs to say that the occupation of young children is play and acquiring skills and the occupation of students is learning. OTs teach play and learning skills, as well as ADLs such as oral feeding and swallowing, crawling, sitting, standing, and walking. OTs are well known for providing sensory integrative therapy and perceptual motor therapy in the schools. Their knowledge of and programs for handwriting are well accepted in the schools as well. OTs also are skilled in the use of adaptive devices that augment skills or provide alternative means for accomplishing school tasks. To meet the challenges of serving infants, toddlers, and their parents, the AOTA offers specialty certification in pediatrics.

Often therapists from the three disciplines work together collaboratively on related services teams to support teachers and improve classroom learning for students at the local level. They provide educationally relevant services. Their intervention skills are complementary and closely interrelated, and these therapists are trained to work together in an interdisciplinary fashion. Each therapy discipline uses a multiskilled, multilevel workforce that incorporates the use of well-trained aides and assistants.

Aides and Assistants: Distinctions in Therapy Services

Within the disciplines of occupational therapy, physical therapy, and speech–language pathology, there are clear distinctions between the roles of aides and assistants (see Table 4.1). These two paratherapist categories differ in the amount of preservice education or training required for their positions, required credentials, the extent of their scope of practice, the amount and type of supervision they require, and the pay and fringe benefits they receive.

Aide is a paratherapist title given to individuals with a minimum level of training and a limited scope of practice in student treatment. The aide is typically an unlicensed, uncertified school employee who works under the direction of the licensed therapist. On-site and close or continuous supervision by the

Table 4.1
Distinctions of Aides and Assistants

Therapy Aides

1. Minimum level of formal training
2. Limited scope of practice
3. Uncertified, unlicensed
4. Prescribed, specifically *assigned* routine tasks
5. On-site, continuous supervision when working with students
6. Usually hourly pay, often near minimum wage and with fringe benefits

Therapy Assistants

1. Associate degree from accredited program
2. Expanded scope of practice
3. Certified, licensed
4. *Delegated,* expanded treatment functions
5. Supervised but may provide treatment without therapist present
6. On-site and distant work settings
7. Usually a salaried employee with fringe benefits comparable to therapist's

therapist of sessions where an aide is in contact with a child or youth is recommended for best practice. The aide carries out designated or specifically assigned routine tasks. These tasks include transporting, transferring, and positioning students; maintaining, cleaning, and assembling materials, devices, and equipment; performing clerical duties; and working with students as assigned in a closely monitored and supervised therapy environment. Continuous supervision means the therapist is in sight of the aide who is performing client-related tasks. In most circumstances, the aide is required to have a high school diploma or GED, to be at least 18 years of age, and to have completed some occupational training in high school, in a postsecondary training facility, or during on-the-job training in the work setting. Aides are often hourly employees with pay near minimum wage and few fringe benefits. Some states recognize additional training or experience through pay grades or levels (I, II, III) within the aide category.

Assistant is a paratherapist title given to individuals with an associate's degree (or equivalent) from a physical therapist assistant (PTA), accredited occupational therapy assistant (OTA), or approved speech–language pathology assistant (SLPA) technical training program. Currently, there are about 250 PTA programs and 300 OTA programs nationwide. There are only about 15 associate's degree programs in speech–language pathology, although the number will continue to increase as more colleges develop associate's degree programs. ASHA approves training programs and registers SLPAs. PTAs and OTAs are typically certified and in most states are licensed or registered employees of either the school district, private therapist, or agency that contracts with the school. Thirty states certify or license SLPAs, and ASHA is planning to offer national registration for SLPAs. ASHA has developed guidelines for supervision of SLPAs (ASHA, 1996) and has also developed practical tools and forms for supervising SLPAs in educational settings (ASHA, 1999).

Assistants only work under supervision of the therapist. In many cases the therapist is not present while the experienced assistant is working with students. An assistant's scope of practice is significantly expanded from that of the aide. Assistants' education, expertise, and clinical training allow them to focus their efforts on executing treatment protocols with students and their families. Although they do not diagnose, develop, or change treatment protocols without permission, experienced assistants may work somewhat independently in carrying out treatment protocols planned by the therapist.

Distinctions in Team Roles

Therapists, aides, and assistants work as a team. Although each has his or her own scope of practice, they share many duties and work together to accomplish common goals and objectives.

Responsibilities of therapists fall into two basic categories: (a) assessing and developing, implementing, and modifying treatment plans, and (b) providing supervision and on-the-job training to paratherapists. Responsibilities defined in the scope of practice of therapists are outlined in Table 4.2. The professional organizations representing the three disciplines (AOTA, APTA, and ASHA) have specific guidelines for the training and experiences of therapists prior to supervising aides or assistants.

The therapist who will be responsible for supervising an aide or assistant should participate in interviews with potential aide and assistant employees. Participation in this process encourages involvement of the therapist because he or she is helping to select the paratherapist(s) with whom he or she will work. It is also the therapist's responsibility to inform students, families, teachers, and administrators of the training and scope of practice of the paratherapist.

The therapist has primary responsibility for making all decisions related to referrals, diagnosis, eligibility for therapy, prognosis, assessment, proposed frequency and duration of therapy, plan development, implementation, modification, and eventual dismissal from therapy. The therapist represents the team in meetings and prepares, edits, and signs all correspondence and reports. Specific intervention tasks are assigned to the aide or delegated to the assistant, first through written prescription and then through weekly and daily protocols. The therapist is responsible for discipline-specific on-the-job training, mentoring, and supervision of paratherapists. The responsibility for ensuring that paratherapists only provide services consistent with their level of training and experience and within the established scope of practice is an important respon-

Table 4.2
Therapist's Responsibilities

1. Complete supervisor training and participate in continuing education.
2. Participate in interviewing paratherapist.
3. Document preservice training and credentials of paratherapist.
4. Inform students, families, and coworkers about paratherapist's roles.
5. Determine frequency and duration of therapy.
6. Represent the team in meetings, correspondence, and reports.
7. Make significant clinical decisions.
8. Determine caseload assignments.
9. Communicate with students and family members regarding diagnosis, prognosis, eligibility, and dismissal.
10. Conduct diagnostic evaluations and interpret results.
11. Initiate treatment.
12. Prepare the intervention plan and approve modifications with other team members.
13. Delegate specific intervention tasks.
14. Review intervention plan implementation.
15. Refer to and communicate with other professionals.
16. Provide on-the-job training and mentoring to paratherapists.
17. Approve and document paratherapist inservice training and continuing education.
18. Provide and document paratherapist supervision.
19. Ensure that paratherapist provides services within the scope of practice.

sibility of the therapist. The therapist should participate in ongoing and annual performance evaluations of paratherapists conducted by building or district administrators. Although these administrators provide overall employee supervision, discipline-specific supervision should be provided only by qualified therapists.

As shown in Figure 4.1(a), treatment duties of paratherapists at either the aide or assistant level are subsets of therapists' responsibilities. The aide is assigned only a very small portion of the therapist's treatment duties. Typically aides assist the therapist with tasks such as maintaining and generalizing already learned behaviors and the therapist is physically present to provide close or continuous supervision. Assistants are delegated a significant portion of the therapist's treatment duties and can work more independently (if experienced) in expanded functions consistent with their more extensive training and experience when compared to the aide. With regard to nontreatment duties, such as clerical and housekeeping tasks, the aide and the assistant perform most of these tasks, leaving time for the therapist to com-

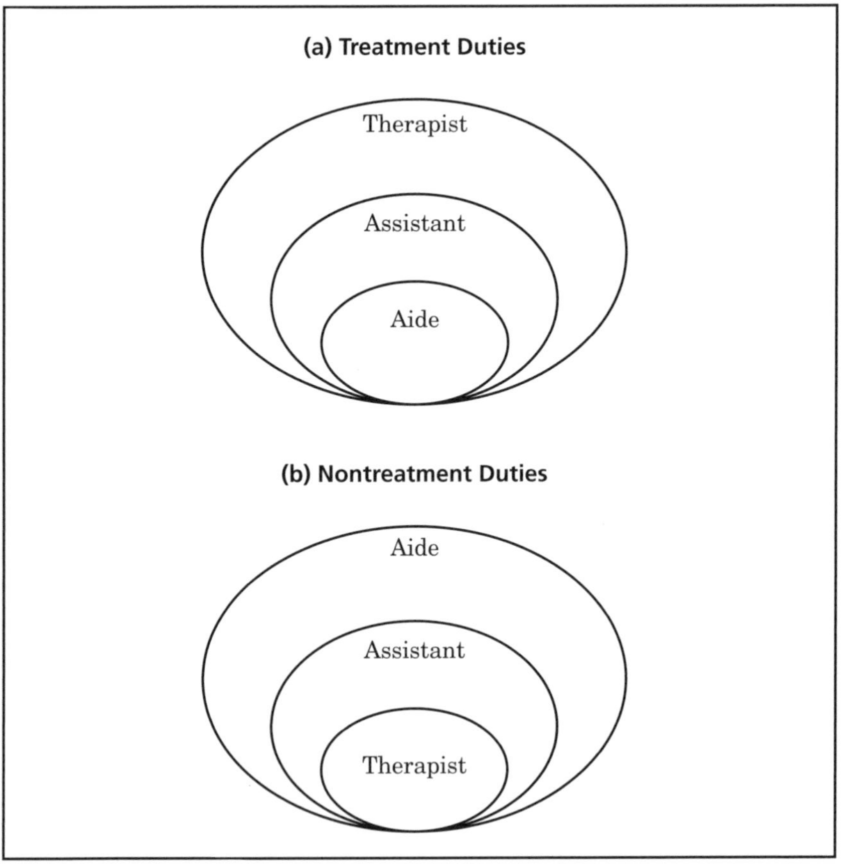

Figure 4.1. Team members' duties.

plete those duties that are exclusively his or hers. Figure 4.1(b) shows how the team is responsible for nontreatment duties.

Therapists and paratherapists share many responsibilities (see Table 4.3). All team members must know and adhere to legal, ethical, and confidentiality standards when interacting with students, family members, and their coworkers. They must demonstrate effective communication skills, appropriate human relations skills, advocacy skills, and respect for their coworkers. All are responsible for providing a healthy and safe therapy environment and for dealing appropriately with emergencies.

With regard to treatment, all members of the team must understand their respective scopes of practice and carry out their responsibilities within prescribed boundaries. All team members must work together to provide efficient and effective

Table 4.3
Shared Responsibilities of Therapy Team Members

1. Knowledge of typical growth and development
2. Knowledge of developmental and acquired disabilities
3. Knowledge of educational service system
4. Ethical conduct
5. Effective communication
6. Human relations skills
7. Leadership and advocacy skills
8. Infection control, safety precautions, and procedures for dealing with emergencies
9. Appropriate behavior management
10. Efficient and effective intervention
11. Observation and reporting skills
12. Intervention documentation skills
13. Ability to use assistive devices
14. Psychosocial support to students and families
15. Administrative and clerical skills
16. Participation in continuing education and professional growth

intervention services in support of educational goals for students and families. All participate in on-the-job training, inservice training, and continuing education within the schools or through colleges or universities, and all participate in their respective state and national professional organizations.

Each team member needs to be aware of the hierarchy of the responsibilities of team members. For example, communication with students, family members, and other service providers regarding referrals, diagnoses, intervention, and other programmatic decisions, such as eligibility and dismissal, are the therapist's responsibility. An aide or assistant should refer questions or comments about these matters to the therapist by saying, for example, "Ms. Jones will be here tomorrow at 2:00 and I'm sure she would be happy to answer that question for you," or "Mr. Rivera, my supervisor, is available at this telephone number and he can answer that question for you." Also, representing the therapy team in staffings is the responsibility of the therapist, although aides or assistants may participate at the request of the family, student, or therapist. Another example of how shared duties may be applied at different levels is that, although all team members must practice ethical conduct and work within school regulations and legal standards, the therapist is ultimately responsible for all activities performed by his or her paratherapist in the work setting. Many duties are primarily paratherapist responsibilities, although they too are shared by the therapist who has responsibility for overall management. Clearly, many therapist duties with respect to intervention can be carried out by trained and experienced paratherapists when they are assigned or delegated and supervised by the therapist. Maintaining a safe and healthy work environment is an important task for all team members. Paratherapists may assist with cleaning and disinfecting work surfaces, materials, and equipment. They may also collect and construct materials and maintain bulletin boards. They help with organizing therapy materials and keeping equipment and therapy apparatus in good working order. They also collect or construct equipment designed by the therapist and team.

In addition, paratherapists contribute significantly to the team's efficiency and effectiveness by performing clerical duties such as scheduling appointments and meetings, answering the telephone and documenting messages, requesting preevaluation documents, filing and retrieving reports and charts, photocopying documents, and word processing. They also help in training students, teachers, and family members to use assistive devices and AAC systems. As members of the team, paratherapists must have a general knowledge of typical patterns of child growth and development, as well as disabilities of both a developmental and acquired nature. Behavior management, treatment protocol implementation, and intervention procedure skills are critical paratherapist competencies, as well as skillful nonjudgmental observation, documentation, and reporting to the therapist. Both aides and assistants need to be knowledgeable about assistive and adaptive devices within their discipline and across the therapies. The ability to provide psychosocial support for children and youth and their families is also a very important skill, when applied within the paratherapist's scope of practice. Paratherapists are also expected to develop personally and professionally to maintain their employability and to facilitate team success by assisting with a variety of administrative functions. Enabled through their training and experience, and consistent with their aide or assistant scope of practice and under the supervision of the therapist, paratherapists supplement the therapist's ability to work with the sizable caseloads typical in the schools. Therapists thereby have more time to fulfill responsibilities that are exclusively theirs.

Standards for Paratherapist Training and Utilization

All three therapy professions recognize paratherapists at the aide and assistant levels to make their team treatment more productive and efficient. Each of the three professions, through AOTA, APTA, and ASHA, has established a formal scope of practice statement and personnel preparation standards for aides and assistants. These standards have been used successfully for over four decades. AOTA and APTA, as well as individual states, recognize paratherapists through formal credentials and accredited training programs. Appropriate assignment of paratherapist roles in all three therapy disciplines is addressed in state practice acts, licensure statutes, or certification regulations, as well as scope of practice statements of the AOTA, APTA, and ASHA or individual states.

Granting credentials such as certification, registration, or licensing is a formal method of recognizing individuals' education and experience, whereas accreditation and approval are processes of recognizing educational training programs that meet minimum standards of space, faculty, learning resources, and practica for training individuals. Certification may be in the form of a completion certificate that documents that a student has completed a course of study. Certification can also mean the individual has completed formal training and passed a board examination, such as that for becoming a certified occupational therapy assistant (COTA). Certification may be administered either nationally or by a specific state agency or even a training program. Licensure or registration is typically awarded through state statute or through a regulatory board. Licensure legally protects the public from untrained practitioners and prohibits persons from using the title or designation without first having met all of the requirements (education, clinical experience, and board examinations). Registration is a less stringent form of credentialing than certification or licensure but serves many of the same purposes.

Until recently, the profession of speech–language pathology has had much less formal guidelines than occupational or physical therapy, with no nationally recognized credentialing or program accreditation procedures. Recently, ASHA approved formal guidelines for speech–language pathology assistants (SLPAs) at either the associate's degree level (or equivalent) or bachelor's degree level (ASHA, 1996).

Physical Therapist Assistant (PTA)

Training Outcomes

An example of a model for PTA training outcomes developed by the Idaho Board of Vocational Education (IBVE, 1994d) is shown in Table 4.4. More detailed information regarding the PTA's competencies and roles may be found in APTA (1999) or on the APTA Web site (www.apta.org).

Table 4.4
Training Outcomes for Physical Therapy Assistants (PTAs)

1. Demonstrate a basic understanding of typical human development.
2. Describe the educational service system and the role of the PTA.
3. Assist with administration and clerical functions.
4. Perform written, oral, and nonverbal communication techniques effectively.
5. Perform student services, including the following:
   a. Instruct student, family, and other personnel in use of assistive and supportive devices that improve mobility.
   b. Position and instruct student, family, and other personnel in correct positioning.
   c. Perform therapeutic modalities.
   d. Perform and instruct student, family, and other personnel in therapeutic exercise with or without equipment.
6. Perform any lifting and transferring of student with correct body mechanics to ensure the safety of the student and self.
7. Describe typical joint range of motion.
8. Demonstrate ability to implement treatment procedures for rolling, crawling, sitting, standing, and walking, and the movement to get from one position to the next.
9. Demonstrate safety precautions as regards to safety harnesses, walkers, and other adaptive equipment.
10. Assess each student's progress and effectiveness of treatment plan.
11. Provide psychosocial support to students and families.

Note. Adapted from *Technical Committee Report and Curriculum Guide for Physical Therapy Assistant* (Vocational Education No. 285), by Idaho Board of Vocational Education, 1994, Boise, ID: Author.

There is an extensive and very successful history of educating and utilizing PTAs. The fields of occupational therapy and physical therapy have many basic similarities, as well as some major differences. PTs or OTs often explain the differences as follows: "The PT team focuses on improving strength, range of motion, and mobility, whereas the OT team focuses on using that developed strength, range of motion, and mobility to develop skills in activities of daily living." In the schools these ADLs include all of the fine and gross motor skills needed to facilitate educational opportunities for students.

PTAs complete a 2-year, associate's degree in an accredited program. Much of the first year is devoted to general education coursework in humanities, oral and written communication skills, mathematics, natural sciences, and biological sciences with emphasis on psychology and sociology. The second year focuses on PTA coursework and laboratory work, as well as clinical education experiences.

Most states regulate PTAs through state statute, board regulation, or both, and credential PTAs through licensing, certification, or registration. The APTA accredits PTA programs and provides guidelines for clinical education as well as considerations for developing PTA training programs. More specific information is available at the APTA Web site (www.apta.org).

Services

The PTA is a qualified paratherapist in the practice of physical therapy who delivers services to children and youth as delegated by and under the supervision of the licensed PT. There is provision for expanded functions through a PTA career ladder (PTA I, II, and III) within the PTA category. After the PT has evaluated the student's record, interviewed the student and family, physically assessed the student, and designed the student's treatment, the actual treatment is often then delegated to the PTA. The PTA will communicate any observed changes in the student's condition, which may require that the PT reassess the student and then modify the treatment program. PTs and PTAs work in a variety of clinical settings. In the schools, PT services are likely to be delivered through a school contract with a PT. Under these contracts, the PTA may be employed by the PT or may be employed by the school and supervised by a PT under contract.

The preservice curriculum for the PTA is designed to prepare the PTA to work under the supervision of a qualified PT who has responsibility for the learner's treatment. Once the learner has been evaluated by the PT, the PT delegates specific aspects of treatment to the PTA and the PTA is required to practice only within those prescribed boundaries. Delegation is typically done based on the following factors as noted by Watts (1971): (a) the situation is predictable and the consequences of the treatment are not perilous to the student; (b) the stability of the situation is great and dramatic change is unlikely to occur; (c) the observability of basic indications of problems with the student's treatment is immediately apparent and readily experienced; (d) basic indicators of problems with the student are clear and unambiguous and the indicators are not easily confused with other phenomena; and (e) the consequences of an inappropriate choice by the PTA will not seriously endanger the student. If a student needs both physical and occupational therapy services, and both are included in his or her plan, these services are often administered in a very collaborative fashion with the PT and OT team working together to meet common educational goals.

Occupational Therapy Assistant (OTA)

Training Outcomes

A specific model for training outcomes for certified occupational therapy assistants (COTAs) developed by the IBVE (1994e) is shown in Table 4.5. Competencies for and role delineation between OTs and COTAs may be found in Johansson (1999) and on the AOTA Web site (www.aota.org). The AOTA Council for Occupational Therapy Education (ACOTE) also periodically publishes guidelines for accreditation of OTA programs which present in detail the approved training standards for OTAs. Gitlow (1997) has provided a description of the prerequisites for OTA training programs. An important clue to the overall role of OTs and OTAs is found in the AOTA Web site subtitle, Occupational Therapy: A Vital Link to Productive Living.

OTAs complete a 2-year associate's degree program in an ACOTA-accredited program or may complete somewhat shorter training to receive a certificate only. The first year is focused on general education comparable to that of the PTA. The second year is devoted to OTA coursework and laboratory work as well as fieldwork. Graduates pass a national examination prior to being certified.

Table 4.5
Training Outcomes for Certified Occupational Therapy Assistants (COTAs)

1. Demonstrate a basic understanding of typical human development.
2. Describe typical fine motor and play development.
3. Describe the educational service system and the role of the COTA.
4. Assist with administration and clerical functions.
5. Effectively perform written, oral, and nonverbal communication techniques.
6. Perform student services, including the following:
   a. Instruct student, family, and other personnel in use of assistive and supportive devices that improve mobility.
   b. Position and instruct student, family, and other personnel in correct positioning.
   c. Perform therapeutic activities.
   d. Perform and instruct student, family, and other personnel in therapeutic exercise with or without equipment.
7. Assist in determining effective adapted equipment needs or classroom modifications.
8. Demonstrate ability to execute an oral feeding program.
9. Assess each student's progress and effectiveness of treatment plan.
10. Provide psychosocial support to students and families.

Note. Adapted from *Technical Committee Report and Curriculum Guide for Certified Occupational Therapy Assistant* (Vocational Education No. 284), by Idaho Board of Vocational Education, 1994, Boise, ID: Author.

Services

The OTA is a qualified paratherapist in the practice of occupational therapy who delivers services to students under supervision of an OT. OTs and OTAs work in a variety of settings. OT services in the education setting are often contracted by the OT, and the OTA may be employed by the school or agency or be an employee of the OT. Much like the PTA, an OTA carries out treatment after the OT has evaluated the learner and designed the treatment. The occupation of children and youth is playing (Couch, Deitz, & Kanny, 1998), being a student, and achieving academically, and, as they get older, learning to drive and holding a part-time job. OTs and OTAs look at the student as a whole person, including individual lifestyle and interests, and they focus on improving the student's "occupational" skills. The OT and OTA help the student attain or regain more independence in ADLs. When working with a student with disabilities, the goal is to build on individual strengths to ensure success in all life activities such as education, recreation, and vocation.

The OT team focuses on sensory processing (how an individual receives and perceives information through a variety of sensory systems), somatosensory perception (awareness of sensations from joints, muscle, and skin receptors), and praxis (motor planning and smoothly and effortlessly executing motor behaviors during learned tasks; AOTA, 1997b). The OT team is especially useful in the schools helping children and youth with visual-perceptual and motor problems in reading and writing (Vreeland, 1999). They also help students who have hyper- or hyposensitivity to touch; students with concentration, attentional, or hyperactivity problems; students with balance and clumsiness problems; and those with dyspraxia (significant difficulty in planning and executing motor behaviors) that can negatively impact every aspect of the student's life requiring fine or gross motor skills (AOTA, 1997a). The OT team is also skilled at working with students with complex health care needs (Lowman et al., 1999).

The OT team typically uses ADLs as the vehicle for their therapy, breaking down these activities into small, manageable steps. Two of the most critical activities are interpersonal communication and feeding–swallowing, activities in which OT and SLP team practices clearly overlap. Preservice interdisciplinary training and training to work together on the job are increasingly recognized as best practice (Giuffrida & Kaufman, 1999).

Speech–Language Pathology Assistant (SLPA)

Training Outcomes

The issue of whether to use support personnel in speech–language pathology has been debated for over 25 years. Generally speaking, those who favor their use feel that access to services will improve, the SLP's specialized skills and time will be put to better use, and the best interests of students and families will be served. Those who oppose their use feel that quality of services will suffer, services of SLPs will be devalued, and students and families will be misled. Idaho has established a model for SLPA training outcomes (IBVE, 1994f), listed in Table 4.6. Longhurst (1997b) described the development of these guidelines and curriculum in more detail. More detailed information may be found in the ASHA guidelines for SLPAs (ASHA, 1996).

In addition to the training standards established by ASHA, a consortium of seven national professional organizations, working collaboratively, have developed guidelines for SLPAs employed in various educational settings. These consortium members included representatives from ASHA; the Council of Administrators of Special Education (CASE); the Council for Exceptional Children (CEC) and two of its subdivisions, the Division for Early Childhood (DEC) and the Division for Children's Communication Development (DCCD); the Council of Language, Speech, Hearing Consultants in State Education Agencies; and the National Association of State Directors of Special Education (NASDE).

SLPAs complete a 2-year accredited associate's degree program. Most of the first year of the SLPA curriculum is devoted to general education coursework in oral and written communication skills, biology, psychology, linguistics, mathematics, multicultural and diversity studies (which are also infused in other courses), and introduction to communication disorders. The second year is focused on SLPA coursework and fieldwork. All SLPA students are expected to develop and demonstrate computer skills, including word processing, data entry and retrieval, records systems, and basic computer applications to clinical intervention.

Services

The SLPA is a qualified paratherapist in the practice of speech–language pathology who delivers services to students as delegated by and under the supervision of the SLP (Paul-Brown & Goldberg, 2001). The SLPA carries out the treatment of the student after the SLP has assessed the student, developed the treatment plan, and initiated intervention. After therapy is initiated by the SLP and a maintenance and monitoring stage is reached, the SLPA takes over day-to-day therapy and carefully observes and reports changes that

Table 4.6
Training Outcomes for Speech–Language Pathology Assistants (SLPAs)

1. Describe an overview of developmental and acquired disabilities.
2. Demonstrate ethical standards of conduct.
3. Describe the educational and related services delivery system.
4. Demonstrate a knowledge of distinctions of SLP and SLPA roles.
5. Practice effective communications.
6. Practice infection control and safety precautions.
7. Demonstrate phonetics skills.
8. Describe the anatomy and physiology of speech–language production and the impact of various illness, injury, malformation, and surgery.
9. Describe typical processes of speech and language development.
10. Describe typical processes of hearing development and principles of hearing measurement.
11. Demonstrate ability to implement treatment procedures for phonological disorders, delays, and differences.
12. Demonstrate ability to implement treatment procedures for language and communication disorders, delays, and differences.
13. Describe the treatment for hearing disorders and the professions that provide the treatments.
14. Demonstrate ability to implement aural habilitation and rehabilitation treatment procedures.
15. Assist with speech and language screening procedures.
16. Demonstrate behavior management skills.
17. Assist with treatment plan implementation.
18. Observe, record, and report students' specific behaviors.
19. Assist students with hearing aids and other communication devices.
20. Assist with routine maintenance and cleaning of equipment and storage areas.
21. Assist with provision of psychosocial support to students and families.
22. Assist with administrative and clerical duties.

Note. Adapted from *Technical Committee Report and Curriculum Guide for Speech–Language Pathology Assistant* (Vocational Education No. 292), by Idaho Board of Vocational Education, 1994, Boise, ID: Author.

may require modification of the treatment plan by the SLP after further assessment.

The associate's degree in speech–language pathology curriculum is designed to prepare the SLPA to work only through delegation and under the supervision of a qualified SLP who retains all legal, ethical, and programmatic responsibility for the students' treatment. SLPA roles or scope of practice will become more refined, although current guidelines (ASHA, 1996; CEC, 1997) specify these roles reasonably well.

There are only minor differences between the ASHA guidelines and the consortium guidelines described previously. ASHA registers SLPAs and approves SLPA training programs. The consortium guidelines suggest that state departments of education credential speech–language paratherapists. ASHA acknowledges the aide level; however, the ASHA guidelines do not include the aide level. ASHA does recognize those with bachelor's degrees in SLP, if recommended by an ASHA-approved SLPA program, as SLPAs with no officially described expanded functions consistent with their higher level of education. The consortium guidelines have a tiered system with different roles at each level. A multitiered system of speech–language paratherapist service delivery is effective and efficient because it delineates tasks that can be performed by basic-, intermediate-, and advanced-level paratherapists (Longhurst, 1997b). ASHA's guidelines suggest generic training and paratherapist utilization in a variety of work settings, while the consortium guidelines focus more on early intervention and school practice. A more basic difference between the two sets of guidelines is that ASHA recognizes as supervisors only SLPs with a certificate of clinical competence (CCC) from ASHA, whereas the consortium guidelines suggest state certification for SLPs who supervise.

Physical, Occupational, and Speech Therapy Aides

As much as possible, all aides who work with students with disabilities and their families should receive a common core of competency-based values training (see top section of Table 4.7). In Idaho this is accomplished through application of a statewide curriculum for training providers of services to persons with developmental disabilities (commonly called DD aide; IBVE, 1993). The applied program of this curriculum is *Creating Visions: Direct*

Table 4.7
Core Competencies for Developmental Disabilities (DD) Aides

1. Discuss an overview of disabilities.
2. Demonstrate a knowledge of the following:
   a. ethical treatment
   b. methods of building positive behaviors
   c. IFSP/IEP implementation and monitoring
3. Provide for health and safety needs.
4. Explain roles and needs of family.

Individuals completing discipline-specific aide training should be able to do the following:

1. Describe typical growth and development processes.
2. Describe developmental and acquired disabilities.
3. Explain discipline-specific aide role and responsibilities.
4. Practice ethical and effective communication.
5. Assist with the following:
   a. transport, transfer, and positioning students
   b. assistive devices
   c. maintenance and cleaning
   d. general treatment procedures
   e. group sessions
   f. observations and reporting
   g. treatment documentation
   h. clerical duties
6. Assist therapist or assistant with discipline-specific treatment and procedures.
7. Observe, document, and report.
8. Apply job-keeping skills.

Note. Adapted from *Technical Committee Report and Curriculum Guide for Providers of Services to Persons with Developmental Disabilities, Level 1* (Vocational Education No. 269), by Idaho Board of Vocational Education, 1993, Boise, ID: Author.

Care Service Provider Training Manual by Burton, Gee, and Overholt (1992) and an accompanying instructor's guide (Burton & Seiler, 1992). Other programs (Rast, 1992; Robinson, 1987; Vassiliou, 1991) have been developed to serve similar purposes.

This initial training consists of didactic training, in-class activities, and about 16 hours of supervised observation and practicum in the schools. The goals of this training are to help the aide understand the characteristics of students with developmental or acquired disabilities and then to demonstrate appropriate skills for working with them and their families during therapeutic interactions. Through this training, aides learn definitions and appropriate use of categorical labels, ethical behavior, how to build positive behaviors, how to implement basic treatment plans, and how to facilitate educational development of students with disabilities. They learn how to provide a clean, safe, and healthy environment and to prepare for emergencies. They also learn the benefits of peer and family support; how to positively involve family members in treatment; and how to communicate effectively with students, their families, and coworkers. This DD aide training is required as a prerequisite to OT, PT, or SLP aide training in Idaho.

Discipline-specific (OT, PT, or SLP) aide training builds on skills learned in the DD aide training and then develops additional competencies (see lower section of Table 4.7; IBVE, 1994b, 1994c, 1994e). Many of the competencies needed by OT, PT, or SLP aides are common to all three disciplines, but each field has additional competencies that are discipline specific. All three types of aides develop knowledge and skills in describing typical developmental sequences and processes in infants, toddlers, children, and youth. All aides also develop competencies in basically describing developmental, sensory and physical, and acquired disabilities such as cerebral palsy, autism, mental retardation, learning and behavioral disabilities, hearing and communication impairments, and traumatic brain injury.

After the introduction to fine motor, gross motor, personal–social, cognitive, and language development, and a basic survey of disabilities, training for aides centers on discipline-specific content. For example, OT and PT aides focus on fine and gross motor development, such as rolling over, sitting, grasping, crawling, balancing, feeding, swallowing, standing, and walking. SLP aides learn more about early language development, auditory discrimination and perception skills, oral-motor skills such as feeding and swallowing, and communication assistive technologies.

Each aide learns to explain discipline-specific roles and responsibilities and is taught how to practice ethical standards and effective communication. Although there is some commonality of training across the three disciplines, much of the remaining aide training focuses on the training procedures, materials, equipment, and devices specific to each discipline. In most cases, procedures for observations, reporting, and treatment documentation are unique to the discipline. The aide must learn to work alongside and assist the therapist as assigned in individual and group sessions. Typically the therapist is present and providing continuous supervision.

Career Pathways for Paratherapists

All three therapy disciplines use a multitiered system. A career pathway for paratherapists is a preplanned and articulated system of advancement within or across therapy disciplines (Longhurst, 1997a). The career pathway for paratherapists in Idaho is provided in Figure 4.2 as an example of an articulated system that facilitates paratherapist mobility. A career pathway helps to remove barriers for advancement through the discipline levels. The potential is that paratherapists are provided opportunities for increased maturity, experience, on-the-job training, and continuing education, as well as financial support to move through the career pathway, possibly terminating at the level of therapist within the discipline. Opportunities for training across disciplines are also inherent in a career pathway. For example, training an individual as both an OT aide and a PT aide, or as an OT aide and an SLP aide, would facilitate the delivery of therapy services.

Managing Paratherapists

In Chapter 3, French provides an excellent overview of how to manage paraeducators that is entirely appropriate in content to managing paratherapists. The executive functions of therapists include planning for paratherapists, managing schedules, training, assigning or delegating tasks, and creating and maintaining standards of practice. In addition, therapist licensure standards, national certification standards, formal professional practice statements, and

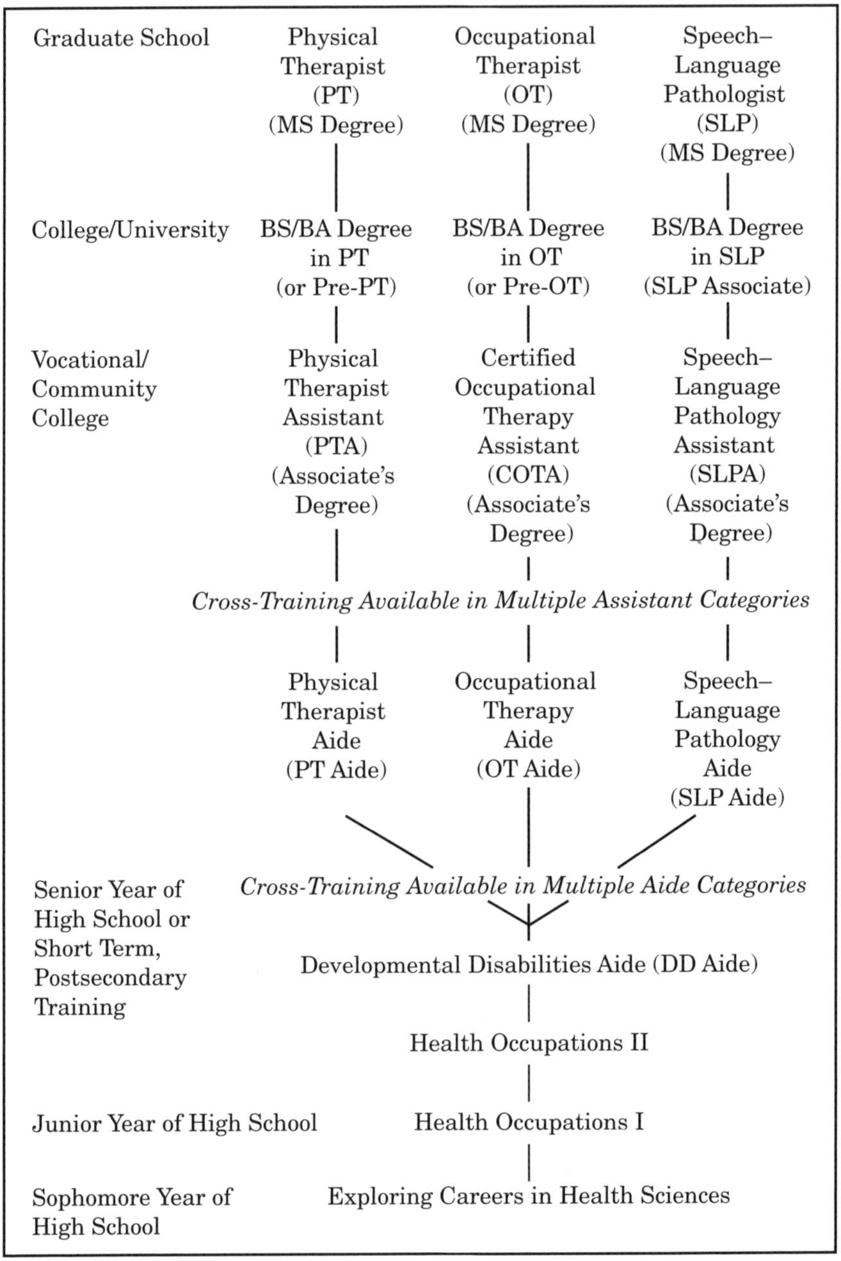

Figure 4.2. Idaho Career Pathways for Paratherapists. *Note.* From "Career Pathways for Related Service Paratherapists Working in Early Intervention and Other Education Settings," by T. M Longhurst, 1997a, *Journal of Children's Communication Development, 18,* p. 30. Copyright 1997 by PRO-ED, Inc. Reprinted with permission.

codes of ethics require specific frequency and duration of supervision by therapists (see Table 4.8 for a summary of these requirements). The supervision requirements stated in these documents are typically viewed as minimum requirements. They specify that it is the therapist's responsibility to design, provide, and document a supervision scheme that protects students' rights and maintains the highest standards of quality care. Higher levels of supervision would be required based on the paratherapist's training and experience, the children and youth served, the specific work setting, and the proximity to the supervisor. For example, more intense, close supervision is required in the orientation of a recently hired paratherapist, or during the initiation of a new program or change in student status. The degree of learner contact by the paratherapist, the complexity of the tasks, the technical nature of the tasks, and even the level of interpersonal interaction required may help determine the appropriate level and type (direct vs. indirect) of supervision (McFarlane & Hagler, 1995). These factors, as well as others, also determine the level of supervision (close, routine, general, or minimal).

The different disciplines generally agree that a therapist should supervise a maximum of three full-time paratherapists. More than one supervisor may provide supervision of a given paratherapist, but not for the same student, and a single therapist should be assigned as the supervisor of record that has responsibility for a given student.

A plan and schedule that summarize the services of the therapist and paratherapist(s) should be used to help organize the team duties. An example of such a plan is shown in Figure 4.3. The assumption inherent in Figure 4.3 is that it documents the schedule of one SLP supervising one of her three SLPAs (the other two work at different schools). The SLP–SLPA team sees 31 clients and has the hour from 3:00 to 4:00 available for staffings and other duties. The SLP is on-site on Fridays to conduct diagnostic evaluations; meet with the SLPA, teachers, and parents; participate in combined (SLP–SLPA) therapy sessions; and supervise the SLPA. She oversees comparable caseloads at her other two schools.

The quality of supervision, including on-the-job training and mentoring by the therapist, has a direct impact on the quality of services provided by paratherapists. The higher the quantity and quality of supervision, the better the services.

Table 4.8
Supervision Requirements for Assistants

Criteria	COTA	PTA	SLPA
Requirements for supervisor	Properly credentialed and licensed in state	Properly credentialed and licensed in state	CCC-SLP designation and licensure; 2 years of experience post-CCC; course or continuing education unit in supervision
Amount and type of supervision	First session and then as needed or as conditions dictate (close supervision for inexperienced and then moving progressively to routine, general, or minimal)	First visit and then as needed but at least once a month	30% for first 90 work days (20% direct, 10% indirect), then adjusted as appropriate but no less than 20%
Off-site assistant contact with therapist	Must be accessible at all times COTA is treating students	Must be accessible by telecommunications at all times when PTA is treating students	Must be reachable by personal contact, phone, pager, or other immediate means during all student contact time
Therapist–assistant conferences	Regularly scheduled and documented	Regularly scheduled and documented	At least every 2 weeks and documented

Note. Supervision requirements may vary from jurisdiction to jurisdiction depending on state rules, regulations, and practice acts. Generally it is assumed that aides work only on-site with the supervisor and under continuous supervision.

School district administrators should be fully aware of the supervision guidelines of the AOTA, APTA, and ASHA and support their therapists in meeting these standards of supervision. Therapists working in the schools are knowledgeable about these standards and welcome the opportunity to help "educate" their administrators. High-quality supervision will help ensure that the highest quality of services is delivered to

Student Information		Speech Therapy Schedule School: Edahow Elementary SLP: Diane Franks Week: 12/4/02–12/8/02 SLPA: Terry Madsen		
Name	**Diagnosis and severity**	**SLP**	**SLP–SLPA combined services**[a]	**SLPA alone (with SLP monitoring schedule)**[b]
T. Smedley *R. Schow* *J. Brockett* *R. Bishop*	hearing impairment and aural rehabilitation (moderate)		M-W-F 1:00–1:50 SLPA M-W; SLP F group	
B. Malepeai *T. Longhurst*	fluency (mild)			T-Th 9:30–10:00 (maintenance)
B. Bain	language disorder (severe)	F 8:15–9:00 (new client diagnosis)		
T. Bradshaw *L. Kline* *N. Bowen* *R. Bowen*	language disorder (mild)			T-Th 10:15–10:45 (maintenance)
K. Lewis *J. Willer* *J. Stokes*	articulation (moderate–severe)		M-F 2:00–2:50 SLPA M-W; SLP F group	
D. Sorenson *W. Johnson*	fluency (mild)			T-Th 11:00–11:30 (maintenance)
A. Weston	voice (abuse) (mild)			T-Th 1:00–1:30 (maintenance)
P. Boysen *E. Mitchell* *J. Batte* *S. Robbins*	articulation (mild–moderate)			M-F 8:20–9:10 group
T. Seikel	voice (abuse) (moderate)	F 9:30–10:00 (new client diagnosis)		
K. Kangas	traumatic brain injury (moderate)	F 10:30–11:00 (dismissal diagnosis)		
K. Edwards *J. Coe-Smith* *S. Lang* *J. Hamilton*	articulation (mild)			M-W-F 9:30–10:20 group (maintenance)
D. Towsley *J. Loftin* *D. Kristky* *A. Seikel*	language disorder (mild)			M-W-F 10:40–11:30 group (maintenance)

[a] The SLP and SLPA are concurrently providing services to the same student group.
[b] When the majority of services are provided by the SLPA alone, especially in maintenance, the supervising SLP must include a schedule of supervision and direct student contact to maintain accountability and quality of service, for example every other week.

Figure 4.3. Sample SLP and SLPA weekly schedule.

infants, toddlers, children, and youth with disabilities in the schools and their families.

Summary

In each of the therapies, there are clear distinctions between aide and assistant titles in preservice education or training, credentials, scope of practice, amount and type of supervision, and pay and fringe benefits. The scopes of practice for both aides and assistants are subsets of therapists' scopes of practice. When appropriately assigned or delegated, the support that paratherapists provide to therapists can increase the efficiency and effectiveness of the therapy team. Therapists in all fields must wrestle with the issue of which therapeutic or educational activities within their scope of responsibility must be performed only by themselves and which can be assigned or delegated to paratherapists under the direction and supervision of the therapist.

Discussion Questions

1. Compare and contrast the credentialing terms *registration, certification,* and *licensure* as used for paratherapists (or therapists). Do you see any inconsistencies in the different disciplines, such as between OT and SLP?
2. The chapter author feels that there are three major determiners of successful paratherapist utilization in the schools. Name them and discuss how the system could have problems if all three factors are not present.
3. There are many positive aspects of increased utilization of paratherapists in the schools, but there are also reasons for concern. List the pros and cons of increased employment of paratherapists to provide clinical services to preschool and school children.
4. Contrast the terms *aide* and *assistant,* including training, duties, and supervision needs.

5. List the responsibilities of the team that are typically performed only by the therapist. Discuss why it is important that paratherapists not perform these tasks.

EXERCISES

1. Make arrangements, possibly through your course instructor, to observe and interview a PTA, an OTA, and an SLPA in the schools or early intervention agency. During your interview, ask about
   a. their typical day-to-day activities;
   b. if they have a written schedule you could see;
   c. the protocols they work from and ask to see an example; and
   d. the procedures they use to document progress and ask to see examples of the form(s) they use.
2. Make arrangements, again through your course instructor, to observe and interview a PT, OT, and SLP who are supervising paratherapists in the schools or early intervention agency. During your interview, ask about
   a. their training experience;
   b. their typical weekly schedule;
   c. what kinds of activities take up most of their time; and
   d. how they work with their aide(s) or assistant(s).
3. After consultation with your instructor, invite a PT, OT, or SLP to talk to your class about utilization of aides and assistants in his or her school district or agency.
4. Search the World Wide Web sites of the three primary associations discussed in the chapter (www.apta.org, www.aota.org, www.asha.org). Some have a "members area" section that you must have a member number to access. Peruse the main menu and then search the site for the following:
   a. mission statement
   b. membership information
   c. credentialing
   d. job outlook/careers
   e. current news/issues
   f. practice guides
   g. information for students
   h. practicum/fieldwork
   i. program accreditation
   j. ethics

5. You might also want to search the site www.ideapractices.org, which contains everything you want to know (and then some) about the Individuals with Disabilities Education Act (IDEA).
6. Make arrangements, again possibly with the help of your course instructor, to visit a training program in a community college or vocational–technical school for PTAs, COTAs, or SLPAs. Ask an administrator or instructor in the program to give you a tour of the laboratories or other learning environments and request literature they give to prospective students. APTA, AOTA, and ASHA Web sites have listings of accredited or approved programs.
7. Therapy services, like many other professions, use a lot of acronyms. Make a list of the acronyms (ADL, FAPTA, etc.) used in this chapter and then write out the interpretation of each.

Glossary of Key Terms Associated with Therapy Services

Accreditation (program approval). Process of recognizing educational programs that meet minimum standards of space, faculty, learning resources, and practica for training individuals.

Activities of daily living (ADLs). Everyday activities in which persons engage that require mobility, strength, and range of motion, such as walking, writing, keyboarding, speaking, feeding, and swallowing.

Aide. Paratherapist title given to individuals with a minimum level of training (typically in high school, on the job, or through short-term vocational training), a very limited scope of practice in student treatment, and continuous, physically present supervision.

Assigned task. A form of direction to aide-level paratherapists by therapists that is more specific and formal than "delegated."

Assistant. Paratherapist title given to individuals with an associate's degree (or equivalent) from a physical therapist assistant, certified occupational therapy assistant, or speech–language pathology assistant program; compared with an aide, can work more independently in expanded functions consistent with more extensive training and experience.

Associate. Paratherapist title that may be given to individuals with a bachelor's degree, such as the title speech–language pathology associate for a worker with a preprofessional BS degree in speech–language pathology.

Career pathway. A preplanned and articulated system of advancement within or across therapy disciplines.

Certification. Typically used to designate that the individual has completed formal training and passed a board examination administered nationally, by a specific state agency, or even by a training program.

Clinical efficacy. A process of being efficient and effective in clinical treatment and of using procedures to document success or lack thereof (accountability).

Delegated task. A form of direction to assistant- or associate-level paratherapists by therapists that is less specific and less formal that *assigned;* assumes the assistant has been well trained to perform the duties and needs only general direction to follow the therapist's treatment protocol.

Executive functions. Activities of therapists including student assessment, planning for the paratherapists, managing schedules, training, assigning or delegating tasks, adopting and developing treatment protocols, creating and maintaining standards of practice, and supervision.

Expanded functions. Duties and tasks that appropriately exceed the typical scope of practice because the worker has additional training and experience.

Licensure. A credential that legally protects the public from untrained practitioners and prohibits persons from using the title or designation without first having met all of the requirements (education, clinical experience, and board examinations).

Minimum supervision requirements. Specifications that it is the therapist's responsibility to design, provide, and document a supervision scheme that protects students' and families' rights and maintains the highest standards of quality intervention. These minimum standards should be exceeded with a new paratherapist, for initial student interventions, and when problems arise.

Nontreatment duties. Typically viewed as clerical and housekeeping tasks, most of which are performed by the aide and assistant, leaving time for the therapist to complete those duties that are exclusively his or hers.

Paratherapists. A generic term for aides, assistants, or associates (or similar titles) who work alongside professional-level therapists to accomplish common team goals.

Physical therapist (PT). A professional therapist who, in the schools, helps students develop strength, mobility, and range of motion in joints and muscles to facilitate activities of daily living. PTs often have at least a bachelor's degree but the master's degree is now the minimum practice requirement for new PTs.

Praxis. Motor planning and smoothly and effortlessly executing motor behaviors during learned tasks.

Protocol. A written therapy plan that includes specific instructions to the paratherapist from the therapist.

Registered occupational therapist (OTR). A professional therapist who works, in the schools, with students in improving skills in activities of daily living, such as walking, writing, keyboarding, speaking, eating, and swallowing. OTRs often have a bachelor's degree, and the profession is moving toward requiring a master's degree for new OTRs.

Registered speech–language pathologist assistant (R-SLPA). A graduate of an ASHA-approved technical training program who has successfully completed a competency evaluation by a qualified supervisor.

Registration. A less stringent form of credentialing than licensure but serves many of the same purposes.

Scope of practice (or scope of responsibility). A delineated set of tasks or responsibilities of a paratherapist or therapist that is consistent with his or her training, experience, and credential(s).

Sensory processing. How a student receives and perceives information through a variety of sensory systems.

Somatosensory perception. Awareness of sensations from joints, muscles, and skin receptors.

Speech–language pathologist (SLP). A professional therapist in the schools who has the primary responsibility of working with students who have communication problems that adversely affect learning and academic progress. SLPs typically hold a master's degree and many have a certificate of clinical competence in speech–language pathology (CCC–SLP) from ASHA.

Supervision, close. Requires daily, direct contact at the site of work.

Supervision, continuous. Requires an on-site, physically present supervisor anytime the paratherapist is working with a student.

Supervision, direct. Requires that the therapist observe and provide directional feedback to the paratherapists and be physically present for all or part of the treatment session.

Supervision, general. Requires at least monthly direct contact, with supervision available as needed.

Supervision, indirect. Enables the therapist to watch videotapes of sessions, review written materials (plans, treatment notes), and communicate with the paratherapist through phone, e-mail, or other means in which directional feedback is provided without the therapist being physically present.

Supervision, minimal. Supervision provided only on an as-needed basis, which may be less than monthly.

Supervision, routine. Requires direct contact at least every 2 weeks at the site of work, with interim supervision occurring by other methods, such as telephonic or written communication.

Supervisor of record. In school or agencies where there may be several SLPs, for example, who provide therapy supervision to a given SLPA, one supervisor is designated as the supervisor of record and accepts ultimate responsibility for specific students.

Support personnel. A generic term, similar to *paratherapist*, sometimes given to workers who provide support to professional-level therapists.

Therapists. A generic term to describe professional-level workers in the three therapies discussed in this chapter: physical therapists (PTs), registered occupational therapists (OTs), and speech–language pathologists (SLPs).

Treatment duties. Tasks that involve specific intervention with the student or the family, such as home programming, exercise, drills, eliciting responses, providing consequences, and charting behaviors that are included in treatment protocols.

Values training. General orientation to disabilities and ethical behavior with persons with disabilities and their families.

References

American Occupational Therapy Association. (1997a). *Occupational therapy services for children and youth under the Individuals with Disabilities Education Act.* Bethesda, MD: Author.

American Occupational Therapy Association. (1997b). Statement: Sensory integration evaluation and intervention in school-based occupational therapy. *The American Journal of Occupational Therapy, 51,* 861–869.

American Physical Therapy Association. (1999). Guide to physical therapy practice. *Physical Therapy, 79,* 1079–1084.

American Speech-Language-Hearing Association. (1996). Guidelines for the training, credentialing, use, and supervision of speech–language pathology assistants. *Asha, 38*(Suppl. 16), 21–34.

American Speech-Language-Hearing Association. (1999). *Practical tools and forms for supervising speech–language pathology assistants.* Rockville, MD: Author.

Burton, S., Gee, R., & Overholt, J. (1992). *Creating visions: Direct care service provider training manual.* Moscow: University of Idaho, Curriculum Dissemination Center.

Burton, S., & Seiler, R. (1992, January). PTA career ladders. *PT Magazine,* pp. 56–61.

Couch, K. J., Deitz, J. C., & Kanny, E. M. (1998). The role of play in pediatric occupational therapy. *The Journal of American Occupational Therapy, 52,* 111–114.

Council for Exceptional Children. (1997). *Consortium guidelines for speech–language paraprofessionals.* Reston, VA: Council for Exceptional Children.

Gitlow, L. (1997). Prerequisites for academic occupational therapy assistant programs. *The American Journal of Occupational Therapy, 51,* 385–387.

Giuffrida, C., & Kaufman, K. (1999). The early intervention interdisciplinary field experience. *The American Journal of Occupational Therapy, 53,* 529–532.

Goldberg, L., & Paul-Brown, D. (1999). Strategies for the effective use of speech–language assistants in the classroom. Proceedings of the Seventh Annual CSPD Conference on Leadership and Change, Arlington, VA.

Idaho Board of Vocational Education. (1993). *Technical committee report and curriculum guide for providers of services to persons with developmental disabilities, Level 1* (Vocational Education No. 269). Boise: Idaho Board of Vocational Education.

Idaho Board of Vocational Education. (1994a). *Technical committee report and curriculum guide for certified occupational therapy assistant* (Vocational Education No. 284). Boise: Idaho Board of Vocational Education.

Idaho Board of Vocational Education. (1994b). *Technical committee report and curriculum guide for occupational therapy aide* (Vocational Education No. 282). Boise: Idaho Board of Vocational Education.

Idaho Board of Vocational Education. (1994c). *Technical committee report and curriculum guide for physical therapy aide* (Vocational Education No. 293). Boise: Idaho Board of Vocational Education.

Idaho Board of Vocational Education. (1994d). *Technical committee report and curriculum guide for physical therapy assistant* (Vocational Education No. 285). Boise: Idaho Board of Vocational Education.

Idaho Board of Vocational Education. (1994e). *Technical committee report and curriculum guide for speech–language pathology aide* (Vocational Education No. 294). Boise: Idaho Board of Vocational Education.

Idaho Board of Vocational Education. (1994f). *Technical committee report and curriculum guide for speech–language pathology assistant* (Vocational Education No. 292). Boise: Idaho Board of Vocational Education.

Johansson, C. (1999, April 15). New standards for a new millennium. *OT Week,* pp. 7–9.

Longhurst, T. M. (1997a). Career pathways for related service paratherapists working in early intervention and other education settings. *Journal of Children's Communication Development, 18,* 23–30.

Longhurst, T. M. (1997b). Idaho's three-tiered system for speech–language paratherapist training and utilization. *Journal of Children's Communication Development, 18,* 57–64.

Lowman, D. K., Simons, D. F., Shepherd, J. T., Fiocca, J. T., Ernouf, H. S., & Hundley, B. S. (1999). Occupational therapists in the school setting: Working with students with complex health care needs. *The American Journal of Occupational Therapy, 53,* 519–523.

McFarlane, L., & Hagler, P. (1995). *Collaborative service provision by assistants and professionals: A manual for occupational therapists, physical therapists and speech–language pathologists.* Edmonton, Alberta, Canada: Alberta Rehabilitation Coordinating Council.

Paul-Brown, D., & Goldberg, L. R. (2001). Current policies and new directions for speech–language pathology assistants. *Language, Speech, and Hearing Services in the Schools, 32,* 4–17.

Rast, J. (1992). *Values and visions: An introduction to developmental disabilities.* Parsons: Kansas University, University Affiliated Program at Parsons.

Robinson, C. (1987). *Training direct care workers in non-institutional family scale residential environments for the developmentally disabled/handicapped person.* Cincinnati, OH: Cincinnati University Affiliated Program, Cincinnati Center for Developmental Disorders Interface Project.

Vassiliou, D. (1991). *Guidelines and coursework syllabus for the North Dakota statewide MR/DD staff training program.* Minot, ND: Minot State University, Center for Disabilities.

Vreeland, E. (1999, March 25). Teaching teachers to teach handwriting. *OT Week,* pp. 8–10.

Watts, N. T. (1971). Task analysis and division of responsibility in physical therapy. *Physical Therapy, 51,* 23–35.

Team Building and Communication

5

Kent Gerlach

OVERVIEW

It is usually not very difficult to prove that "two heads are better than one." Almost everyone can buy into that statement. Respect for the roles of every team member and the desire to make the team relationship work are key elements of the team building process.

In today's schools and other educational settings, the focus is on improving the performance of individuals and teams through improved communication and collaboration. There are many definitions for teams in education and business. Collectively, these definitions convey that a team is two or more people who work together to achieve a shared goal. Their mission and purpose must be clear and understood by all members of the team. The common goal and coordinated efforts to achieve the goal make them a team. To be successful, teachers and paraeducators must view themselves as a team. They need to form a relationship that is built on good communication, trust, respect, and recognition of the values of the contributions of team members. In program implementation teams, no matter what program or learning environment they work in, the team leader is always a licensed and certified professional practitioner.

Merriam-Webster's Collegiate Dictionary (1993) defines *collaboration* as "to work jointly with others or together, especially in an intellectual endeavor; to cooperate" (p. 224). Collaboration for the purpose of this text is defined as the process of joining together to work on tasks in a cooperative, respectful, and purposeful manner.

A common thread across definitions of teams includes the notion that teamwork is both interactive and dynamic. It is a process among partners who share mutual goals and work together to achieve the goals. Teamwork is the main ingredient for facilitating change and solving problems because it allows people to discuss their work together and, as a result, to grow professionally.

To be successful, it is important that professionals and paraeducators view themselves as partners in the educational process. Input from all team members needs to be solicited. Questions need to be asked. Ideas need to be shared and appreciated.

One of the best examples of team building exists in athletics. Individual team members may have different backgrounds, attitudes, and roles. They develop into teams when their common purpose is understood by all of the members. For the most part, the purpose is to "win" the game or event. Within effective teams each member plays important roles, using his or her strengths and talents to best advantage. When the members integrate their skills to accentuate strengths and minimize weaknesses, team objectives are achieved much easier.

In sports, feedback is immediate. When the players are individually focused, success as a team is impossible to achieve. Like their athletic counterparts, teachers, other school professionals, and paraeducators can accomplish far more when they work well together. Unfortunately, many team leaders fail to recognize and apply the principles used in athletics. Some leaders do not always know how to transform a group into an effective team. A former coach at the University of Alabama, Paul "Bear" Bryant, said it best when he stated that there are five things a winning team member needs to know:

1. Tell me what you expect from me.
2. Give me the opportunity to perform.
3. Let me know how I am getting along.
4. Give me guidance when I need it.
5. Reward me according to my contribution.

Another example of teamwork is the surgical team, which is headed by a surgeon and includes surgical assistants, nurses, the anesthetist, and technicians. Each person knows his or her role and each person knows that his or her success is dependent on the other members of the team. All are committed to achieving a single objective, the well-being of the patient. Like all successful teams, the operating group has taken a substantial amount of time to develop its effectiveness. The topics for this chapter include characteristics critical to successful teams, effective leadership, interpersonal communication skills, problem solving, and conflict resolution.

Instructional Objectives

After studying this chapter and participating in discussions and case studies, the reader will be able to do the following:

1. Define effective teamwork and describe its characteristics.
2. Identify communication skills critical for working effectively with paraeducators and other colleagues.
3. Define components of effective listening and name the factors that can interfere with meaningful listening.
4. Identify methods of improving listening skills.
5. Define attending and responding skills and give an example of each.
6. Explain the importance of joint problem solving as it applies to school professionals and paraeducators.
7. Identify and apply an eight-step problem-solving process to strengthen professional and paraeducator teams.
8. Discuss the nature and possible sources of conflict among team members.
9. Identify and apply a six-step conflict resolution strategy to a variety of situations that might occur among teachers, other school professionals, and paraeducators.

Characteristics of Successful Teams

The characteristics of successful teams can be found throughout social science, business, literature, and research. The most common characteristics are discussed in the following sections.

Members Must View Themselves as a Team

Individuals cannot be effective team members unless they see themselves as important to the team effort (Friend & Cook, 1996). Extending that notion further, individual members must also be viewed by others as valuable contributors to the work of the team (Feldman, 1985). Additionally, all members must be committed to making the team process work.

When team members work well together, many individual and group benefits emerge as a result of the process. Tables 5.1 and 5.2 synthesize currently recognized advantages to teaming and characteristics of effective teams.

Teams Are Goal Focused

All team members must be focused in the same direction, with their efforts supporting one another. Successful teams have a clear understanding of their goals. The elements of a goal include (a) defining what is to be achieved, (b) establishing a measure of accomplishment (How will we know when the desired outcome has been reached?), and (c) setting the time factor (When precisely do we want to have the goal completed?).

When writing goals, the teacher, other school professionals, and paraeducators must keep their focus on the needs of children and youth being served. All team members must agree on the goals of their efforts. These efforts also include supporting one another. Typical goal-directed questions include the following: What are the goals of Title I? What are the goals of inclusion? What are the goals for this particular learner? How can we work together to achieve the goals for this learner?

Most local education agencies (LEAs), other education agencies, or school buildings have clearly defined mission statements (see Table 5.3 for a list of terms commonly used in mission statements). Through a mission statement, an organization specifies overall strategy or intent that governs the team's goals and objectives. The mission statement serves as the foundation on which all staff can build to establish goals and related actions. By focusing on goals, priorities can be determined much more easily. Together, teachers, other professional practitioners, and paraeducators decide what needs to be done, how it will be done, who will do it, and by what deadline.

Table 5.1
Advantages of Teaming

1. Teams build an awareness of interdependence. When people recognize the benefits of helping one another and realize it is expected, they will work together to achieve common goals.
2. When people work together to achieve common goals, they stimulate each other to higher levels of accomplishment; fresh ideas are generated.
3. Teamwork builds and reinforces recognition and mutual support within a team. People have an opportunity to see the effect of their effort and the efforts of others on student achievement.
4. Collaboration leads to commitment to support and accomplish student and team goals.
5. Teams develop unique, creative, and flexible solutions to problems.
6. Teams foster professional and personal growth by sharing knowledge and skills.
7. Teams reduce the feeling of isolation that is common in education.
8. Teams support and mentor each other.
9. Teams maximize each member's potential, strengths, and contribution.
10. Teams establish goals together. Members feel a sense of ownership toward goals. Input is solicited from all team members.
11. Members are encouraged to openly express ideas, opinions, disagreement, and feelings. Questions are welcomed.
12. Team members practice open and honest communication. They make an effort to understand each other's point of view. They operate in a climate of trust and respect.
13. Members participate in discussions affecting the team but understand their supervisor or leader must make the final decision.
14. A team spirit develops when members work well together.

Teams Clarify Roles

To create an effective team, team members need to discuss and clarify the role distinctions. As noted previously, teachers, other school professionals, and paraeducators need to be aware of and understand their roles in getting tasks done and teachers need

Table 5.2
Characteristics of a Successful Team

1. Teams use their time and talents effectively.
2. Teams are committed to skill development.
3. Members build morale by showing respect and recognition to one another.
4. Members give one another feedback.
5. Members cooperate rather than competing.
6. Members maintain positive attitudes toward each other's ideas.
7. Teams communicate openly.
8. Members mentor and learn from one another.
9. Teams resolve conflicts effectively.
10. Teams accept challenges.

Table 5.3
Terms Commonly Used in Mission Statements

Term	**Definition**
Mission	A statement of what the school district or team is about and the unique contribution it can make.
Goal	A result to be achieved.
Objective	A specific outcome that the team intends to meet in pursuit of its goals.
Strategy	A set of rules and guidelines to assist orderly progression toward meeting a team's goals and objectives.
Plan	A time-phased action sequence used to guide and coordinate strategies in pursuit of objectives.

to know how to use the skills and expertise of each team member most effectively. Several factors need to be considered in determining the roles and responsibilities of team members. They include experience, training, comfort level, time constraints, and knowledge and skill levels of individual team members. In determining roles for the paraeducator team, professional and ethical considerations are important.

Effective Leadership

Leadership is a critical factor for team success. The leader is always the teacher or another licensed school professional who has been designated as the paraeducator's supervisor. The supervisor's role is similar to that of a coach. It involves assessing the paraeducator's skills and helping the paraeducator use them to the fullest. Paraeducators contribute more effectively when they are "coached" and encouraged to make optimal use of their strengths and resources. A supervisor provides direction and ideas, helps identify alternatives, raises questions, and supplies feedback.

Whenever possible, the supervisor seeks input from the paraeducator. Effective team leaders have a sense of mission and purpose, and they lead by example. They are committed to improving their performance as leader, supervisor, or manager; they have good communication skills; and they clarify roles and expectations for team members. A team leader provides on-the-job training and mentors others, respects team members, is enthusiastic, and demonstrates organizational skills. Team leadership skills are outlined in Table 5.4.

Team Effectiveness Is Established Through Shared Norms and Support

A team is an organized system of individuals whose behavior is regulated by a common set of norms or values (Friend & Cook, 1996; Sherif & Sherif, 1956). Conflict or differences of opinion are dealt with openly; authority, responsibility, and decision-making lines are clearly understood. In addition, team meetings have clear agendas and are organized for productivity and efficiency.

Shared norms, or team member expectations or "rules," include such things as arriving on time, being prepared, asking questions, listening to one another, respecting the views of one another, and maintaining a positive attitude. Other expectations for success include providing support for each other professionally and personally, dealing with each other honestly and truthfully, and serving as good role models for learners. More than ever before, children and youth need to see two adults working well together. Teachers, other professionals, and paraeducators

Table 5.4
Team Leadership Skills

Teamwork skills: The ability to interface with the paraeducator in a manner that promotes teamwork and develops commitment.

Technical and management skills: The ability to understand the mission of the team and program. The supervising professional must schedule, plan, and manage time, and handle the unexpected.

Communication skills: The ability to provide and receive information in an effective manner.

Problem-solving skills: The ability to identify problems and propose, evaluate, and analyze alternative solutions in order to develop ways of implementing the plan.

Interpersonal skills: The ability to recognize and demonstrate appropriate social behaviors, work with different interpersonal styles, appreciate the uniqueness of others, and manage conflict.

Feedback skills: The ability to monitor performance of the paraeducator through appropriate observation and feedback to ensure team effectiveness.

Managing and delegating skills: The ability to communicate responsibilities effectively to the paraeducator.

Coordinating and planning skills: The ability to see that roles and responsibilities are scheduled appropriately, resources are available when needed, and conferences and meetings are used to their fullest advantage.

must always demonstrate the skills of effective communication, respect, and integrity.

Norms or team rules are the shared beliefs of the team regarding appropriate behaviors for members. In other words, norms delineate the expectations of all team members. Team norms help maintain a behavioral consistency among members. For team norms to influence a person's behavior, team members must recognize that the norms exist, be aware that other members accept and follow the norms, and must accept and follow them. Members more readily accept and practice norms for which they have a sense of ownership. Generally, team members will support and accept norms that they have helped create or that they consider valid. Table 5.5 lists sample norms from one team. These norms could be applied to the department of a school professional and paraeducator team.

Table 5.5
Sample Expectations of Team Members

1. Team members will be present and punctual at all meetings.
2. Team members will come prepared to meetings.
3. Team members will ask questions if issues are unclear.
4. Team members will listen to one another's ideas.
5. Team members will contribute to the development of trust and openness.
6. Team members will assume the responsibility to address concerns or ask for clarification.
7. Team members assume the responsibility that their verbal contributions will move the team forward and will be pertinent to the topic.
8. Team members will contribute to the goals of the team.

Team effectiveness can be achieved by sharing expectations with one another, by allowing paraeducators to participate in the planning process when appropriate, by appreciating each other's unique personality traits, by respecting diversity, and by demonstrating a positive attitude. Once a team works well together, the job is less stressful, more enjoyable, and more rewarding for all team members.

Effective Teams

According to Soloman (1977), an effective team is one in which group members

- truly listen to each other in order to understand and empathize, rather than to defend, explain, or counteract;
- speak openly, honestly, and spontaneously about the ways in which their interaction is or is not fulfilling organizational objectives;
- deal with specific task-related behaviors; and
- openly inquire into ways in which they might improve their work together as a team.

According to Smith (1985), any improvement effort needs sustained support to flourish. In the context of teacher–paraeducator teams, support means more than giving permission. It means

1. setting expectations,
2. controlling competing priorities,
3. allocating time, and
4. developing staff capabilities.

Characteristics of New Teams

According to a review of research on team effectiveness done by Abelson and Woodman (1983), a team that has just formed usually has some or all of the following characteristics:

1. There is considerable confusion as to the roles that team members must assume.
2. There is confusion as to the social relationships among members of the team.
3. Individuals have assets or competencies relative to the team's purpose. However, some people may be unaware of how their skills or knowledge relate to team goals. Perhaps more important, some individuals may be unaware of (or may not value) the competencies of others, or may not appreciate their relationship to team goals.
4. Although team members may understand short-range goals (e.g., why the group was brought together), understanding of long-range goals is likely to be more elusive.
5. In the absence of established norms, there is considerable confusion about group processes: how the team will operate, how decisions will be made, and so on.
6. Team members (and particularly leaders) do not pay much early attention to social relationships, being more likely to focus initially on the task.

If a team is to be effective, the team must agree on why it exists—that is, what its purpose is. Members must see the benefits of teamwork. The team's mission must be developed with input from all team members. Responsibilities of each member must be clearly defined, and the supervisor's role must be made clear. The importance of listening to one another is stressed and clear expectations are given in order to get the job done. Information is shared in a timely manner, and the time the team meets together is productive. (Table 5.6 lists considerations that are important in developing teams.) Members of the team must be flexible, trusting of the other team members, and wholeheartedly supportive of other members during the team's progress toward its goals. (Table 5.7 lists considerations the team should use to assess its effectiveness.)

Interpersonal Communication Skills

Teamwork depends on effective interaction. Communication skills are both verbal and nonverbal. Through effective communication, a speaker expresses his or her beliefs, ideas, needs, or feelings. The listener must assimilate this information in such a way that there is agreement between what the listener understands and what the speaker intended to communicate.

What exactly is communication? *Merriam-Webster's Collegiate Dictionary* (1993) says that *communication* is a noun meaning "a process by which information is exchanged" (p. 233). For effective team performance, communication must facilitate the free flow or exchange of ideas, information, instructions, and reactions that contribute to common understanding. This flow should be a continual give-and-take, free from hindrances. The flow may be up,

Table 5.6
The Process of Team Development

1. Define the purpose, mission, and goals of the team.
2. Establish team composition and roles.
3. Clarify team rules (norms) and responsibilities.
4. Integrate individual personalities and strengths.
5. Direct and manage team performance.
6. Evaluate team effectiveness and give feedback.

Table 5.7
An Assessment of Team Effectiveness

1. Goals for the team are established.
2. Team members are committed to those goals.
3. The team shares a clear vision of what needs to be done to accomplish the goals.
4. Roles and responsibilities of each team member are clearly established. (Leadership role is clear.)
5. Team expectations are communicated in a climate of trust, openness, and respect.
6. Members keep one another informed of issues affecting the team.
7. Problems are solved together.
8. Team members listen to one another. Effective communication strategies are employed. Questions are asked and input is solicited.
9. The meeting time is effective and productive.
10. Team members are recognized and appreciated for the work they do.

down, or sideways; within teams, it goes in all directions. When ideas are shared through communication, there is opportunity for evaluation and input that can build even better ideas. From each new experience, more ideas can be developed and tried.

The dictionary definition says that ideas must be exchanged before any instruction can take place. If the receivers do not understand what is being said, the words are useless. Successful communication results in a mutual understanding of what information was given and what was heard. Reactions are crucial. Unless people respond to the stimulus of the communication, nothing has occurred. It is best when this reaction happens instantaneously.

Building Trust Among Team Members

Trust is defined as an assured reliance on the character, ability, and strength or truth of someone or something. Trust is built in teams by promoting open communications, providing fair leadership, and supervising with sensitivity. Building trust is essential and not always easy. For team members to gain trust in each other, the following conditions are necessary:

- Paraeducators must perceive their supervisors as open, fair, honest, and willing to listen.
- Supervisors must be decisive and stand by their decisions in difficult situations.
- Paraeducators must have the confidence that their supervisors will support them and take responsibility for decisions and actions.

Trust is necessary to have a productive working environment. It is essential for all personnel to practice open, honest communication to increase awareness and build cooperation. This environment of trust promotes loyalty and commitment to achieve the team's goals and objectives.

Effective Listening

Team members must have effective listening techniques to promote the essential understanding required for successful intervention. Good communication starts with the ability to listen effectively. In effective team communication, listening is especially important. Listening is a primary way of getting information, as well as a means of conveying interest in the messages of others. Listening establishes rapport. Attention, willingness to listen, and desire to understand are important elements in establishing rapport, but accurate understanding is required to build and maintain a trusting relationship. When team members demonstrate precise knowledge of what a person has said, they are then perceived as being competent (Friend & Cook, 1996). All team members need to develop listening skills so that they can obtain sufficient and accurate information necessary for an effective working relationship. Because many paraeducators have received little training or orientation for their job, it is especially important that the supervisor accurately and clearly describe the goals and needs of the learner being served.

Factors that Can Interfere with Effective Listening

Several factors can interfere with effective listening. Examine the following situation: Marla, the supervising teacher, met with

Alison, the paraeducator, at the end of a typical workweek. Marla had planned for the meeting. She gave what she thought was a clear and precise description of next week's activities. Alison, on the other hand, left the meeting not sure of what had been said. She was not sure what she was to do next week and regretted that she did not ask questions. What went wrong here? DeVito (1994) describes several obstacles for effective listening, as discussed in the following subsections.

Daydreaming

Daydreaming can interfere with listening and receiving information. Minds sometimes wander from listening to thoughts of picking up the children, getting to a meeting on time, or other personal concerns. Perhaps this is what happened to Alison when Marla was speaking. She may have lost track of Marla's message because she was thinking about another problem. It is important to concentrate on what a speaker is telling us. Giving undivided attention is not always easy and takes practice.

Stumbling on Trigger Words

Effective listening can stop when the listener's awareness is "triggered" by a particular word. Alison may have reacted to a word that she did not know the meaning of, a descriptor that could influence a change in her role or duties, or a term that was used in such a way that it created a response that distorted other things Marla was telling her.

Being Distracted

Any distraction may interfere with effective listening. Alison could have been distracted by a child in the room or a noise outside on the playground or in the hall. Distractions can be physical, verbal, mental, or environmental, such as an uncomfortable chair or temperature, or lack of sleep.

Filtering Messages

Friend and Cook (1996) pointed out that a frame of reference may cause a person to selectively attend to specific parts of a message and ignore others, thereby causing the listener to inaccurately perceive the message. Some people may simply not want to listen to a particular message and they "tune out." People tune out for various reasons. Alison may have found part of the message irrelevant because she felt she already knew what was being said, or it had little relevance to what she perceived as her responsibility. She might have felt the message contained too many details or too much information at once. Whatever the reason, when a listener filters the message, misunderstandings between speaker and listener may result.

Thinking About a Response or Questions

When Marla was speaking, Alison may have been thinking about what she would say when she had the opportunity to speak. Alison may have thought about some questions she wanted to ask Marla. Prior to the meeting she wrote these questions down and was reviewing her notes as Marla spoke. This caused her to miss some of the things Marla was saying.

Tips for Improving Listening Skills

To improve listening skills, it helps to consider how people comprehend verbal messages. Comprehension involves patience, openness (being nonjudgmental and unbiased), and having an intense desire to understand information from another point of view. Friend and Cook (1996) listed several ways to improve listening:

1. *Mentally rehearse the information.* The listener can identify the main themes or keywords and practice repeating these themes as the speaker shares information. Sometimes repeating a keyword over and over helps the listener to remember it.

2. *Categorize the information.* The listener can develop a scheme that helps to "map" the ideas (e.g., by classifying information about learners according to behavior or instructional needs).

3. *Use the listening process.* The listening process involves both attending and responding skills. This process will save time in the long run, even though it may seem

time-consuming at first. By developing the process of listening, both parties may prevent having to go back and redo things or correct misunderstandings.

The Process of Listening: Attending Skills

Attending skills or active listening can be defined as the nonverbal things or behaviors the listener exhibits to show that he or she is listening. A person's behavior can communicate to colleagues a clear message that shows interest in what they have to say. The opposite message can be sent when the listener's behavior indicates lack of care and interest.

The following example demonstrates effective listening: Connie, the paraeducator, asked the supervising teacher about a student who has become withdrawn, unresponsive, and appears to be depressed. The supervising teacher, Robert, without pause said, "Let's sit down and talk about this." Robert, who was correcting papers at the time, put the papers aside and focused on what Connie was telling him about the student. What does this example indicate about this team and their ability to communicate?

This next story demonstrates the importance of nonverbal cues: Ann, the paraeducator, asked the supervising teacher about a student she was working with who is having difficulty with math. Although Sharon, the teacher, said she had several ideas, at the same moment she looked at her watch. Then she pointed to the math material cabinet and said as she stepped out the door, "Help yourself to any of the materials. They should help. Let me know at our next meeting if he shows any improvement." What does this example show about this team and their ability to communicate? What did the teacher's body language and nonverbal cues communicate?

The following attending skills can help to keep team members on track and are powerful tools for influencing others:

- eye contact
- facial expressions
- body language
- gesturing
- waiting to respond

- leaning forward
- resisting distractions and interruptions
- nodding head

The Process of Listening: Responding Skills

The act of responding also includes both verbal and nonverbal skills. Responding skills can encourage people to check the accuracy of the message being communicated. DeBoer (1995) defined responding skills as behaviors that people use when they are listening well. These responding skills include paraphrasing, reflecting, clarifying, summarizing, and perception checking. Occasionally, these skills can be used to seek more information. To use these skills effectively, the listener should avoid editorializing or adding any additional comments or information.

Paraphrasing

In paraphrasing, the listener attempts to restate his or her interpretation of what the other person just communicated. The main purpose of paraphrasing is for the listener to check the accuracy of his or her interpretation of the speaker's information, thoughts, and stated feelings. After the listener states the person's ideas, the speaker approves and clarifies the paraphrase. Note the following example:

SPEAKER (TEACHER): This was a great day today. We got everything done that was on my list. Thanks for your help.

LISTENER (PARAEDUCATOR): We got a lot accomplished today. I'm really glad you feel I contributed to the success of the day.

People are able to listen to themselves through paraphrasing by providing a restatement of their thoughts and ideas. Paraphrasing starts with phrases such as, "You are," "You believe," "It seems like you," and "What you are saying is." By restating the main points, the listener shows attendance to and accurate understanding of what the speaker was relating and thus conveys interest in the issue and in the speaker.

Reflecting

Reflecting involves careful listening, understanding, and concentration. The listener describes what the other person has said and then tries to state (reflect) the meaning of the message. To do this, the listener reflects the speaker's feelings. Note the following example:

SPEAKER (TEACHER): How can I possibly get all this paperwork done? I don't have time to teach anymore.

LISTENER (PARAEDUCATOR): You are really frustrated with the paperwork, aren't you?

SPEAKER (TEACHER): Yes, I really am.

LISTENER (PARAEDUCATOR): What can we do together to reduce the paperwork load? How can I help?

A reflection focuses on the emotional side of communicating. Sometimes this can be an important tool for the person speaking because it captures a message that the listener can note through voice tone, quality, pitch, volume, speech rhythm, and pacing or tempo. Sometimes people are not aware of their feelings or how they are coming across without the listener's help. Both the supervisor and the paraeducator become mutually supportive by demonstrating careful listening, which leads to shared understanding.

Clarifying

Clarifying is the skill of requesting more information. The listener can show interest in the speaker, as well as ensure understanding of what is said, by seeking clarification through questioning. For example, if the speaker says, "This was a great day today. I completed many of the items on my list," the listener's response could be, "What did you get done today that you are so happy about?" The question is not a judgment of the statement but rather a search for clarity.

Summarizing

Summarizing pulls together the key points in a discussion. It helps participants to see the whole picture, and to refocus and clarify decisions. It also acts as a point for further discussion, reviews progress, and pulls together important facts or ideas. The following is an example of this:

> TEACHER (SUPERVISOR): Let me review what we have discussed so far.

Summarizing consists of one or more comments that restate in a concise way several preceding statements made by the individuals or team members involved in the discussion. It is a means to ensure that all individuals understand what is being said, and it functions in much the same way as a chapter summary section in a book or an abstract of a journal article.

Friend and Cook (1996) stated that summarizing differs from paraphrasing in at least two significant ways. When you paraphrase, you are simply restating what another person has just said. Paraphrasing is usually immediate, and it is a response to a discreet self-contained piece of information. On the other hand, summarizing is a response to several pieces of information. Summarizing generally occurs at the end of a meeting or conversation to address the main points covered.

Perception Checking

Perception checking is similar to reflecting; however, instead of making a statement that reflects what the listener senses a person is feeling, the listener checks his or her perceptions by asking questions. If the speaker says, "This was a great day today. I accomplished everything on my list," the listener's response could be, "Are you feeling really proud of your work today?" Or if the speaker says, "I get so upset when parents don't show up for a conference," the listener's response could be, "You sound really frustrated with the parents. Are you frustrated with them?"

Problem Solving with Paraeducators

As teachers, other school professionals, and paraeducators work together, problems will arise. Some of these problems are related to meeting the needs of individual children and youth, many involve behavior management issues, some are related to building issues and policies, others are related to parental or family concerns, and still others are connected to interpersonal relationships. When these problems are approached in a systematic manner, everyone benefits.

When teachers, other school professionals, and paraeducators work together as a team to solve problems, they build a respectful way of settling their differences. Teachers often use a step-by-step problem-solving process with students more frequently than with adult colleagues. In classrooms and educational settings, teachers take time to help students analyze problems, identify and weigh possible solutions for potential success, and then choose one to implement. The same problem-solving steps can be used effectively as educational professionals and paraeducators face the challenges of their work.

Most problem-solving processes consist of a series of steps. Many problem-solving strategies have been developed that can be adapted to meet the needs of school professionals and paraeducators who are working together (Dewey, 1993; Elgin, 1989; Gordon, 1977; Margolis & Brannigan, 1978; Schrage, 1990; Senge, 1990). This section examines an eight-step problem-solving process that applies strategies from the various sources:

1. Define the problem.
2. Determine the cause of the problem.
3. Determine the needs and desired outcomes.
4. Brainstorm possible solutions.
5. Select the solution that will best meet the needs.
6. Develop a plan of action.
7. Implement the plan.
8. Evaluate the solution and the problem-solving process.

By following each step, identifying the importance of each step, and developing ideas for accomplishing each step, participants will learn how the work of the team can be strengthened.

▶ Step 1: Define the Problem

A situation must be clearly understood before it can be dealt with. It is not always easy to put a problem into words, but if it cannot be stated clearly, it will be impossible to choose a course of action that will lead to a satisfactory solution. Each person sees the problem from a unique perspective and each perspective contributes to developing team understanding. Each person should describe the problem in his or her own words and from his or her own point of view. Answering questions such as the following promotes development of a common understanding of the problem:

1. What is the problem?
2. What is not working in this situation?
3. What factors are contributing to this problem?
4. Who is involved (students, staff, parents)?
5. Who is affected and how are they affected?

Team members should individually consider these questions and prepare answers to be used in a discussion. Having each member participate in defining the problem promotes respect for all contributions. Because the problem needs to be thoroughly described before a solution is implemented, it is important that no one feels he or she is suggesting the ultimate solution.

Once all team members have had a chance to contribute to identifying the problem, the team can draft a problem statement. This process brings the team to a consensus on just what it is they are attempting to solve.

▶ Step 2: Determine the Cause of the Problem

It is not enough to define the problem. It is essential to determine what causes the problem to exist and persist. For example, the problem may be caused by "outside conditions" (contractual agreements, a lack of financial resources) that the team may have little ability to change, or it may result from a lack of understanding of the distinction in the roles and duties of the teacher and paraeducator. Other factors that may influence how a problem is defined include differences in values and attitudes, age, work experience and education, cultural heritage, and other personal traits. It is important that the team identify those areas of agreement and disagreement.

▶ Step 3: Determine the Needs and Desired Outcome

Determining the needs of a situation requires the team to examine and clarify what the desired outcomes will be. This is not the same as developing a solution; rather, it is a chance to talk about what should happen in the situation. In doing this, it is helpful to address questions such as these:

1. What do we want to happen?
2. What is needed to improve our communication with each other?
3. What is needed to improve our communication with colleagues, parents, and students?
4. What is the desired outcome in this situation?

By answering these or similar questions, a team can focus on what they want to achieve. This helps bring team members to a positive and future-oriented approach.

▶ Step 4: Brainstorm Possible Solutions

Brainstorming is a method for generating as many solutions as possible that might help to solve a problem. One way this can be accomplished is to have team members think of possible solutions for the problem at hand. Then the supervisor and paraeducator share their solutions to the problem. A list of the brainstormed solutions is written so that all participants can see the various ideas. To conduct a good brainstorming session, the following suggestions should be followed:

- Establish a time frame.
- Write ideas on paper or use a computer.
- Generate and accept all ideas; do not evaluate.
- Make sure everyone participates.
- Take more time if creativity is high or more ideas are needed.

▶ Step 5: Select the Solution That Will Best Meet the Needs

The team should select a solution that will have the greatest chance for achieving the desired outcomes. The following questions can help team members arrive at mutually agreed upon solutions:

1. Which solution will meet the needs and achieve the desired outcomes?
2. Which solution is the easiest to implement?
3. Which solution is within the team's control?
4. Which solution would be least disruptive?

Discussion of these or similar questions will help to identify a solution that will be acceptable to all team members. Sometimes it is possible to combine two or more solutions to find a workable answer.

▶ Step 6: Develop an Action Plan

After the team members have agreed on a solution, an action plan should be developed so that everyone knows what is to be done and by whom. It is best if the action plan is written out and copies distributed to everyone involved. This increases the likelihood that members will understand the solution and be accountable for clarifying their role in achieving the goals of the plan.

A sample form for an action plan is shown in Figure 5.1. The action plan provides a record of the decision, is a communication tool among team members, and serves as a reference for follow-up activities.

▶ Step 7: Implement the Plan

By now each team member should know who is responsible for each action or task and what the time frame is for carrying out the activity. Next team members discuss what support or resources are needed to achieve the goals of the plan. Questions to guide this discussion follow:

1. What resources are needed to implement the plan?
2. Who should know about this plan (students, parents, teachers, staff)?
3. Do any schedules need changing?
4. When will the team meet to review the plan?

ACTION PLAN

Date ______________________________

Supervising Teacher ______________________________

Paraeducator ______________________________

Other Staff ______________________________

____

Action	Person Responsible	Deadline

Figure 5.1. Sample action plan form.

Each team member who participates in testing the solution should keep a record of how it is working. Observations about what is and is not working well will help the team determine whether or not the goals of the plan are being achieved. These observations can be analyzed at the next meeting to determine what is more or less effective.

▶ Step 8: Evaluate the Solution and the Problem-Solving Process

It is important to complete the problem-solving process in two ways. First, the team needs to determine whether the plan effectively achieved the desired outcome. This evaluation process should be carried out periodically, and part of the results should be used to develop new strategies or alternative solutions. Questions that can guide this discussion follow:

1. What has been accomplished by the action plan?
2. Have there been any unexpected outcomes?

3. Does the plan need to be revised to address these outcomes?
4. Is there any sign that the actions are resolving the original problem?
5. Have any new problems arisen that need to be addressed?
6. When will this action plan need to be reviewed again?

Second, the team needs to review the problem-solving process itself. This means that all team members who participated in Steps 1 through 6 should now assess how well the process worked. The point of this evaluation is to determine whether the problem-solving steps were helpful to the team and whether there are any suggestions for improving them. The following questions can be used to guide this discussion:

1. How well did this problem-solving process work?
2. What should be changed next time, if anything?
3. What were the benefits to the team and students of a process for problem solving?
4. What have we learned from solving the problems this way?

The answers to and discussion of these questions will provide direction for the next time professionals and paraeducators have problems to solve.

Summary

Problems are a natural part of team relationships. It is helpful for teams to use a problem-solving process to address various issues, which may include communication breakdown, parental concerns, student behaviors, scheduling conflicts, interpersonal relationships, and building or district practices and policies. Such a problem-solving approach respects the individual differences and the collective wisdom that exists on any educational team. The use of this mutual problem-solving process fosters cooperative working partnerships between school professionals and paraeducators and results in better services for students.

Conflict Resolution

Conflict is a natural, though sometimes unwelcome, occurrence in any working relationship. In educational settings, conflicts may arise at any point. Potential areas of conflict are identifying the needs of students, integrating parental desires, scheduling, using different teaching methods, working with other staff, and measuring student success. When teachers, other professionals, and paraeducators understand the nature of conflict and use a conflict resolution strategy, much of the confusion and personal misunderstanding can be avoided.

People who work together will often experience conflict as a result of opposing ideas or interests. For example, the paraeducator and the teacher might have different beliefs about the level of support a student needs to be successful. The professional might believe that a student needs less attention from adults and the paraeducator might believe the student needs more attention. When such a disagreement occurs, it is imperative that a conflict resolution strategy be implemented so that the student receives consistent support. Nearly all conflicts have an emotional component, especially when any of the parties involved feels strongly that he or she is right and knows what is best. Using conflict resolution strategy lessens the emotional response and proves to be a more objective approach that is respectful of everyone.

When conflict is present, team members should realize that conflict results from

- differences in needs, objectives, and values;
- differences in perceiving motives, words, actions, and situations;
- differing expectations of outcome (favorable vs. unfavorable); or
- unwillingness to work through issues, communicate, or compromise.

Negative conflict becomes a problem when it is avoided or approached on a win-or-lose basis. Animosities will develop, communications will break down, trust and mutual support will deteriorate, and hostilities will result. When sides are chosen, productivity will diminish or stop. The damage is usually difficult, and sometimes impossible, to repair.

When conflict is appropriately addressed, it can help the parties to explore new ideas, test their position and beliefs, and stretch their imagination. When conflict is dealt with constructively, people can be stimulated to greater creativity, which will lead to a wider variety of alternatives and better results.

As in problem solving, conflict resolution strategies have a series of steps that assist in bringing the situation into focus and reaching a mutually satisfying outcome. The strategy outlined in Table 5.8 can be used by all who are involved in the conflict or by only one of the people. Each step is described in the following text.

▶ Step 1: Pause

Stepping back and pausing helps to put the conflict into perspective and is the first step to resolving it. This step will help the team focus the energy in a productive manner rather than getting caught up in the emotions of the issue at hand. The conflict may not have to be resolved at that very moment, and some time away gives people a chance to reorganize their thoughts.

This step is very important for defusing the emotions of a conflict. In the fast pace of the school day, a disagreement can become exaggerated, as people feel pressed to get their work done and to get along well with their coworkers. Stepping back from the situation will offer each person the chance for a new perspective and prevent the conflict from escalating.

Table 5.8
Conflict Resolution Strategy

1. Pause.
2. Name the conflict or source of the conflict.
3. Consider what part individuals play in the conflict.
4. Consider options.
5. Choose the best option.
6. Develop an action plan together.

▶ Step 2: Name the Conflict or Source of Conflict

Conflict can result from many sources as team members work together for the best interests of their students and clients. It is important to recognize just what the source of the conflict is. The questions that follow will assist school professionals and para-educators in assessing the sources of conflicts:

1. Do team members all have the same information?
2. Do all team members understand their roles and responsibilities?
3. Is the information the team has complete?
4. Are the team members' goals compatible?
5. Are the methods the team is using effective?
6. Is it comfortable for team members to disagree openly with one another?

If the answer to any of the above questions is no, it indicates where the source of the conflict may be. In addition, the team members should consider who is involved in the disagreement, how it is affecting the people in their work, and what effect it is having on the students.

Naming the conflict or source of conflict can be done by all parties involved or by only one individual who believes that there is a conflict and wants to think it through on his or her own. When this step is done in a thoughtful manner, there is more chance that the resolution will be effective and that the real conflict will be addressed. If this step is not carried out, the result can be a reactive, narrow-sighted response, which serves to confuse the issue and create further conflict.

▶ Step 3: Consider What Part Individuals Play in the Conflict

In the third step, the individuals involved in the conflict analyze what part they have in it. Each person has varying responses to conflict and different approaches to dealing with it. Thomas and Kilmann (1974) identified five typical responses to conflict: avoidance, accommodation, compromise, competition, and collaboration. Each of the five responses is useful in its own right and can contribute to productive conflict resolution.

Avoidance. People avoid conflict for various reasons. Some people may find conflict emotionally upsetting; others may not wish to expend the time or energy needed to resolve issues; still others may choose to have a cooling off period so that the issue can be approached in a more rational manner. It is important to recognize when avoidance is being used as the response to conflict and for what reason.

Accommodation. When people accommodate during a conflict, they tend to go along with the desire of another and give up their own. This is done when a person seeks to preserve harmony in the relationship, or when the issue is not of great importance to the individual, or when the individual is hesitant to assert a view that will be in disagreement with another. Although on the surface accommodation may appear to resolve a conflict, it may not be the best method for team effectiveness. In the paraeducator–teacher team, it is important to emphasize that the supervisor has the ultimate responsibility in decision making.

Compromise. Compromise is characterized by individuals giving up some of their own demands and making concessions for the common goal. When using compromise, individual team members are willing to put aside some of their own outcomes and incorporate some of the other team members' ideas or suggestions into a mutually acceptable solution. The benefits of a compromise are many because each team member contributes to a resolution that is agreeable to all.

Competition. When competition is used in conflict resolution, individuals are certain that they are right and rarely incorporate the thinking of others into their own. Sometimes this comes about as a matter of perceived authority (e.g., "I'm responsible for this program, so I need to be the primary decision maker"). At other times competition is used so that a quick solution can be reached. If competition is being used, it is helpful to recognize this and determine its effectiveness.

Collaboration. Collaboration is the most cooperative and creative form of conflict resolution. In using collaboration, team members contribute their individual ideas and are open to the ideas of others. A solution reached through collaboration is one that none of the individual team members could have developed without the others. Thus the outcome is mutually satisfying and all team members feel involved in the resolution.

▶ Step 4: Consider Options

During Step 4 of conflict resolution, it is important to determine what alternatives are available and to thoughtfully consider and evaluate the potential of each. Typically, team members can do one of three things:

1. **Let things continue as they currently exist.** When teams choose to let things continue as they currently exist, the conflict may increase or it may disappear after a certain amount of time. The team should consider the benefits and liabilities of letting the current situation remain the same.
2. **Address the issue with the key people involved in the situation or conflict.** Teams may choose to address the issue with the key people involved so that the conflict is out in the open and discussion can be held to ascertain each person's experience and point of view. Not every conflict needs to be addressed in this manner. The team should consider the benefits and liabilities of addressing the issue with key people involved.
3. **Develop a new way of thinking about the conflict.** Sometimes all that is needed is a shift in attitude about the conflict. Perhaps the conflict is not as intense or as important as team members have made it. Rethinking or reframing a situation can result in a new approach that allows the individuals to proceed with other daily responsibilities. The team should consider the benefits and liabilities of developing a new way of thinking about conflicts.

▶ Step 5: Choose the Best Option

After evaluating the potential benefits and liabilities of the alternative choices, the team should deliberately and specifically choose the one that is most likely to resolve the conflict effectively. Which choice is best suited to this situation? If the team chooses to address this with other people, who are the key players? Has the team exaggerated this conflict? If so, how can the team think about it differently? The team needs to make a plan to take whatever steps are necessary to implement its choice.

▶ Step 6: Develop an Action Plan Together

Whether a choice has been made to let things continue as they are, to address the conflict with others involved, or to develop a new way of thinking about it, putting the plan into action is the final and most important step. After the first five steps have been accomplished, the conflict is usually acted on in a more neutral and less emotional fashion. Such an approach shows respect for all team members.

Summary

Conflict may occur when people work together. Having a conflict resolution strategy will assist team members in working through the problem in a way that is beneficial. It is important to discover the sources of conflicts, to identify one's own part in the conflict, and to think through possible ways of resolution. As school professionals and paraeducators learn to work through their conflicts, they grow in their strength as a team and the students are the benefactors.

Discussion Questions

1. List teams of which you have been a member (e.g., athletic team, committee). Think about the teams that were most effective and describe why. Think about the teams that were least effective and list why.
2. Think about any situation that you have been involved in where collaboration and teamwork were valued, encouraged, and demonstrated. Use this as a basis for a discussion with others to generate specific examples of the characteristics of good teamwork.
3. Define leadership. What are the characteristics of an effective leader?

4. List the factors that could interfere with listening and give examples.
5. Review the tips for improving listening skills and give examples. Give examples of attending skills and responding skills that you have observed people using.
6. List the stages in the problem-solving process. Set up a role-playing situation where a problem has been identified. Develop a role play that uses the problem-solving process.
7. Think about conflicts you have experienced in your personal life or a work situation. How were these conflicts resolved? Now that you know about the problem-solving and conflict resolution strategy, explain how you would handle things.
8. Identify two issues that school personnel might encounter where the problem-solving or conflict resolution strategy could be used.
9. Think about a small group meeting in which you participated that did not go as well as it might have. List the various blocks or hindrances that kept the meeting from being more successful.
10. Discuss the importance of a positive school environment and how an effective paraeducator–teacher team can enhance this learning environment.
11. Discuss why the following are important for good communication and team effectiveness.
    a. Developing an ongoing dialogue on how best to use team time.
    b. Providing complete information and clear instructions when coaching, and checking to be sure your team members really understand everything.
    c. Giving paraeducators plenty of advance notice for team meetings, deadlines, and so on.
    d. Making sure that expectations are reasonable and clear.
    e. Discussing goals, objectives, priorities, and plans with team members.
    f. Setting aside a regular time period for meeting with team members.

g. Following a written agenda to make sure your team meetings are productive.

EXERCISES

Review each of the following case studies and answer the questions that follow.[1]

CASE STUDY 1: A PROBLEM-SOLVING EXERCISE

Paraeducator Julie Brown

I am Julie Brown and I have been working as a paraeducator in special education for the past 3 months. I completed high school and was married soon after I graduated. My two children are now in high school and I decided to accept this job to supplement our income so that they can go to college. I really like working with children and have been active in elementary school PTA, was a Girl Scout leader, and taught in our local religious school. In fact, there was a boy in my class who had a developmental disability and I liked the challenge of finding ways to make him feel as though he was part of the group.

When I took this job, I was briefed on district policy with regard to salary, fringe benefits, working hours, vacation, and so on. In addition, I was told about the chain of command in the schools and the supervisor very briefly described my role and responsibilities as a paraeducator. I was told that Mr. White would be the classroom teacher I would be working with and that I would meet him when I reported to work. The supervisor said Mr. White would give me information about the specific tasks I would be expected to perform and the methods and strategies he would expect me to use to carry out the activities.

From the day I walked into the classroom, we have never had a formal discussion about what he expects me to do; there is always some reason why we can't sit down and talk. We can

[1]The case studies are adapted from *A Core Curriculum and Training Program to Prepare Educators to Work in Inclusive Classrooms Serving School Age Students with Disabilities*, by A. L. Pickett, K. Faison, and J. Formanek, 1999, New York: National Resource Center for Paraprofessionals in Education and Related Human Services, Center for Advanced Study in Education, Graduate School, City University of New York.

never meet during his prep periods because he is always too busy doing lesson plans to talk to me. When I suggested we meet after school, he told me that would be impossible because he either has graduate classes or meetings to attend. Then on one of the days when he was "free," I really had to get home to take one of my kids to the doctor.

I never know in advance what he wants me to do or how he wants it to be done. Just before he does something in the class, he will say, "Julie, take this group and follow my plans." I have no real idea about what to do, except to try to do what I see him doing while I sit in the back of the room watching him teach the lessons as he has asked me to do. When I am teaching, he frequently breaks into what I am doing and corrects me right in front of the students. I don't have the guts to tell him how this makes me feel—so I save it up until I get home, and my family bears the brunt of all my frustrations.

But what really has me worried is what his correcting me in front of the students might be doing to my ability to work with them. Today it came to a head when he had to leave the room and I was left alone with the group.

I asked one of the students who is rather difficult to work with to join us for an activity. He responded by looking straight at me and saying, "No, I don't want to, and I don't have to because you're just the 'para,' and you can't tell me what to do." I wanted to cry and quit right then—but I didn't. Where do I go from here?

Teacher Ken White

I am Ken White, a high school teacher who has been assigned my first paraeducator after teaching for 12 years. This was done because several special education students were assigned to my class as part of the district's efforts to place them in what the district calls the "least restrictive" environment. I wish they had asked me whether I wanted someone or not because I am really a loner and have very strict rules about how things are to be done in my classroom. I've never worked with anyone before in my classroom and I'm not really sure that I think it is worth the time to plan for another adult, especially someone who is not trained to be a teacher, much less to work with students with special needs.

At any rate, Julie walked into my room 3 months ago, just before school began, and said she was the paraeducator assigned to me. I asked her if she had been told what her duties were and she informed me that they had been explained to her at a meeting at the district office. I wish they had told me what I could expect her to do because I have no idea what goes on in those "briefing" sessions, nor have I seen a copy of a job description for paraeducator. I asked her to sit in the back of the room and watch for a while so she could get the hang of how I work. I told her that we'd get together later when I had some free time to talk to her.

During the first few days, I never had time to talk to her. I had lesson plans to develop. I have four different preparations, which really take a lot of time. I'm also taking a second master's and I have to leave 3 days a week almost immediately after school, so for me, just sitting down to talk is a problem. I wish there was time during the day to do this, but I'm just too busy with the kids and the planning to talk to her.

I finally decided that I'd let her review some of the skills I had already taught the students. So I gave her my plans and told her to follow them religiously. But she never did it exactly the way I wanted it to be done—she apparently thought it didn't make much difference how she did it as long as she felt comfortable. So what was I to do? I told her to do it the way I had written it and not to use her own methods.

Three months have gone by and I'm still as harried as I was before, if not more so. And to make matters worse, she seems to be having problems controlling the kids in the classroom. It started when I had to leave for an emergency meeting and Julie was left in charge. I'm not sure what she did wrong but she is having real trouble dealing with one of the kids and it seems to have an impact on the way some of the other students are responding to her. Maybe I should find the time to talk to her about how she deals with the problems of integrating the paraeducator into the program.

Case Study Discussion Questions

a. Describe the problem from the paraeducator's point of view. (This may include attitudes, actions, and other factors described in the case study.)

b. Describe the problem from the teacher's point of view.

c. What behavior(s) does the teacher need to change?

d. What behavior(s) does the paraeducator need to change?
e. Discuss and list desired goal(s) for the team.
f. How can they work together to achieve the goal and to be a better instructional team? What additional information, skills, or other resources will they need to achieve the goal?

CASE STUDY 2: A PROBLEM-SOLVING EXERCISE

Paraeducator Sharon Ferguson

I'm Sharon and I have been a paraeducator for almost 25 years. I started working in an elementary school and did lunchroom duty, monitored the playground, and helped the teacher in the classroom. About 15 years ago the principal asked me how I would feel about working in a new special education program. I've worked in several special education classes—everything from programs for kids with severe and multiple disabilities to resource rooms. I've seen teachers come and I've seen them go. But I'm still around because I love working with special education children and have made a lot of good friends in the building. Over the years I've had a chance to learn about what works and what doesn't work.

I've worked with some really terrific teachers and some that were not so good. In some cases, I was always the one who had to do all of the dirty work or the jobs that bored them—even though my title is instructional assistant and I'm supposed to work directly with the students. Other teachers thought they were being "good" to me by treating me as an equal with exactly the same responsibilities as theirs—even though I'm paid a whole lot less than they are. The folks that really drove me crazy were the ones "who had all the answers" and expected me to follow their rules to the "T." Despite these problems, if they were willing to take time to get to know me and discuss their expectations, we were usually able to work out our differences and get along well.

This year I've been assigned to work with a new teacher fresh out of college with no experience and a lot of new theories and bright ideas. On the first day of school we had a conference and she outlined what she wanted me to do. Basically, as I see it, she expects me to return to the status that I had when I first started 20 years ago. I am supposed to escort the children to the lunchroom, the playground, speech therapy, and so on; keep the attendance records; do the toileting; keep the room neat; and generally stay out of her way. She does let me play records and tell stories during the rest period.

Now she has developed a "new" program plan for James and all of a sudden has asked me to help implement it. I don't think it's going to work because Mrs. Adams tried something similar last year and we had to change it several times. By the way, Mrs. Adams was one of the best teachers I've ever worked with. She had a great sense of humor, always included me in on the fun things, changed diapers herself once in a while because she believed that toilet training was part of the instructional process, asked me what I thought about her ideas and what was going on in the class, and when I talked, she listened.

I'd like to talk to Ms. Brown about James—but I've got a couple of problems. She hasn't asked me about what I think and she really seems more interested in trying out her theories than she is in hearing from me. In fact, if I had to describe her, I'd say she is very dictatorial. Besides, the older I get, the nicer it is to just do my job and go home rather than taking orders from someone who doesn't know half as much as I do about teaching special education kids. On the other hand, with a few minor changes, the goals and activities she has planned for James would probably work—maybe.

Teacher Anne Brown

My name is Anne and this is my first teaching job. My undergraduate degree is in special education and I have a master's as well. I have had some teaching experience, but only as a student teacher. I've really been looking forward to being in charge of my own classroom, and putting the techniques I've worked so hard to learn to work. There was one thing, however, that no one prepared me for when I was in college—that is, that I would be expected to supervise someone old enough to be my mother who also has more than 25 years experience. But I do think I'm lucky to have an aide to help out with all of the little things that have to be done in the classroom so I can spend a lot of individual time with the students.

I really feel that as the teacher, I am the person who is responsible for what goes on in the classroom and that I will be held accountable for the good and the bad. That is why, after thinking it over, I decided that the best way to use my aide was to have her do the noninstructional chores and clerical duties. Besides, since Sharon is so much older than I am and really has a lot of experience, I decided that it was very important to establish myself as the authority figure. This isn't always easy because working with Sharon can be a little intimidating. She really gets along well with the other teachers in the building, and they all rave about her and tell me how lucky I am to have her.

There is a child in the class who seems to fit an almost textbook picture of a syndrome that I've read about but have never seen. I'm sure that he will benefit from a new technique that has been developed to cope with such a youngster and his behavior. I have laid out, in great detail, the type of interventions that I want to use and have started to follow the program. I've decided, however, that if it is going to work, Sharon is going to have to be involved as well because everything has to be done consistently and systematically.

When I asked her to help implement the program she didn't ask any questions or say anything—she just smiled a Mona Lisa smile. Later that day she started telling me about how terrific Mrs. Adams was and what a terrific teacher she was. She's done this before and I'm getting a little tired of it. In any event, I'm really more concerned about James and meeting his needs. I'd like to talk to Sharon about it. But I don't want her to think I don't know what I'm doing and I certainly don't want to diminish my authority in the classroom. What can I do?

Case Study Discussion Questions

a. Describe the problem from the paraeducator's point of view. (This may include attitudes, actions, and other factors described in the case study.)
b. Describe the problem from the teacher's point of view.

c. What behavior(s) does the teacher need to change?
d. What behavior(s) does the paraeducator need to change?
e. Discuss and list desired goal(s) for the team.
f. How can they work together to achieve the goal and to be a better instructional team? What additional information, skills, or other resources will they need to achieve the goal?

CASE STUDY 3: CONFLICT RESOLUTION STRATEGY

The following case study applies the six-step conflict resolution strategy to a situation that might be encountered by school professionals and paraeducators.

The Situation

Dan is a speech–language pathologist who works with Madeline, a speech–language assistant. Madeline works with students in small groups to reinforce their practice of articulation skills. Dan has become increasingly frustrated because Madeline has been arriving late to work with the students. The regular classroom teachers have told Dan that Madeline often comes to their classrooms 10 to 15 minutes late, then works with students for only 10 minutes instead of the scheduled 20-minute session. Dan wishes that Madeline would recognize the importance of being punctual and giving students their full time, but he realizes that she may not change if he continues to avoid the situation. Knowing that he needs to intervene, Dan believes that it will probably be more positive if he thinks though the conflict resolution steps he has leaned.

Case Study Discussion Questions

a. How does the conflict resolution strategy help Dan in this situation?
b. How does the strategy support Madeline in this situation?
c. What would you do if this does not resolve the situation?

CASE STUDY 4: PROBLEM SOLVING

Apply the problem-solving approach, as discussed in this chapter, to the following case study.

The Situation

Jeff, a student who has a reading disability, is in fourth grade. The Title I teacher has worked closely with the fourth-grade teacher so that Jeff does most of his schoolwork in the fourth-grade classroom. Recently Jeff has had difficulty staying on task for more than a couple of minutes. He can be a behavior problem. The fourth-grade teacher is at a loss as to what to do and asks the special education teacher and the paraeducator who support Jeff in the regular classroom to help solve this problem. The special education teacher tells the paraeducator about the fourth-grade teacher's concern and sets a time for a meeting that is convenient for all three of them. At this meeting, the special education teacher asks the fourth-grade teacher to share details of her concern.

Group Activity

Role-play this case study using the collaborative problem-solving process. Then answer the following questions based on the team's experience.

Case Study Discussion Questions

a. How well did this problem-solving process work for the team?
b. What would the team change next time, if anything?
c. What were the benefits to the team and to Jeff?
d. Are all seven steps necessary all of the time?

CASE STUDY 5: DEVELOPING EXPECTATIONS

To develop expectations for communications is to think ahead about the desired outcomes of an interaction, to anticipate behaviors that might interfere with or enhance mutual understanding, and to predict possible needs that will arise. With that in mind, discuss the following case study.

The Situation

Sue, a speech–language professional, is going to meet with Monica, a paraeducator, for their first planning meeting. She wants them to "get off on the right foot" and wants Monica to feel free to ask questions as they come up. She knows that Monica is a bit shy and may be hesitant to speak up.

Case Study Discussion Questions

a. What can Sue do so that Monica will feel comfortable?
b. How can Sue approach the meeting so that they begin as partners, not as boss and employee?
c. What behaviors might intimidate Monica?
d. What are the issues they need to discuss at this first meeting?
e. How many issues should Sue try to cover at this meeting?

CASE STUDY 6: UNDERSTANDING PERSPECTIVES

To understand perspectives during communication is to recognize that people see issues, situations, and ideas through their own points of view and that knowing and respecting these diverse views can serve the discussion in positive and productive ways. With that in mind, discuss the following case study.

The Situation

Beth, a resource teacher, works with Joseph, a paraeducator, who assists her with students when they are in the regular classroom. She believes that Joseph is becoming frustrated in trying to adapt to so many different classroom teachers' expectations of him. She wants to have a discussion with Joseph and two of the classroom teachers so that a common understanding can be reached.

Case Study Discussion Questions

a. What should Beth tell the teachers when she invites them to the meeting?
b. How should Beth approach Joseph so that he knows the purpose of the discussion?
c. What can Beth do at the meeting to get everyone's perspective of the current situation?
d. How can Beth make sure that each person is heard and understood?
e. How can Beth facilitate the development of a mutually accepted plan?

CASE STUDY 7: ASKING QUESTIONS

Asking questions during interpersonal conversations is to inquire further and demonstrate a sincere interest in learning from another. With that in mind, discuss the following case study.

The Situation

Sabrina, a vision specialist who is in the elementary school only once a week, relies on Ryan, a paraeducator, to provide three students with practice sessions in Braille. As part of her weekly visits, Sabrina meets with Ryan for a half hour. Lately she has felt that she has done too much of the talking and that Ryan is not contributing as much as he used to. She hopes that the next meeting will be more balanced in participation.

Case Study Discussion Questions

a. What can Sabrina do at the next meeting to solicit Ryan's participation?
b. What questions would encourage Ryan without putting him on the spot?
c. How can Sabrina make sure that she doesn't end up doing all of the talking?
d. If Ryan gives a brief response, what can Sabrina ask to get him to say more?

e. How can Sabrina find out about the students' progress from Ryan?

CASE STUDY 8: LISTENING

Listening actively is making a conscious effort to hear the words and understand the meaning of a spoken message. It is one of the most empowering communication skills a person can learn. With that in mind, discuss the following case study.

The Situation

Ralph has become aware that whenever Yuko, the paraeducator, is explaining something to him, he is distracted by trying to get several other things done in his classroom. Consequently, he doesn't remember what she says and has to ask her to repeat herself. He wants to give her his full attention next time.

Case Study Discussion Questions

a. What could Ralph do to make sure that he is paying attention to Yuko?
b. What should Ralph stop doing to improve his listening?
c. How will better listening skills improve his relationship with Yuko?
d. How can Ralph make sure that he doesn't lapse back into his old nonlistening habits?
e. How will Ralph know if he has become a better listener?

CASE STUDY 9: SPEAKING CLEARLY

Speaking clearly in conversation is to express oneself in such a manner that the receiver's understanding closely matches what the speaker meant to convey.

The Situation

Jami, an occupational therapist, is to meet with the paraeducator, Connie, who works with her. They have been discussing an inservice they will present on serving students with special needs in the regular classroom.

Jami wants to be sure that they are coordinated in an efficient and effective manner. She has been leading most of the conversation and Connie has been appearing to agree. Now she wants to be sure that she has made herself clear and that Connie has understood what Jami meant.

Case Study Discussion Questions

a. How can Jami check to see if Connie is understanding what has been said?
b. What questions can Jami ask that will elicit Connie's perspective?
c. How will Jami know if she got her points across?
d. What should Jami do if Connie has misunderstood some of the discussion?
e. How frequently should Jami check for Connie's understanding?

References

Abelson, M. A., & Woodman, R. W. (1983). Review of research on team effectiveness: Implications for teams in schools. *School Psychology Review, 12,* 125–136.

DeBoer, A. (1995). *Working together: The art of consulting and communicating.* Longmont, CO: Sopris West.

DeVito, J. A. (1994). *The interpersonal communication book* (7th ed.). New York: Harper Collins.

Dewey, J. (1993). *How we think.* Boston: Heath.

Elgin, S. (1989). *Success with the gentle art of verbal self-defense.* Englewood Cliffs, NJ: Prentice Hall.

Feldman, R. S. (1985). *Social psychology: Theories, research, and applications.* New York: McGraw-Hill.

Friend, M., & Cook, L. (1996). *Interactions: Collaboration skills for school professionals* (2nd ed.). White Plains, NY: Longman.

Gordon, T. (1977). *Leader effectiveness training.* New York: Wyden Books.

Margolis, H., & Brannigan, G. (1978). Problem solving with parents. *Academy Therapy, 22,* 423–425.

Merriam-Webster's collegiate dictionary (10th ed.). (1993). Springfield, MA: Merriam-Webster.

Pickett, A. L., Faison, K., & Formanek, J. (1999). *A core curriculum and training program to prepare educators to work in inclusive classrooms serving school age students with disabilities.* New York: National Resource Center for Paraprofessionals in Education and Related Human Services, Center for Advanced Study in Education, Graduate School, City University of New York.

Schrage, M. (1990). *Shared minds.* New York: Random House.

Senge, P. (1990). *The fifth discipline.* New York: St. Martin's Press.

Sherif, M., & Sherif, C. (1956). *An outline of social psychology.* New York: Harper & Row.

Smith, R. M. (1985). *The high school department: A new force for excellence.* Portland, OR: Northwest Regional Educational Laboratory. (ERIC Document Reproduction Service No. ED265162)

Soloman, L. N. (1977). Team development: A training approach. In J. W. Pfeiffer & J. E. Jones (Eds.), *The 1977 annual handbook for group facilitators* (pp. 181–193). La Jolla, CA: University Associates.

Thomas, K., & Kilmann, R. (1974). *Thomas–Kilmann Conflict Mode Instrument.* Tuxedo, NY: Xicom.

Paraeducators in Educational Settings: Administrative Issues

6

Stan Vasa, Allen Steckelberg, and Anna Lou Pickett

OVERVIEW

Administrators at state, district, and building levels play critical roles in establishing effective education and related services programs. This is especially true for programs in which paraeducators are employed. In this chapter, the focus is on the responsibilities of district and building administrators.

Although schools and other education agencies have considerable latitude in the development and administration of paraeducator training programs and personnel practices, common concerns and tasks must be addressed. Securing funding, allocating budgets, determining wages and fringe benefits, conducting needs assessments, and developing procedural and policy handbooks are major responsibilities for district administrators. In addition, district and building administrators work together to provide leadership in the development of paraeducator performance standards and opportunities for systematic competency-based training. They also have responsibility for ensuring that teachers are aware of and are prepared for their roles as supervisors of paraeducators.

Policies and procedures established by district and building administrators are important in creating a climate that promotes and increases the value of the services provided by paraeducators. Administrative leadership is necessary to clearly establish roles for paraeducators and to provide the support and training necessary to ensure they are prepared to work with children and youth. Administrators must also support teachers and other certified and licensed professionals so that they can be effective program and instructional managers, and supervisors of paraeducator performance. This chapter addresses policies and administrative issues in establishing and maintaining quality education and related services programs that include paraeducators. Topics discussed include establishing district and building policies and practices, conducting needs assessments, developing job descriptions, selecting and assigning paraeducators, developing training policies and programs, developing supervisory policies, and evaluating the impact of paraeducators on education and related services programs.

Instructional Objectives

After studying this chapter and participating in discussions and exercises, the reader will be able to do the following:

1. Explain how district policies and standards for paraeducator roles, supervision, and training contribute to more effective schools.
2. Describe why needs assessments are important tools for determining policies and standards and facilitating administrative decision making.
3. Describe the need for and components of three levels of job descriptions: (a) district, (b) program, and (c) personalized assignments for individual paraeducators.
4. Discuss effective procedures for paraeducator recruitment, selection, and placement.
5. Describe district and building administrators' responsibilities for developing supervisory procedures and evaluation criteria for paraeducator performance.
6. Describe district and building administrators' responsibilities for developing and implementing systematic staff development opportunities for paraeducators and school professionals.
7. Explain the importance of a districtwide handbook designed to share information about policies and procedures connected with paraeducator employment.

Establishing Policies and Standards

Guiding Principles

District and school administrators have operational responsibility for establishing policies and procedures that promote the appropriate and effective utilization of paraeducators in the protection of rights of learners and their families, and recognition of paraeducators as vital members of the school's educational team. The first step in establishing policy is to examine the reasons for employing paraeducators. As part of the strategic planning process, district and school staff must work together to identify expected benefits that will result from the placement of paraeducators in programs and different educational settings. This information is then used to guide the development of policies and the allocation of human and fiscal resources.

Establishing policies for paraeducator roles and responsibilities as part of a common vision for all school personnel provides direction in allocating resources and setting standards for employment, training, supervision, and evaluation of paraeducators. Typical outcomes of paraeducator employment include (a) extended instructional options, (b) increased learning opportunities for students, (c) reduction in adult-to-student ratios, and (d) more efficient use of resources.

These benefits will be achieved only when programs that utilize paraeducators are carefully planned and include appropriate training, supervision, and monitoring for paraeducators. The many benefits of well-designed policies and systems for integrating paraeducators into education and related services teams include, but are not limited to,

- increased availability of positive adult role models for students;
- expanded student learning opportunities;
- increased availability of individual and small group instruction;
- additional time for professionals to plan, provide instruction and related services, and evaluate program outcomes;

- increased on-task student behaviors;
- improved teacher morale; and
- better monitoring and evaluation of the educational process.

The ultimate goal in employing paraeducators is the improvement of quality educational programs for all learners. Development of a set of guiding principles provides the foundation and vision for effectively utilizing paraeducators in educational settings. A vision statement also serves as the framework for the development of needs assessment activities and paraeducator job descriptions. Table 6.1 provides an example of a statement of guiding principles for paraeducator employment, roles, preparation, and supervision.

Needs Assessment

Conducting a systematic needs assessment is a valuable tool for administrative decision making regarding the employment, placement, training, and supervision of paraeducators. Issues commonly addressed include (a) needs of students for individualized attention, (b) extent of professional and supervisory staff needs for paraeducator support, (c) training required by teachers to supervise paraeducators, and (d) paraeducator training needs.

Establishing the educational needs of students and the support required by school professionals to meet these needs is critical. In tandem, these activities provide the basis for determining whether paraeducator employment should be initiated, expanded, or reduced. Determining where and how paraeducators should be assigned is affected by many factors, including the number of children and youth served by the district or agency who may (a) have learning, physical, and sensory disabilities; (b) have limited English proficiency; and (c) come from economically or educationally disadvantaged families or other backgrounds that place them at risk. Changes in programs related to inclusion of children and youth with special needs in general education have placed increased classroom, program, and curriculum management responsibilities on school professionals. In many situations, the increasing demand for extended services warrants additional support through utilization of paraeducators. With changing programs also comes the need for pre- and

Table 6.1

Guiding Principles for Paraeducator Employment, Roles, Preparation, and Supervision

1. Skilled paraeducators are employed to improve the quality of education and services and to help ensure supportive, inclusive, safe, and healthy learning environments for children, youth, and staff.
2. Administrators and teachers create environments that recognize paraeducators as valued team members and effectively integrate them into teams.
3. Members of program planning and implementation teams participate within clearly defined roles in changing, dynamic environments to provide learner-centered, individualized experiences and services for all children and youth and their families.
4. Paraeducators are respected and supported in their team roles by policymakers, administrators, teachers, and families.
5. Standards for paraeducator roles and professional development ensure that paraeducators are assigned to positions for which they are qualified and have the skills required to assist teachers to provide quality learning experiences and related services for all children and youth and their families.
6. Paraeducators receive pre- and inservice professional development provided by the district and are provided opportunities for continuing education or career advancement offered by institutions of higher education.
7. All school professionals responsible for supervising the work of paraeducators have the skills necessary to plan for, direct, provide on-the-job training for, monitor, and evaluate the performance of paraeducators.
8. Paraeducators have an occupational and professional identity and contribute to learner-centered activities that help to achieve the mission of the school.

Note. These guiding principles are based on research activities conducted by the National Resource Center for Paraprofessionals and paraeducator development efforts in Utah, Minnesota, Iowa, Washington, Rhode Island, and Nebraska. Adapted from *Strengthening and Supporting Teacher/Provider–Paraeducator Teams: Guidelines for Paraeducator Roles, Supervision, and Preparation,* by A. L. Pickett, 1999, New York: National Resource Center for Paraprofessionals, Center for Advanced Study in Education, Graduate Center, City University of New York. Copyright 1999 by National Resource Center for Paraprofessionals. Adapted with permission.

inservice training as well as on-the-job coaching. Training needs of paraeducators and professionals and the resources available to support staff development programs can also be identified through a needs assessment.

Paraeducator Job Descriptions

A natural outgrowth of a needs assessment is the development or amendment of current job descriptions for paraeducators. Job descriptions validate the importance of paraeducators, clarify teacher–paraeducator role distinctions, serve as a reference point for evaluating paraeducator performance, and identify skills and training needs for paraeducators. Written job descriptions at both district and program levels help to promote job satisfaction by eliminating paraeducator and teacher concerns about what is expected of team members.

Job descriptions are often constructed at three levels to provide guidance to staff and paraeducators.

- **Districtwide job descriptions** provide guidelines for duties, outline supervision of paraeducators, and establish minimum educational and experiential requirements for employment. Included are the duties that paraeducators may perform as dictated by school district policy and ethical and legal considerations. Administrative concerns such as working conditions, training requirements, supervision procedures, and evaluation should appear in a written job description.

- **Program-level job descriptions** are used to delineate paraeducator roles in unique settings and programs that may include general, bilingual, Title I, and special education; early childhood programs; community-based training; and related services (i.e., occupational and physical therapy, speech–language pathology). These job descriptions serve as both communication instruments and organizational tools. In contrast to district-level statements, roles can be delineated more specifically and expectations for on-the-job training and performance indicators can be more directly related to the specific duties performed by individual paraeducators in program job descriptions.

- **School professional–developed personalized job assignments** allow teachers to communicate to paraeducators information about how the job description applies in their classrooms and about their philosophies for teaching and management style. Paraeducators themselves often take an active role with the supervising teacher in the development and interpretation of an individualized assignment. This collaboration provides an opportunity for discussion and the development of understanding and ownership of the roles and responsibilities for the team. (Development of program and individualized job assignments are also discussed in Chapter 3.) Figure 6.1 provides an example of a districtwide job description.

Selection and Hiring of Paraeducators

Services provided by schools are directly affected by the quality of all personnel, including paraeducators. Procedures for recruitment, selection, and placement of paraeducators require attention from policymakers and district and building administrators. By establishing policies and systems that recognize the need for paraeducators and the contributions they can make to improving education and related services, administrators will be able to attract and retain a skilled paraeducator workforce. Recruitment efforts should describe assignments that encompass a variety of interesting duties, opportunities for personal growth and career advancement, various benefits offered by districts, and intrinsic rewards that come from working with children and youth. Sources for recruitment of paraeducators include parent–teacher associations, senior citizen centers, civic and community organizations, school volunteer programs, community colleges, high school occupational and vocational training programs, and retired military personnel.

An important component of school policies regarding paraeducator employment is the creation of educational and experiential qualifications for their employment. Establishing qualifications is essential for ensuring that candidates have the education, the life or work experiences, or both that will enable them to carry out assigned duties, protect learner and parent rights, and respect diversity among learners and their families and staff. Employment

PARAEDUCATOR JOB DESCRIPTION

Position Title: Instructional Paraeducator

Position Setting: Elementary/Secondary Classroom

Qualifications for the Position:

1. Must be 18 years of age or older.
2. Must meet experiential and education criteria established by the district.

Purpose: Assist the teacher in providing learning experiences for students.

Duties and responsibilities:

1. Carry out instructional activities with students as planned and directed by the teacher.
2. Assist the teacher in implementing the classroom behavior management program.
3. Provide objective feedback to the teacher on student progress and behavior.
4. Assist in the preparation and care of instructional materials and equipment.
5. Perform clerical duties assigned by the teacher.
6. Follow district procedures for maintaining healthy and safe environments for learners and staff.
7. Practice legal and ethical standards of conduct established by the district.

Training Requirements:

Attend a 3-day orientation session at the beginning of the school year and a minimum of 20 hours of inservice training during the school year.

Supervision Guidelines:

The teacher will supervise the daily work of the paraeducator, provide a schedule and daily plans, and conduct regularly scheduled planning conferences. The paraeducator will be responsible to the teacher in instructional support role matters. The paraeducator will be responsible to the building principal in district policy matters.

Evaluation Guidelines:

Paraeducators are responsible for performing all tasks assigned to them and for following the instruction of the supervising teacher or building administrator. Paraeducators will be continuously evaluated with a written evaluation by the supervising teacher or administrator. Each paraeducator will develop an individualized training plan for the year in conjunction with the supervisor.

Figure 6.1. Sample district paraeducator job description.

standards promote the hiring of quality personnel but should not create unnecessary barriers. Previous work experience, references, educational level, literacy, language and writing skills, and skills applicable to the specific position (e.g., word processing, computer knowledge, understanding of students' cultural and ethnic heritages) are important in selecting the best qualified candidate. Research shows that interpersonal skills and attitudes of applicants and an interest in self-improvement may also serve as effective indicators of how well a candidate will fit into the team (Kansas State Department of Education, 1983; Vasa, Steckelberg, & Ulrich-Ronning, 1982).

Although it is difficult to assess objectively a potential employee's attitudes, values, and interpersonal skills, they are important to the paraeducator's ability to work effectively in the classroom. The importance of conducting a systematic interview cannot be overstated as a tool for assessing self-confidence, patience, empathy, concern for children, and other personal qualities that help to identify an effective team member. Including the supervising professional in the interview whenever possible can help to minimize potential sources of conflicts between team members and ensure that the applicants clearly understand the duties they will be expected to perform. As part of the interview process, the candidate should be given the job description, and interviewers should provide information about the school's organization and the types of students to be served. A written set of performance indicators, ethical responsibilities, and duties expected of the prospective employee should also be available.

In addition, interviewers need to know how to use techniques that will enable them to draw out information about skills and unique talents of applicants who may never have thought of themselves in those terms. Figure 6.2 contains examples of interview questions that assist with making hiring decisions and matching teachers and paraeducators.

Paraeducator Supervision Policies

Both district and building policies and administrative practices need to acknowledge and support the supervisory roles of teachers. Developing standards and guidelines for paraeducator supervision involves determining the roles and duties of teachers in

INTERVIEW QUESTIONS

- Why did you apply for this position and to this district?
- Why do you want to work with children and youth?
- What do you think you can offer the learners? The staff? The parents?
- What are your talents? Your skills? What do you do in your spare time (hobbies)?
- What work have you done before? What did you like and dislike about your previous job(s)?
- What did you like and dislike when you were in school?
- What is your long-range career goal?
- What could students learn from you that will help them grow?
- What is your work style? Do you prefer to initiate activities or be assigned tasks?
- Are you likely to ask for help or let your supervisor know when something is unpleasant, or will you avoid talking about it?
- How do you think you would feel about being supervised by teachers?

Figure 6.2. Sample interview questions.

(a) selecting paraeducators; (b) planning, assigning, and delegating tasks to individual paraeducators; (c) identifying a paraeducator's skills and training needs; (d) planning and providing on-the-job training for paraeducators; and (e) participating in formal (annual) paraeducator performance evaluations. Figure 6.3 provides an example of a district-level policy statement that addresses these issues. It is divided into two parts. Part I describes the supervisory roles of classroom teachers. Part II describes the supervisory roles of school professionals who direct paraeducators assigned to vocational or other community-based programs.

Principals and program administrators, in particular, play critical roles in enabling and supporting teachers, occupational and physical therapists, and speech–language pathologists to carry out their supervisory responsibilities and to effectively

District-Level Supervision Policy Statement

I. Supervision of Paraeducators in Building-Based Programs

1. Teachers are responsible for planning and assessing all aspects of instructional programs.
2. When supervising paraeducators, teachers shall
   a. plan and assign paraeducator duties;
   b. direct and delegate paraeducator responsibilities;
   c. establish methods for evaluating and communicating student needs and progress;
   d. provide systematic on-the-job training, related to the tasks performed by the paraeducator; and
   e. evaluate the impact of activities carried out by the paraeducator on student performance.
3. The supervising professional shall keep written records of paraeducator evaluation and training and provide copies to the paraeducator and building principal.

II. Supervision of Paraeducators in Nonschool Sites

The utilization of paraeducators in vocational, traditional, and other community-based programs is critical to the successful implementation of these programs. To ensure that paraeducators are appropriately supervised, the supervising teacher is responsible for the following:

1. Providing on-the-job training before the paraeducator accompanies a student to any site. Training should focus on detailed instructional plans, prepared or approved by the supervising teacher, and data collection methods documenting student performance.
2. Making regularly scheduled on-site visits to community placements. The time will be spent observing, evaluating, planning, and/or training with the paraeducator and on-the-job training for the paraeducator.
3. Monitoring student progress. Supervisors will review data and make changes in instructional plans as required. All changes in the student programs will be discussed with paraeducators.
4. Maintaining a clear line of communication with the paraeducator. Emergency communication procedures should be developed, implemented, and monitored by building principals.
5. Sharing relevant information about the paraeducator's performance and training needs with principal and paraeducator.

Figure 6.3. District-level supervision policy statement. *Note.* Adapted from job descriptions in *Policy and Regulation Manual,* by Lincoln Public Schools, 1993, Lincoln, NE: Author. Copyright 1993 by Lincoln Public Schools. Adapted with permission.

integrate paraeducators into education and related services teams. The Iowa Department of Education (1998) and Pickett, Vasa, and Steckelberg (1993) identified scopes of responsibilities for building and program administrators. Table 6.2 describes the roles of program administrators and principals in implementing district policies that are designed to ensure that paraeducators are appropriately prepared, supervised, and evaluated.

Evaluating Paraeducator Performance

Evaluation of paraeducator performance is twofold: (a) informal evaluation of paraeducator performance by the supervising teacher, which occurs throughout the school year, and (b) formal (annual or semiannual) evaluation that involves the observations and ratings of principals or designated program personnel in addition to those of the supervising teacher. When effective supervision is provided, informal (functional) evaluation combined with feedback from the teacher takes place almost daily. In fact, the supervision and evaluation processes are almost inseparable and provide a basis for on-the-job training. Regularly scheduled conferences are important components of the functional assessment process because they provide opportunities for the supervising teacher to discuss how well the paraeducator implements program strategies and objectives, follows instructions, and establishes rapport with students. Conferences also provide an opportunity to discuss the teacher's observations regarding strengths and readiness of the paraeducator to take on new tasks. The monitoring checklist shown in Figure 6.4 is an example of a format for recording the results of observations.

Standardized performance indicators for assessing the adequacy of supervision are helpful to both administrators and teachers as they work together to ensure that paraeducators are appropriately directed and monitored. The following points are important to the development of effective supervision of paraeducators: (a) the teacher manages personnel resources in the classroom; (b) the teacher must have sufficient information and control to make appropriate educational decisions; and (c) the teacher is responsible for the students' learning outcomes (Pickett, 1999; Vasa & Steckelberg, 1998). This approach applies

Table 6.2
Roles of Program and Building Administrators in the Management of Paraeducators

- Ensure that teachers and paraeducators understand the distinctions in their roles and are aware of school and district policies.
- Inform parents about the roles of paraeducators in implementing their child's program.
- Involve teachers in the selection of paraeducators.
- Schedule opportunities for teachers and paraeducators to meet regularly for on-the-job training and planning.
- Provide support that will help team members to resolve interpersonal or other problems that may occur in classrooms or other learning environments.
- Ensure that paraeducators are appropriately prepared to carry out assigned tasks.
- Provide clear guidelines for the supervision of paraeducators.
- Provide leadership in the evaluation and systematic improvement of teacher supervision and monitoring of paraeducators.
- Develop, in collaboration with teachers, performance indicators and instruments for assessing the performance of paraeducators and guidelines for involving teachers in annual performance reviews of paraeducators.
- Assess emerging training needs for teacher and paraeducator team members.
- Provide teachers and paraeducators with information about career development opportunities and support services available through the district or institutions of higher education.

Note. Adapted from *Guide for Effective Paraeducator Practices in Iowa,* by Iowa Department of Education, Division of Early Childhood, Elementary and Secondary Education, 1998, Des Moines, IA: Author; and *Using Paraeducators Effectively in the Classroom* [Fastback 358], by A. L. Pickett, S. F. Vasa, and A. L. Steckelberg, 1993, Bloomington, IN: Phi Delta Kappa Educational Foundation.

to a broad range of settings and types of programs and more adequately reflects the intended use of paraeducators than do policies that tend to dictate physical location or direct observation time.

In contrast to functional assessment activities, formal evaluations are usually more standardized and take place either annually or semiannually. The formal evaluation process is frequently shared by administrators and teachers (Vasa et al.,

MONITORING CHECKLIST

Instructions: This form is completed by the supervising teacher to provide feedback after observing the paraeducator conducting an instructional activity. Write notes on the blanks.

Date ______________ Activity ______________________

Skills Comment	Well Developed	Needs Improvement
1. Prepares for the session ______________________	☐	☐
2. Establishes rapport with student ______________________	☐	☐
3. Gives clear instructions ______________________	☐	☐
4. Uses appropriate questions and cues ______________________	☐	☐
5. Uses materials effectively ______________________	☐	☐
6. Keeps lesson focused on objective ______________________	☐	☐
7. Keeps student on task ______________________	☐	☐
8. Gives appropriate feedback to student ______________________	☐	☐
9. Uses reinforcement effectively ______________________	☐	☐
10. Records student responses ______________________	☐	☐
11. Follows lesson as planned ______________________	☐	☐
12. Stays on task, uses time effectively ______________________	☐	☐

Figure 6.4. Sample monitoring checklist.

1982). Components of a formal evaluation process include (a) preobservation activities, including defining concerns, using standardized indicators of acceptable paraeducator performance developed by the district; (b) data gathering through formal observations, rating scales, questionnaires, or other instruments; (c) analysis of results and identification of current skills and those that need to be improved; and (d) conferencing with the paraeducator who is being evaluated to provide positive feedback about performance and outline plans or strategies to improve performance of the paraeducator when required.

Items appearing on observation forms and rating scales should correspond with duties and responsibilities outlined in the district and program job description. Local needs and expectations determine the specific content of evaluation instruments. Figure 6.5 is a sample paraeducator rating scale to be completed by a principal or program administrator. (Teachers may also be included in the formal assessment process.)

Evaluating the Quality of Supervision of Paraeducators

In addition to assessing the performance of individual paraeducators, an equally important outcome of the evaluation process is the determination of how well the paraeducator is supervised and integrated into the instructional team. Questions and issues that require the attention of principals or program administrators to determine the effectiveness of supervision include the following:

1. Are district and building guidelines and procedures for supervision in place?
2. Is there a set time in daily or weekly schedules for a teacher and paraeducator to meet?
3. Does the teacher provide appropriate direction and support for the paraeducator?
4. How does the presence of the paraeducator impact the productivity of the teacher?
5. How does the presence of the paraeducator impact the students?

PARAEDUCATOR PERFORMANCE INDICATORS

Name ______________________________ Worksite ________________

Evaluator ______________________________________ Date ___/___/___

Directions: Complete the following form for each paraeducator employed in the district. The rating scale of 1 to 5 is employed: 1 indicates that the paraeducator does not know how to perform the task; 5 indicates that skill is well developed and that the task may be performed with little guidance. Make narrative comments where they would be appropriate in evaluating the paraeducator.

Team Participation

The paraeducator

1. Follows teacher/provider instructions for carrying out an assigned task **1 2 3 4 5**
2. Asks for clarification of instructions that are not fully understood **1 2 3 4 5**
3. Shares information objectively about learners and their families with teachers **1 2 3 4 5**
4. Uses communication and other interactive skills that demonstrate respect for other staff, learners, and families **1 2 3 4 5**
5. Responds to differences of opinions among team members with openness and respect **1 2 3 4 5**
6. Responds appropriately to feedback about performance . . . **1 2 3 4 5**

Maintaining Learner-Centered Environments

The paraeducator

1. Follows district procedures for protecting the safety and health of learners and staff **1 2 3 4 5**
2. Uses universal health precautions and proper body mechanics for lifting learners and heavy objects **1 2 3 4 5**
3. Follows teacher plans for engaging families in their child's learning activities and environment **1 2 3 4 5**
4. Interacts appropriately with families **1 2 3 4 5**

(continues)

Figure 6.5. Sample paraeducator performance indicators. *Note.* Adapted from *Strengthening and Supporting Teacher/Provider–Paraeducator Teams: Guidelines for Paraeducator Roles, Supervision, and Preparation,* by A. L. Pickett, 1999, New York: National Resource Center for Paraprofessionals, Center for Advanced Study in Education, Graduate Center, City University of New York. Copyright 1999 by National Resource Center for Paraprofessionals. Adapted with permission.

Organizing Learning Environments

The paraeducator

1. Prepares materials and learning centers before an activity is scheduled to begin	1 2 3 4 5
2. Prepares materials following teacher/provider instructions	1 2 3 4 5
3. Uses computers, copy machines, and other equipment appropriately and correctly	1 2 3 4 5
4. Uses adaptive equipment and assistive technology as prescribed by teachers or other supervising professional	1 2 3 4 5
5. Modifies, in consultation with teachers, learning activities and materials to accommodate individual needs	1 2 3 4 5
6. Shares relevant information with teachers that assist the planning process	1 2 3 4 5

Engaging Children and Youth in Learning Experiences

The paraeducator

1. Develops and maintains effective interactions with all students	1 2 3 4 5
2. Follows teacher plans for individuals and groups	1 2 3 4 5
3. Follows teacher plans and strategies for managing student behavior	1 2 3 4 5
4. Follows teacher plans and methods that facilitate learning for children and youth with challenging behaviors	1 2 3 4 5
5. Follows teacher plans and methods for providing vocational and other community-based learning experiences	1 2 3 4 5
6. Previews a learning activity to ensure that individuals and groups understand the objective of the activity	1 2 3 4 5
7. Encourages learners to work independently	1 2 3 4 5
8. Provides assistance, when appropriate, to ensure that learners stay on task	1 2 3 4 5
9. Engages learners in one activity at a time	1 2 3 4 5
10. Provides clear and concise directions to learners	1 2 3 4 5
11. Uses learning activities developed by teachers that accommodate individual needs	1 2 3 4 5
12. Uses learning strategies that support peer interaction among all students	1 2 3 4 5
13. Documents the results of learning activities and shares relevant information with teachers	1 2 3 4 5

(continues)

Figure 6.5. *Continued.*

Assessing Learner Performance

The paraeducator

1. Uses teacher-developed functional assessment instruments as directed 1 2 3 4 5
2. Shares results of functional assessment activities objectively with teachers 1 2 3 4 5
3. Scores informal reading, spelling, and math tests accurately 1 2 3 4 5
4. Accurately documents information about learner performance as required by state, district, or agency policy 1 2 3 4 5
5. Accurately completes attendance, truancy, and suspension records following district or agency policies and practices 1 2 3 4 5
6. Accurately files student information 1 2 3 4 5

Practicing Professional and Ethical Standards of Conduct

The paraeducator

1. Performs only tasks for which he or she is appropriately prepared 1 2 3 4 5
2. Follows work rules and procedures established for district personnel 1 2 3 4 5
3. Maintains confidentiality about all personal information, assessment results, medical history, and other records concerning students and their families 1 2 3 4 5
4. Follows procedures that protect the safety and well-being of students and staff 1 2 3 4 5
5. Uses interactive and communication methods that demonstrate respect for cultural diversity and individuality among students, their families, and staff 1 2 3 4 5
6. Participates in professional and career development opportunities 1 2 3 4 5

Figure 6.5. *Continued.*

The list in Table 6.3 provides a guide for administrators to use in planning and evaluating the supervision and integration of paraeducators into education and related services teams.

Training Policies

Administrators at the district and building levels are responsible for ensuring that both teachers and paraeducators have the skills and knowledge base they need to work as members of

Table 6.3
Performance Indicators for Effective Paraeducator Supervision

1. Are there established district or building policies and procedures for paraeducator supervision that include
   - roles of teachers in supervising paraeducators?
   - time in daily or weekly schedules for team meetings?
   - guidelines for functional (informal) assessment?
   - performance indicators for conducting formal (annual) evaluations?
   - procedures for conducting paraeducator evaluations?
   - plans for structured inservice linked to on-the-job training?
2. Do supervising teachers
   - demonstrate awareness of distinctions in teacher and paraeducator roles?
   - plan assignments for paraeducators based on their qualifications and identified ability to perform a task?
   - model standards for professional and ethical conduct for paraeducators?
   - develop paraeducator work plans that (a) specify the individual(s) or groups the paraeducator will assist, (b) describe the learning or behavior management strategies that the paraeducator will use, (c) identify the materials or equipment required to perform the task, (d) designate where the activity will occur, and (e) describe how information on student performance will be documented and shared with the teacher?
   - describe methods the team will use to maintain supportive, safe, and healthy environments for learners and staff?
   - use interactive and communication skills that demonstrate respect for and recognition of cultural and other differences that may influence paraeducator actions and performance?
3. Does the presence of a paraeducator provide the teacher with more time for tasks that include
   - consulting with other education and related services personnel?
   - assessing and diagnosing student needs?
   - planning lessons?
   - modifying curriculum and instructional strategies for individual students?
   - achieving student goals and objectives?
   - providing personalized attention to all students?
   - assessing program outcomes?

Note. Adapted from *Using Paraeducators Effectively in the Classroom* [Fastback 358], by A. L. Pickett, S. F. Vasa, and A. L. Steckelberg, 1993, Bloomington, IN: Phi Delta Kappa Educational Foundation, and *Strengthening and Supporting Teacher/Provider–Paraeducator Teams: Guidelines for Paraeducator Roles, Supervision, and Preparation,* by A. L. Pickett, 1993, New York: National Resource Center for Paraprofessionals, Center for Advanced Study in Education, The Graduate Center, City University of New York.

education and related services teams. This section discusses (a) the components of a comprehensive training system for paraeducators, (b) the roles of district and building administrators and school professionals in implementing the training plan, and (c) the training needs of teachers that enable them to supervise and work effectively with paraeducators.

Components of a Systematic Professional Development Program

To provide a comprehensive system of personnel development for all team members, it is important to use a variety of approaches. Effective training for paraeducators should include professional development opportunities that provide a continuum of experiences, including (a) initial orientation for paraeducators, (b) structured on-the-job coaching in classrooms or other learning environments, (c) formal inservice sessions to supplement the workplace training, and (d) access to postsecondary education based on the individual's career preference. Ideally, training should be provided at the district, building, and classroom levels. Opportunities for professional development for paraeducator staff may include conference attendance, self-instruction using resource materials provided by the district, and distance learning. An emerging tool used by school districts to support paraeducator training is online training resources (Steckelberg & Vasa, 1998). World Wide Web delivery of training assists in alleviating scheduling and access problems often faced in planning training programs. It is important to note that when administrators or personnel developers select instructional resources, particularly those to be used for self-instruction, they must evaluate them to assure that the materials (a) are based on current best education practices, (b) recognize distinctions in teacher and paraeducator roles, (c) demonstrate respect for paraeducators and the contributions they make to improving educaton for all learners, and (d) include strategies that take into account adult learning preferences (Pickett, 1999).

Initial orientation for paraeducators must provide them with an overview of district and building policies (e.g., Who is to be called if a paraeducator will be absent or late? What is the role of the supervising professional? What are the professional and ethical responsibilities of paraeducators? What are the district's emergency procedures? Do the students have special needs, and if they do, what are they?). As noted throughout this chapter, many of the skills paraeducators need to learn are appropriately taught in an on-the-job setting by the supervising teacher. On-the-job training may be particularly effective in strengthening behavior management, instructional, and other skills related to the program or classroom that were learned in pre- and inservice training programs. A planning guide developed by the supervising professional helps organize and document on-the-job training activities.

Establishing a Training Plan

Paraeducator training programs should be long range, comprehensive, and systematic. Often the impact of training is lessened because it is based on speakers from outside the district or the current "hot topic" rather than systematic development of an identified set of knowledge and skills. Paraeducators deserve a well-defined set of training competencies and incentives for achieving them. To develop opportunities for structured approaches to orientation, on-the-job training, and ongoing inservice training programs, school districts should consider establishing a committee of administrators, teachers, and paraeducators to identify competencies and instructional needs for paraeducators. Involving teachers and paraeducators in designing and providing training often results in more relevant training. Their participation has the added benefit of improving job satisfaction, developing ownership of training, and enhancing staff morale.

Training competencies should be based on skills that paraeducators require to carry out instruction and other program duties in different curriculum areas and levels of paraeducator positions. Training must also prepare paraeducators to maintain confidentiality; respect the human and legal rights of children, youth, and their families; and provide safe and secure learning environments. (Paraeducator responsibilities, competencies, and performance indicators are discussed more fully in Chapter 2.)

In addition to establishing competencies, the district must develop a plan for ensuring that paraeducators acquire and use the identified skills. An annual training plan provides a systematic way of focusing on the skill development of paraeducators. The training plan should include competencies, a method for demonstrating mastery, and a time frame for completing the program. Flexibility to allow alternative methods for learning and demonstrating competence and development of skills should be considered and incorporated into the plan.

An annual training plan provides a systematic method for managing and evaluating training programs. A training plan, such as the example in Figure 6.6, can be included in paraeducator personnel records for charting their progress. Completion of all or portions of the planned activities may serve as the basis for advancement to a higher level and receipt of additional benefits.

Training for Supervising Teachers

In addition to developing paraeducator training opportunities, districts must also support the supervisory roles of teachers by preparing them to assume these responsibilities. Teachers must have knowledge and skills that enable them to fully tap the benefits provided by paraeducators. Table 6.4 describes the skills teachers require to serve as effective team leaders and supervisors of paraeducators.

Effective supervisors of paraeducators should have knowledge of management and supervisory procedures that include (a) planning paraeducator tasks based on learner needs, (b) establishing priorities and scheduling resources, (c) clarifying expectations, (d) delegating paraeducator assignments, (e) providing training and support for paraeducators, (f) evaluating paraeducator performance, and (g) providing a supportive work environment. (Teacher supervisory responsibilities are discussed more fully in Chapters 2 and 3.)

It is important for school administrators and professionals to join forces with graduate and undergraduate professional development programs, state departments of education, and other agencies with jurisdiction over credentialing. Making these connections helps to develop standards that will ensure that teachers and other school professionals are prepared to carry out their supervisory responsibilities.

ANNUAL TRAINING PLAN

Name ______________________________ Date __/__/__

Orientation Topics	Target Date	Date Completed	Evaluation
Orientation to the building and introduction to other staff members	__/__/__	__/__/__	
Goals of the school program	__/__/__	__/__/__	
Distinctions in teacher and paraeducator roles	__/__/__	__/__/__	
State regulations and district policies regarding paraeducator employment	__/__/__	__/__/__	
Ethical considerations in working with students and families	__/__/__	__/__/__	
First aid and emergency procedures	__/__/__	__/__/__	
Inservice Topics			
Roles and responsibilities of team members	__/__/__	__/__/__	
Instructional strategies	__/__/__	__/__/__	
Legal, ethical, and confidentiality standards	__/__/__	__/__/__	
Behavior management	__/__/__	__/__/__	
Team building strategies	__/__/__	__/__/__	
Communication and problem-solving skills	__/__/__	__/__/__	
Human growth and development	__/__/__	__/__/__	
Technology and computer skills	__/__/__	__/__/__	
Appreciating diversity	__/__/__	__/__/__	
On-the-Job Training			
General content of instructional materials	__/__/__	__/__/__	
Daily routines and schedules	__/__/__	__/__/__	
Systems of reporting student progress and other record-keeping and clerical duties	__/__/__	__/__/__	
Instructional strategies	__/__/__	__/__/__	
Behavior management	__/__/__	__/__/__	
Classroom management	__/__/__	__/__/__	
Observation and recording strategies	__/__/__	__/__/__	
Other: ______________	__/__/__	__/__/__	

Figure 6.6. Sample annual training plan.

Table 6.4
Supervisory Knowledge and Skill Competencies Required by Teachers

- Awareness of reasons for the employment of paraeducators
- Understanding of distinctions in the roles of paraeducators and supervisory professionals
- Awareness of professional, ethical, and legal factors that impact paraeducator roles and supervision
- Ability to participate in interviewing applicants for paraeducator positions
- Ability to communicate effectively with paraeducators
- Knowledge of problem-solving techniques
- Ability to develop and implement on-the-job training activities for paraeducators
- Ability to plan, assign, and delegate paraeducator tasks
- Ability to monitor paraeducator performance and provide on-the-job training
- Ability to share information with principals about paraeducator performance

No matter what education strategies and practices are incorporated into teacher and paraeducator preparation, to be effective they must take into account the many different ways adults learn. Figure 6.7 provides an overview of the many factors that impact adult learning styles and preferences (Pickett, 1999).

Promoting Adoption of District Policies and Practices

Districts employing paraeducators have the responsibility for developing and implementing policies and procedures that maximize the benefits of paraeducator employment to ensure that student needs are met and their rights are protected. Carefully written policies contribute to an environment that recognizes the contributions and value of all staff, provide a common vision for all school personnel, establish the basis for allocating resources, and serve as a foundation for evaluating education quality and student progress at both the district and building levels.

(text continues on p. 281)

How Adults Learn:
Implications for Paraeducator Preparation

- Adults commit to learning when the goals are realistic and important to them. Therefore, professional development should address areas that paraeducators believe have immediate application in learning environments.
- Adults learn, retain, and use that which they perceive is relevant to their needs. Therefore, professional development must enable paraeducators to see the relationships between what they are learning and their day-to-day activities.
- Adults need to see the results of their efforts and have feedback on how well they are doing. Therefore, professional development should provide opportunities for paraeducators to try out what they are learning and to receive structured feedback.
- Adults are more concrete in the way that they operate than formerly thought. Therefore, paraeducators should have the opportunity for directed experiences in which they apply what they are learning in the work setting.
- Adults who participate in small groups are more likely to move their learning beyond understanding to application, analysis, synthesis, and evaluation. Therefore, professional development for paraeducators should include learning in small groups in which they share, reflect, and generalize their experiences.
- Adults come to learning with a wide range of life experiences, knowledge, interests, and competencies. Therefore, professional development for paraeducators must accommodate this diversity.
- Adults want to be the origin of their own learning. Therefore, professional development opportunities need to give paraeducators some control over the what, why, when, and where of their learning.
- The transfer of learning is not automatic for adults and must be planned and facilitated. Therefore, coaching and other follow-up supports are needed to help paraeducators transfer learning into daily practice.

Figure 6.7. How adults learn: implications for paraeducator preparation. *Note.* Adapted from *Strengthening and Supporting Teacher/Provider–Paraeducator Teams: Guidelines for Paraeducator Roles, Supervision, and Preparation,* by A. L. Pickett, 1999, New York: National Resource Center for Paraprofessionals, Center for Advanced Study in Education, Graduate Center, City University of New York; and "Assumptions About Staff Development Based on Research and Best Practices," by F. H. Wood and S. R. Thompson, 1996, *Journal of Staff Development, 14*(4), pp. 52–57.

Table 6.5
Paraeducator Policy Handbook Outline

Definitions

Statutory provisions
State and district policies

Rationale or need for paraeducators

Purpose of position
Benefits for students
Benefits to school
Benefits for school professionals

Requirements for employment

Education (minimum level)
Age (minimum)
Interest in working with students who have different ability levels and learning needs

Job description

Position title(s) and setting(s)
Duties and responsibilities
Supervision guidelines
Evaluation procedures and criteria

Staff development

State and district training policies and standards
Rationale for training
Training goals and competencies
List of training resources (building, district, community colleges)
Types of training: orientation, on-the-job, inservice

Benefits and working conditions

Salary
Hours
Absence procedures
Benefits (i.e., sick leave, insurance, personal leave, vacations)

Supervision policy

Definition of supervision
Supervision responsibilities (role and responsibilities of school professionals and administrators)

(continues)

Table 6.5 *Continued.*

Evaluation procedures
School district policy
Person(s) responsible
Frequency of evaluation
Criteria for evaluation
Feedback and reporting guidelines
Appeal and grievance provisions
Dismissal procedures
School and emergency procedures
Paraeducator professional and ethical responsibilities
Maintaining confidentiality
Relationship to students
Relationship to supervisors, colleagues, and parents

One of the most effective means of communicating policies and practices is a handbook. Policy handbooks include information about paraeducator duties, ethical and legal responsibilities of paraeducators, supervisory responsibility, personnel practices, and other district policies that are important to staff employed in the district. Table 6.5 outlines the content for a section in a district or school policy handbook connected with paraeducator roles, preparation, and supervision. The components of policy handbooks frequently contain definitions, rationales, job requirements, role descriptions, training provisions, benefits and working conditions, supervision policy, evaluation procedures, emergency procedures, and confidentiality and ethics matters.

Summary

Administrators provide a climate of high expectations for performance and leadership in promoting quality educational programs. Paraeducators can play important roles in education if they are appropriately trained, effectively supervised, and well supported by certified and licensed professionals and administrators.

Paraeducator contributions are directly related to well-planned programs that are based on student needs and that provide appropriate guidelines for performance, necessary training, and supervision. Educational resources are squandered when paraeducators are hired and placed in classrooms with little or no orientation, given schedules that do not include time for planning with the teacher, are not compensated for time spent developing job-related skills, and are assigned to supervising teachers who have little training or support as managers.

Paraeducators should be recognized in district policies as important members of the team and as contributors to increased quality of education and related services. District policies should delineate the roles of paraeducators, identify training requirements, and clarify supervision policies. Administrators have the responsibility for the recruitment, selection, hiring, and assignment of paraeducators. Teachers make positive contributions to the selection process and should be included in paraeducator interviews. Regular evaluation of paraeducator contributions is an important element in determining how to continuously develop the program. Administrators need to establish criteria for evaluation and involve both professionals and paraeducators in the assessment process.

Administrators have a leadership role in establishing training policies and working with school staff to develop a plan for a long-range training program. Systematic training programs include a defined set of competencies and a plan for achieving the competencies. In addition, they provide accountability for both paraeducators and administrators.

Paraeducators cannot be ethically employed in classroom settings without appropriate supervision by school professionals. Clear guidelines for supervision are important to both paraeducators and teachers. Administrators must support supervision by making sure that teacher and paraeducator schedules allow time for planning, on-the-job training, and activities that evaluate classroom duties. Providing professionals with strategies for planning and documenting conferences with paraeducators also supports effective supervision. Recognizing the training needs of professionals to be supervisors and providing them with opportunities to learn skills that will enable them to work with paraeducators can have an impact on both the educational achievement of students and the effectiveness of teams. In the final analysis, effective paraeducator programs rely on direction and support provided by school administrators.

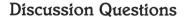

Discussion Questions

1. What are the primary responsibilities of district administrators and principals for creating strategies and mechanisms that support school professional and paraeducator teams?
2. How do responsibilities of administrators differ from the supervisory responsibilities of school professionals?
3. Does your district have job descriptions for paraeducators? When were they developed?
4. Do the job descriptions designate supervisory responsibility? Do they recognize differences in the roles of school professionals and paraeducators?
5. Does your district have standards for assessing the performance of school professionals as supervisors of paraeducators?
6. Does your district have standards for assessing the performance of paraeducators?
7. Who provides the staff development for paraeducators in your district? Is it the district, the supervising school professional, a community college, or a combination?
8. Is the training standardized and competency based? Is it ongoing and part of the district's plan for professional development for all personnel?
9. Has your state, district, or other agency established standards for preparing school professionals to supervise paraeducators?

EXERCISES

1. Assume you have been asked to participate in interviews with candidates for the paraeducator position in your classroom. Develop a list of questions that will help you elicit information in order to choose the person with whom you would prefer to work. Remember that the purpose of an interview is to gather information about an applicant's educational, life, and work experiences, skills, and attitudes. In addition, because interviews should provide the applicant with information about the requirements of the position, the program, and the students, determine what information is important for you to share with the person.

2. Divide into groups of four or five participants. Assume that you are members of a committee that has been asked to plan a 2-day orientation workshop for both new and experienced paraeducators. The goal of the workshop is to prepare paraeducators for assignments in inclusive classrooms and community-based learning settings. What topics and issues should be on the agenda? What type of follow-up training will the paraeducators need during the year? Who should provide the training? (You may want to review information discussed in previous chapters.)

3. Working with your group, use the Job Description Analysis (Worksheet 6.1) to develop a model districtwide job description for paraeducators.

4. Continue to work as a group. Assume that you are members of a committee appointed by the district superintendent to design a section for inclusion in the district's policy handbook. Use the questions in Worksheet 6.2 and the outline in Table 6.5 (earlier in this chapter) as a discussion guide to identify the information that all staff need to know about paraeducator employment, supervision, and training. Then work as a team to develop the contents of the section.

5. Continue to work as a group and identify the most important skills and knowledge that teachers and other school professionals require to effectively supervise paraeducators. Work together to plan a curriculum that will ensure that school professionals acquire the necessary skills. Remember that teachers and other school professionals who supervise paraeducators are responsible for planning the tasks that paraeducators will perform, directing and monitoring their performance, and providing on-the-job training.

6. Assume that your group makes up the shared decision-making council in your school. After you read the following case study, work as a team to develop a list of suggestions the principal could implement to provide regular opportunities for the team to meet. Imagine that your group is holding their second meeting. Brainstorm a list of ideas and strategies that you could suggest to Ilona that might help her find the time for the instructional teams to meet regularly.

CASE STUDY: ESTABLISHING MEETING TIMES

Ilona is the principal of a middle school that serves a student body with diverse education and related services needs. Students with learning, physical, and sensory disabilities are assigned to inclusive classrooms. During the last 3 years, the demographics of the neighborhood where the school is located have changed and now Vietnamese and Korean are the primary languages spoken in many students' homes. Still other students come from family backgrounds that place them at risk and will benefit from personalized attention that will help them master new academic skills. As a result, the instructional team in most classrooms includes one or more paraeducators.

Recently, several teachers and paraeducators spoke to Ilona about a problem that affects their ability to work together effectively: It is a lack of time for team members to meet to share information, plan activities, and discuss student needs and progress.

Shared decision making has proven to be an effective way for school staff and parents to address mutual concerns. Therefore, Ilona has decided to ask the school-based council to discuss ways to schedule opportunities for instructional teams to meet regularly. As the council began to study the situation, they quickly discovered that this problem could not be solved easily or in a vacuum. As they began to study the issues, the council discovered the following information:

a. Paraeducators are paid on an hourly basis, they arrive when the students arrive, and they leave when the students are dismissed.

b. Budgetary cutbacks districtwide make it difficult to extend the number of hours paraeducators work.

c. During teachers' planning periods, paraeducators are assigned other duties (e.g., monitoring the playground or lunchroom; escorting students with special needs to music, gym, math; assisting the librarian).

WORKSHEET 6.1

Job Description Analysis

Directions: Obtain and analyze job descriptions from different districts and programs to determine if they contain the components listed below. Check those items that are included in the job descriptions. Working with your group, develop a list of suggestions to improve one or more of the job descriptions.

1. Are the following items included in the job description?

	Yes	No
Position title	☐	☐
Position setting	☐	☐
Qualifications (educational and experiential)	☐	☐
Rationale or purpose of position	☐	☐
Training requirements (preservice orientation, inservice, on-the-job)	☐	☐
Duties and responsibilities	☐	☐
Hours of employment	☐	☐
Supervisory responsibility	☐	☐
Evaluation procedures and criteria	☐	☐

2. Is the title appropriate and reflective of current trends in paraeducator employment?
3. Do the job descriptions include adequate information about expectations for the position (e.g., what the paraeducator will be doing)?
4. Do the job descriptions present a realistic relationship to tasks that paraeducators are currently performing in classrooms or other learning environments?
5. Are the descriptions of the teacher–paraeducator relationship sufficiently delineated? Are line-staff relations with other personnel described?
6. Are paraeducator responsibilities to students detailed? Are limits to authority identified?
7. Do the job descriptions describe orientation and inservice paraeducator training programs? Are on-the-job training goals identified?
8. Do the descriptions allow for paraeducators to participate in the evaluation process? Is information included on the methods of evaluation of the paraeducator? Are performance indicators described?

WORKSHEET 6.2

Paraeducator Policy Handbook Issues

Directions: Discuss with your group the following questions. Then work together to develop the content either for a section in a district policy manual or for a specific handbook.

1. Why are districtwide policy and regulation manuals important?
2. Should there be a building- or program-specific handbook for paraeducators?
3. How will the information contained in a building- or program-level handbook differ from districtwide procedure and policy?
4. Which handbook do you feel would be most beneficial to team members?

References

Iowa Department of Education, Division of Early Childhood, Elementary and Secondary Education. (1998). *Guide for effective paraeducator practices in Iowa*. Des Moines: Author.

Kansas State Department of Education. (1983). *A manual for the implementation of the facilitator's model.* Topeka: Author.

Lincoln Public Schools. (1993). *Policy and regulation manual.* Lincoln, NE: Author.

Merriam-Webster's Collegiate Dictionary. (1993). Springfield, MA: Merriam-Webster.

Pickett, A. L. (1999). *Strengthening and supporting teacher/provider–paraeducator teams: Guidelines for paraeducator roles, supervision, and preparation.* New York: National Resource Center for Paraprofessionals, Center for Advanced Study in Education, Graduate Center, City University of New York.

Pickett, A. L., Vasa, S. F., & Steckelberg, A. L. (1993). *Using paraeducators effectively in the classroom* [Fastback 358]. Bloomington, IN: Phi Delta Kappa Educational Foundation.

Steckelberg, A. L., & Vasa, S. F. (1998). How paraeducators learn on the Web. *Teaching Exceptional Children, 30,* 54–59.

Vasa, S. F., & Steckelberg, A. L. (1998, February). *Issues and responsibilities of educators in utilizing, training and managing paraeducators who work with students with behavioral disorders.* Paper presented at the Midwest Symposium for Leadership in Behavioral Disorders, Kansas City, MO.

Vasa, S. F., Steckelberg, A. L., & Ulrich-Ronning, L. (1982). *A state of the art assessment of paraprofessional use in special education in the state of Nebraska.* Lincoln: University of Nebraska–Lincoln, Department of Special Education and Communication.

Wood, F. H., & Thompson, S. R. (1996). Assumptions about staff development based on research and best practices. *Journal of Staff Development, 14*(4), 52–57.

Professional and Ethical Responsibilities of Team Members

7

William Heller and Kent Gerlach

OVERVIEW

The role of professional practitioners and their relationship to paraeducators has been described and analyzed in great detail in this text. We make no attempt in this chapter to further delineate the roles of school and agency employees in educational or other settings. The purpose of this chapter is to consider the professional and ethical implications of these roles. This is an important consideration because each individual brings into a setting his or her own values, attitudes, and personalities.

In this chapter, we address several questions: What roles do one's personal values play in interactions with children and youth, parents, and other school personnel? What ethical responsibilities and rights do children and youth, parents, teachers, and paraeducators have? What are the ethical issues that emerge when distinctions in the roles of school professionals and paraeducators are not clear? When tasks are assigned or delegated inappropriately to paraeducators? When opportunities for systematic staff development for paraeducators do not exist? When school professionals are not adequately prepared to supervise paraeducators?

Instructional Objectives

After studying this chapter and participating in discussions and exercises, the reader will be able to do the following:

1. Describe how organizations are dependent on effective relationships among and between those who work within them.

2. Explain the criteria for determining whether or not an occupation warrants recognition as a profession.
3. Discuss why educators are considered professionals as a consequence of the public's perception of their roles, not as members of an occupation meeting the criteria for status as a profession.
4. Describe why the most important characteristic of a profession is a code of ethics.
5. Describe components of a code of ethics developed by several professional organizations.
6. Describe the components of a paraeducator code of ethics.
7. Identify the major sources of ethical dilemmas for school professionals and paraeducators.
8. Discuss the seven steps for making decisions when ethical dilemmas are confronted.
9. Recognize that ethical dilemmas vary in different situations.
10. Recognize that there are not always right or wrong answers to ethical dilemmas.

An Organizational Perspective

Complex internal and external forces affect organizations, including educational systems. These forces include, but are not limited to, laws, litigation, and social, political, and fiscal concerns. The ethical beliefs of our diverse society have an impact on how these forces are changed to meet the needs of learners and their families.

Relationships exist between the individual and the organization in which the individual affiliates. In this chapter, we focus on employing agencies, professional organizations, and unions. The importance of these relationships lies within the organization and has an impact on the individual in proportion to the strength of his or her identification with the organization. Marlowe (1971) summarized this phenomenon as it relates to the individual in the following way: "The organization generally tries to get the individual to absorb certain beliefs as well as do certain things" (p. 477). Marlowe also indicated that a reciprocal relationship needs to exist if the organization and the individual are going to fulfill their respective needs. It is through individuals that an organization achieves its goals and objectives, and it is through the organization that the individual is able to improve and advance. Within this relationship the organization, through key members, enacts policies, procedures, and standards to govern the members at large. Because individuals have differing degrees of identification with an organization, they will also have differing relationships with each other, even in similar roles. That is why some individuals within an organization may complain openly about their organization's leadership, its direction, and other factors, whereas their colleagues do not. The person whose own values and goals are matched most closely with those of the organization will be the most comfortable and supportive of the organization's policies and procedures.

Professional Values and Ethics

Although they are important, personal values alone cannot always serve as the guide to professional behavior. This is the case because each person's experience is different. Not everyone has adopted the same values. Even those who hold the same beliefs may not apply them in the same way in their work with children. These realities make it clear that individuals need more than just their personal values to deal with the ethical issues they encounter in their work.

It is important for the organization to expect behaviors from its members that are considered to be appropriate within the context of the organization. It is just as important for the individual to be informed of these desired behaviors in order to act accordingly (Robbins, 1976). In addition to the relationship between the organization and the individual, relationships also exist among the organization, the individual, and the public. This is especially true in education, which is an enterprise operated by educators for students and supported by public funds. As a consequence of this triadic relationship, the public now requires educators to conduct more research, train more personnel, and provide more services than at any other time in the history of education. The public is demanding accountability, matching the public's expectations for the schools with the behavior (outcomes) of the school as an organization. Clearly stated standards in a code of ethics provide a shared common ground for educators who strive to do the right thing for children, youth, and families.

The principles on which our country was founded are delineated in the U.S. Constitution. Specifically, the 14th Amendment to the Constitution guarantees all citizens of the United States due process and equal protection under the law. According to the Education for All Handicapped Children Act of 1975, which was amended and revised as the Individuals with Disabilities Education Act (IDEA) in 1990, educational services must be provided to all children and youth with disabilities in the United States, without regard to the nature and severity of their disabilities. The implementation necessary to comply with this goal becomes the responsibility of educators. Prior to implementation, educators must establish objectives. Once completed, if educators fail to implement objectives, then they violate the principle of providing education to all children and are, as a consequence, unethical. If education services provided are inappropriate, then, by definition, they also are unethical.

Konnert and Graff (1976) related the establishment of goals and objectives to the individual when they stated,

> With the increasing interdependence of all activities throughout the world, worthy organizational goals cannot be set in isolation, if man is to survive. The value one puts on these interdependent variables directly reflects the feelings and beliefs one has relative to the nature and welfare of man, the nature and uses of knowledge, and other fundamental questions. In short, one cannot establish worthy goals without revealing individual philosophical beliefs and values. (p. 2)

Konnert and Graff further stated that their use of the term *philosophy* and its derivations is interchangeable with such terms as *morality* or *ethics*. If Konnert and Graff's premise is accepted, then it is impossible for personnel in education and related services to establish goals and objectives without revealing their personal ethics.

It is through the implementation of goals and objectives that services are provided. There are differences between development and implementation: Development is an administrative process, whereas implementation is an instructional process. The instructional process is where the service is provided. If an organization or individual develops service goals and objectives and does not implement them, then the organization or individual is merely engaging in the administrative process. If the goals and objectives were developed based on the ethical beliefs of a profession or society, then failure to implement the goals and objectives is unethical.

Education as a Profession

Most educators consider themselves professionals by virtue of their degree and certification or licensure to practice as a teacher, administrator, or counselor, or in another key educational role. However, the field of education does not meet the criteria necessary for earning the distinction of being a profession. If education is not a profession, how can its members be professionals? The answer to this question is one that has concerned the discipline of education for years and continues to do so. A profession is generally defined as an occupation requiring training in a specialized field. Darling-Hammond provided guidance for determining the components of a profession. She stated,

> A profession is formed when members of an occupation agree that they have a knowledge base, that what they know relates directly to effective practice, that being prepared is essential to being a responsible practitioner, and that unprepared people will not be permitted to practice. Until members of the profession band together to articulate and enforce standards, the debate will continue.
>
> In other professions, differentiated roles and responsibilities have gradually emerged as a means of balancing the requirements of supply and qualifications. Those not fully certified or less extensively trained are limited to performing tasks for which they have been prepared, and they practice under supervision. Complex decisions are reserved to those certified to make such judgments. (Darling-Hammond, 1990, p. 269)

It is important that educators and paraeducators understand the characteristics of a profession and the extent to which the discipline of education embodies them.

A review of the literature regarding the characteristics of a profession reveals four that are often cited among authors (American Association of School Administrators, 1960; Leiberman, 1956; Moore, 1970; Myers, 1973). First, the profession must possess a specific body of knowledge. Second, the profession must have an organization that represents the profession. Third, the profession must have a formal code of ethics developed by the members and enforced in cases in which the code is violated. Finally, the profession, through its members, should be dedicated to providing quality service to its clients.

The following list synthesizes the efforts of Heller (1983), Reynolds and Birch (1982), and the National Association for the Education of Young Children (NAEYC; Feeney & Freeman, 1999) to define a profession:

1. The work done is acknowledged to be a vital public service.
2. Learning to do the work calls for extended and specialized education based, in part, on undergirding disciplines.
3. Performance of the activities requires major public trust and accountability.
4. The application of the thinking process to the solution of problems is a predominant ingredient.
5. Decisions and procedures are based on reliable knowledge that is constantly refreshed by new facts and ideas from the arts and sciences and from other professions.
6. The activity has a definite and useful purpose in the eyes of both the practitioner and society.
7. A profession bases its work on a body of knowledge and expertise, which is applied according to the needs of a specific discipline.
8. Procedures exist to ensure that all members are qualified to perform a basic and common body of practice at a safe level.
9. The already qualified members prescribe and apply standards governing admission to their group.

10. Members of the profession have agreed on *standards of practice*—procedures that are appropriate to the solution of ordinary predicaments that practitioners expect to encounter in their work.
11. A profession makes its own decision regarding entry into the field, training, licensing, and standards.
12. The profession exercises internal control over the quality of the services offered and regulates itself.
13. The profession adopts and enforces a code of ethics.
14. Recognized and accredited higher education institutions exist to prepare members for the profession.
15. There are associations made up exclusively of members of the profession that are aimed at maintaining and elevating its standards and its public accountability.

Whether or not education is considered a profession, educators are viewed as professionals. The expectations that parents have for educators are no different from those that parents have for physicians or attorneys. Those expectations are that educators know their subject matter, can effectively teach learners the subject matter, and are accountable for their performance and learner achievement. The public, learners, and parents view education as a profession and they expect its teachers, administrators, and others to be professionals. As long as education remains the domain of the public, the discrepancies between it and non–public-controlled professions will continue, but the fact remains that in the eyes of the public, education is a profession. These expectations are really all that matter. The educator must meet all the expectations that are inherent in the title "professional." It is within this expectation and context that professionalism is defined.

Ethics Defined

In the preceding discussion we have tried to answer the question of whether or not education is a profession. Although it is at best a semiprofession from a criterion-based analysis, it is a profession in terms of the public's expectations. Basic to these expectations, and an element required of all professionals, is a code of ethics. All professions are based on an accepted set of ethical standards or principles set by their members. *Ethics* is defined as the study of right and wrong, duty and obligation. Ethics involves critical reflection on morality. Ethics and other related terms are contained in the glossary at the end of this chapter.

Ethics and associated concepts, such as morals, values, and religion, deal with the conduct of humans. Understanding the differences between various terms associated with ethics requires the examination of definitions.

Ethics may be viewed from three perspectives (Edwards, 1967). First, ethics is viewed from a philosophical perspective called *metaethics*. This perspective focuses on the inquiry *about* ways of life and rules of conduct. Second, ethics may be viewed as a way of life or the manner in which people live. This view is commonly associated with religious beliefs. A third viewpoint is more professional in nature and emphasizes the pursuit of a set of rules, conduct, or a moral code. Examples are found in the various professions, such as law or medicine.

Some philosophers have simply defined ethics as the body of knowledge concerned with the conduct of humankind (Copeland, 1928; Everett, 1918; MacKenzie, 1925; Symonds, 1928). Dewey (1962) viewed ethics as

> the principles that will tell us what is the *right* thing do, or what things are *worth* doing, no matter what people in fact approve or disapprove of and no matter who will be damaged by the decision. It is not concerned with what public opinion on moral matters actually happens to be, just as the scientist is not concerned with what people believe about the shape of the earth but with its actual shape. (pp. 6–7)

The concept of ethics is viewed differently based on the terms associated with it. The purpose of this chapter is to discuss the ethical and professional responsibilities of teachers, other professionals, and paraeducators. Ethics is best viewed from the professional perspective because the teacher and paraeducator are a team. Together, they are the ones responsible for this purpose in the classroom or related environment. The definition for this purpose was developed by Hartoonian (1976):

> Ethics . . . have to do with the relationships that exist between and among people, with the modes of conduct that exist within a profession, and with the moral principles of the cultural heritage to which a society or civilization makes reference. (p. 2)

One characteristic of a profession is the development and governance of a code of ethics. *Code of ethics* is defined as a document that maps the dimensions of the profession's collective social responsibility and acknowledges the obligations shared by individual practitioners in meeting the profession's responsibilities. According to Leiberman (1956), a code of ethics provides several advantages. First, it provides a mechanism to separate the competent professional from the incompetent. Second, it provides the newly trained professional with information regarding rights, privileges, and obligations. Third, it establishes a foundation for the interaction between the professional and the client. Finally, it provides the public with a guide to understand the conduct of the professional. Moore (1970) not only supported Leiberman, but added that a professional code of ethics is equivalent to a private system of law.

Codes of Professional Ethics

A code of ethics for education professionals is based on critical reflection about professional responsibility carried on collectively and systematically by the membership of a profession. It defines the core values of the field and gives guidelines for what professionals should do in situations in which they encounter conflicting obligations or responsibilities in their work. *Core values* are defined as commitments held by a profession that is consciously and knowingly embraced by its practitioners because they make a contribution to society.

A code of ethics may overlap in some ways with regulations and laws, which are important in governing the field and providing basic protections for learners and their parents. A code of ethics describes the aspiration of the profession and the obligations of individual practitioners. It tells professionals how they should approach their work, as well as what they should and should not do. A code of ethics is the tool that guides individuals in the process of practicing professional ethics. Table 7.1 contains components of a code of ethics.

Table 7.1
Code of Ethics Components

• A vision of how the professional should behave
• A statement of commonalities by members of the profession
• Guidance in making choices that best serve the interests of learners and their families
• A tool to help members of the profession articulate their core values and standards of practice
• A resource for generating discussion
• Information for those outside the profession about the profession's beliefs and values and what constitutes professional behavior
• Assurance to the public that professional practitioners will behave in accordance with high moral standards

The National Education Association (NEA) adopted, in 1975, a *Code of Ethics for the Education Profession,* which serves as a guide for the individual educator as well as a basis for enforcement by NEA of any violations of professional conduct. Ethics is basic to professionalism and any judgments made of professional practice must be considered against an established code of ethics approved by educators. The preamble of the NEA code of ethics (Figure 7.1) asks all educators to accept responsibility for adhering to the highest ethical standards.

Education, like many other professions, has numerous specialties. Education specialties include early childhood, elementary, and secondary education; special education; counseling; school administration; and related services, to name a few. Each of these specializations has its own code of ethics. Each also addresses a commitment to learners, to quality practice and performance, and to the profession. Thus, each specialty conforms to the NEA code in content and differs only in terms of its specificity to a group of professionals serving a particular population of children or school system role. The code of ethics for the Council for Exceptional Children (CEC) is shown in Figure 7.2.

The code of ethics developed by the National Association for the Education of Young Children (NAEYC) identifies a number of specific ethical responsibilities for early childhood educators (see Figure 7.3). Behaviors that one must or must not perform are spelled out in the code of ethics. The NAEYC code of ethics

CODE OF ETHICS OF THE EDUCATION PROFESSION: PREAMBLE

The educator, believing in the worth and dignity of each human being, recognizes the supreme importance of the pursuit of truth, devotion to excellence, and the nurture of democratic principles. Essential to these goals is the protection of freedom to learn and to teach and the guarantee of equal educational opportunity for all. The educator accepts the responsibility to adhere to the highest ethical standards.

The educator recognizes the magnitude of the responsibility inherent in the teaching process. The desire for the respect and confidence of one's colleagues, of students, of parents, and of the members of the community provides the incentive to attain and maintain the highest possible degree of ethical conduct. The Code of Ethics of the Education Profession indicates the aspiration of all educators and provides standards by which to judge conduct.

The remedies specified by the NEA and/or its affiliates for the violation of any provision of the Code shall be exclusive and no such provision shall be enforceable in any form other than one specifically designated by the NEA or its affiliates.

Figure 7.1. Preamble of the Code of Ethics for the Education Profession. *Note.* From *Code of Ethics of the Education Profession,* by National Education Association, 1975, Reston, VA: Author. Copyright 1975 by National Education Association. Reprinted with permission.

makes it clear, for example, that educators should never share confidential information about a child or family with a person who has no legitimate need for knowing, should make hiring decisions based solely on the individual's qualifications and ability to do the job, and should adhere to laws or regulations designed to protect children.

The NAEYC code of ethics also includes a statement of commitment that expresses those basic personal commitments that individuals must make in order to align themselves with the profession's responsibilities as set forth in the NAEYC code of ethics. It is a recognition that the ultimate strength of the code rests in the adherence of individual educators.

The ethical responsibilities of paraeducators are basically no different from those of teachers and other licensed and certified professionals. Indeed, the ethical obligations of paraeducators to children and youth, parents, and colleagues are the same as those developed in the NEA, CEC, and NAEYC codes of ethics. A delineation of these obligations by the paraeducator is presented

CODE OF ETHICS FOR EDUCATORS OF PERSONS WITH EXCEPTIONALITIES

We declare the following principles to be the Code of Ethics for educators of exceptional persons. Members of the special education profession are responsible for upholding and advancing these principles. Members of the Council for Exceptional Children agree to judge them in accordance with the spirit and provisions of this Code.

1. Special education professionals are committed to developing the highest education and quality of life potential of exceptional individuals.
2. Special education professionals promote and maintain a high level of competence and integrity in practicing their profession.
3. Special education professionals engage in professional activities that benefit exceptional individuals, their families, other colleagues, students, or research subjects.
4. Special education professionals exercise objective professional judgment in the practice of their profession.
5. Special education professionals strive to advance their knowledge and skills regarding the education of exceptional individuals.
6. Special education professionals work within the standards and policies of the profession.
7. Special education professionals seek to uphold and improve where necessary the laws, regulations, and policies governing the delivery of special education and related services and the practice of their profession.
8. Special education professionals do not condone or participate in unethical or illegal acts, nor violate professional standards adopted by the Delegate Assembly of CEC.

Figure 7.2. Code of Ethics for Educators of Persons with Exceptionalities. *Note.* From CEC Code of Ethics and Standards of Practice, by The Council for Exceptional Children, 1997, Reston, VA: Author. Retrieved August 14, 2002, from the World Wide Web: http://www.cec.sped.org/ps/code.html. Copyright 1997 by the CEC. Reprinted with permission.

in Figure 7.4, a suggested code of ethics for paraeducators developed by Vasa and Steckelberg (1991).

Much of the language used in the model code of ethics for paraeducators is similar to the codes of ethics for several professional organizations presented earlier. The one notable distinction is the area of teacher–paraeducator relationships. Interestingly, the code of ethics for paraeducators addresses the supervising relationship directly, whereas the code of ethics for professional

STATEMENT OF COMMITMENT

As an individual who works with young children, I commit myself to furthering the values of early childhood education as they are reflected in the NAEYC Code of Ethical Conduct.

To the best of my ability I will

- Ensure that programs for young children are based on current knowledge of child development and early childhood education.
- Respect and support families in their task of nurturing children.
- Respect colleagues in early childhood education and support them in maintaining the NAEYC Code of Ethical Conduct.
- Serve as an advocate for children, their families, and their teachers in community and society.
- Maintain high standards of professional conduct.
- Recognize how personal values, opinions, and biases can affect professional judgment.
- Be open to new ideas and be willing to learn from the suggestions of others.
- Continue to learn, grow, and contribute as a professional.
- Honor the ideals and principles of the NAEYC Code of Ethical Conduct.

Figure 7.3. Statement of Commitment. *Note.* From *Code of Ethical Conduct and Statement of Commitment,* by National Association for the Education of Young Children, 1997, Washington, DC: Author. Copyright 1998 by National Association for the Education of Young Children. Reprinted with permission.

school personnel does not at this time. There is reason to believe that this will change. It is already happening in the legal, medical, related services, and allied health professions.

The problem facing educators regarding the role and supervision of paraeducators is one of definition and delegation. The lines of demarcation between the work of school professionals and that of paraeducators are somewhat blurred and difficult to judge on a continuum. Some teachers will delegate more authority and autonomy to one paraeducator than to another. That is why knowledge of the code of ethics established for the profession is so critical. The individuals (teacher and paraeducator) must, in many cases, determine whether or not what has been delegated is within the parameters of the roles of the teacher to delegate the task or within the parameters of the role of the paraeducator to carry out the task. The degree and amount of

PARAEDUCATOR CODE OF ETHICS

1. Practice the standards of professional and ethical conduct approved by the school district or agency.
2. Recognize and respect the roles of teachers as supervisors and team leaders.
3. Recognize and respect the differences in the roles of teachers, other professional practitioners, and paraeducators.
4. Recognize the teachers' responsibilities for planning learner programs, modifying curriculum and instruction, assessing learner progress, and developing behavior management programs.
5. Perform tasks that are within an identified scope of responsibility for paraeducators in different position levels.
6. Share information with parents about their child's performance as directed by the supervising teacher.
7. Refer concerns expressed by learners or others to the supervising teacher or other professional practitioner.
8. Share appropriate information about learner's performance, behavior, progress, or educational program only with the supervising teacher in the appropriate setting.
9. Discuss confidential issues and school problems only with the supervising teacher or designated personnel.
10. Respect the dignity, privacy, and individuality of all learners, families, and staff members.
11. Refrain from engaging in discriminatory practices based on a learner's disability, race, sex, cultural background, or religion.
12. Follow the guidelines established by the district agency to protect the health, safety, and well-being of all learners and staff.
13. Represent the school district or agency in a positive manner.
14. Follow the chain of command established by the district to address policy questions, systems issues, and personnel practices.
15. When problems cannot be resolved, use the agency's grievance procedure.
16. Participate with administrators and other stakeholders in creating and implementing comprehensive systems of professional development for paraeducators.
17. Participate in continuing staff development.
18. Know school policies and procedures.

Figure 7.4. Suggested code of ethics for paraeducators. *Note.* Adapted from *Issues and Responsibilities in Utilizing, Training, and Managing Paraprofessionals,* by S. F. Vasa and A. L. Steckelberg, 1991, Lincoln: Department of Special Education and Communication Disorders, University of Nebraska.

delegation not only determine roles but also, without equivocation, precipitate the formulation of ethical dilemmas.

Preparation of Education Personnel To Deal with Ethical Dilemmas

A variety of instructional materials exists for preparing teachers for the everyday aspects of service delivery to children and youth. At every level, however, there is an absence of comparable materials available for preparing teacher educators, school administrators, supervisors, and teachers to deal with everyday ethical issues in the classroom (Bateman, 1982; Heller, 1982, 1983; Howe & Miramontes, 1992; Kaufmann, 1992; Maple, 1983; Stephens, 1985; Turnbull & Barber, 1984). This lack of information probably has contributed to the current limited focus on ethical issues in preservice and graduate teacher education curricula in special education. "The ethics of special education has so far received scant attention, either as a field of ethical inquiry or as a topic in teacher education" (Howe & Miramontes, 1992, p. 1). Special education professionals are not the only professional educators voicing concern regarding the lack of ethics in education. In *The Moral Dimensions of Teaching*, Goodlad, Soder, and Sirotnik (1990) addressed professionalization issues from ethical perspectives and advocated reorienting teaching and teacher education around ethical relationships. Goodlad et al. (1990) suggested that teachers need to prepare all children to live in a democratic society that embraces dialogue and debate about those things that make lives and living worthwhile.

Although many leaders in education have voiced concern over the lack of attention to ethics in general and special education, only a few empirical studies have been undertaken and the results of those studies are less than encouraging. The results of several studies, as well as the issues involved in "education reform," "restructuring," and "excellence in education," have caused many education professionals to note that

> education, and especially special education, is rife with ethical problems—problems concerning how to treat individual students, how to ensure equal educational opportunity for all, how

> to respect the views of parents, how to effectively work with colleagues, how to supervise and manage paraeducators, how to train paraeducators and how to do all these things while maintaining one's personal integrity and allegiance to the practices of education. (Howe & Miramontes, 1992, p. 1)

Kaufmann (1993), in discussing how radical reform might be achieved in special education, agreed with Sarason (1990):

> Attempts to reform education will make little difference until reformers understand that schools must exist as much for teachers as for students. Put another way, schools will be successful in nurturing the intellectual, social, and moral development of children only to the extent that they also nurture such development of teachers. The notion that what is good for students is also good for teachers applies not only to the conditions under which they work but also to the way they approach problems. (p. 7)

Kaufmann's and Sarason's basic premise is that lasting reform in special education can be achieved only if special education leaders and professionals use the same problem-solving strategies they recommend for special education teachers. Among others, these strategies include "devotion to ethical decision making" (Kaufmann, 1993).

Needed: More Ethics Education

"Presently, most personnel preparation programs provide little if any preparation and information about professional expectations. Evidently, reliance is upon whatever standards students happen to have acquired on their own" (Stephens, 1985, p. 191). Even if it could be assumed that most teacher education preparation programs introduce teacher trainees to the codes of ethics of various specialty groups within education, knowing a code of ethics and knowing how to respond to situations containing ethical dilemmas are not necessarily correlated. Usually, the principles articulated in ethical codes are very general. The resulting problem is that "they provide little by way of guidance regarding what to do in specific cases of ethical controversy" (Howe & Miramontes, 1992, p. 121). The lack of ethics preparation typically has been justified on the basis that the existing curricula are demanding enough given the wide range of educational needs of children. Handelsman (1986) questioned the ethical soundness of this rationale by asking, "Is it ethical to train people to do a variety of skills without training them to perform these skills in an ethical manner?" (p. 371).

The basic premise underlying this chapter is that a knowledge of professional ethics is especially essential for all school professionals with responsibilities for the supervision and management of paraeducators in education and related services. Teachers and paraeducators must follow professional and ethical guidelines in their relationships with learners, their families, colleagues, policymakers, administrators, the public, and each other. Such a diversity of relationships creates an area for competing interests among all concerned that can result in major ethical dilemmas. When dilemmas involve decisions that impact the lives of learners, including their safety, well-being, and quality of education, school professionals cannot afford to resolve them without serious ethical deliberation and appropriate preparation. All team members must be prepared for their roles.

All educators, including related services professionals, paraeducators, and paratherapists, knowingly or not, have responsibility for safeguarding the human and legal rights of children and youth and their families, as well as providing quality services. A code of ethics by itself cannot provide sufficient guidance for educators who are confronted with ethical dilemmas. It is open to serious question whether administrators and supervisors are sufficiently knowledgeable concerning ethics to adequately assist teachers, paraeducators, and related support personnel in dealing with ethical dilemmas.

Sources of Potential Problems for Teams of School Professionals and Paraeducators

The teacher–paraeducator relationship provides numerous opportunities for ethical dilemmas. The following are some potential sources of these dilemmas. The issue of classroom authority and who is the one, to put it in terms of the vernacular, "in charge" remains a major source of professional and ethical problems. Although the teacher is held responsible and accountable by the school system for what occurs in a classroom, the teacher, in reality, may not be in charge. For example, a teacher may be more passive and nondirective and the paraeducator may be more structured and assertive. A potential result is blurred or unclear lines of authority in the classroom. Chances are that anyone observing such a classroom would notice this and perhaps consider the paraeducator to be the authority figure.

The nature of graduate and undergraduate preparation for teachers and other school professionals may create dilemmas. Few teacher education programs prepare their students to work effectively with paraeducators. Many teachers find themselves working with one or more paraeducators before they have ever had a serious thought about what role such an individual might perform in a classroom and other settings. In addition, paraeducators usually receive limited preparation in learning about the roles of their supervisors. The paraeducator may well be versed in the process of instruction, but not in determining educational needs of students, deciding which instructional strategies to implement, or evaluating the effectiveness of these strategies—the things teachers must do many times in a given day. These decisions are based on years of formal preparation by the school professional with a focus on decisions being made unilaterally in a classroom managed by a single individual, the teacher. What a teacher knows and understands about the role of a paraeducator is extremely important and should not have to depend solely on inference or on-the-job experience. Unfortunately, the latter is currently more the rule than the exception.

Team members need to understand their own unique scopes of responsibility. Pickett (1999) has identified a scope of responsibility for teachers that includes

- diagnosing learner needs,
- planning lessons for the entire class,
- aligning and modifying curriculum content with teaching strategies to meet individual learner needs,
- implementing the plans to facilitate learning,
- evaluating learner performance, and

- involving families and caregivers in all aspects of a child's education.

Under the direction of teachers and other school professionals, paraeducators have responsibilities that include

- providing opportunities for one-to-one or small group instruction for learners who can benefit from more individualized attention,
- assisting in maintaining supportive learner-centered environments,
- participating in functional assessment activities,
- assisting with involving families in their children's learning experiences,
- maintaining records about learner progress, and
- facilitating transition from school to work and independent living.

The concept of "team" is important to an effective professional–paraprofessional relationship, yet this is a difficult concept to achieve. The team concept requires sharing, cooperation, effective communication, mutual understanding, shared goals, and a respect for the roles of everyone on the team. It is easy to talk about teaming and teamwork, but achieving a true team practice in reality is seldom easily accomplished.

The human element is a critical variable, especially in classroom settings that constitute a source for possible dilemmas. Not only are there professional–paraeducator relationships, but equally as significant, there are relationships with learners and parents, who may choose to align their affections and judgments with the teacher, the paraeducator, or possibly both. Children and parents may actually vie for the affection or attention of the teacher or paraeducator. Unfortunately, this competition for favor more often than not divides rather than unifies, which could lead to the destruction of a quality professional–paraeducator relationship.

Inclusive settings also frequently require the use of teacher consultants or resource teachers to assist in the accommodation of children with disabilities. Introduction of additional adults, including paraeducators and related services personnel, into a classroom changes the concept of classroom autonomy for the teacher and introduces the need to team or collaborate. The majority of teachers have not been prepared to cope with such situations.

Another situation that can cause professional and ethical concerns is when paraeducators are assigned to a specific student or students rather than to a team of professionals as a program. Frequently in this case, the paraeducator has full responsibility for modifying the plans and works with the student exclusively. This situation can lead to a sense that both the paraeducator and the student are segregated. If a regular teacher feels that the paraeducator has the responsibility for a specific student, planning and supervision by the teacher may be nonexistent. The effect of paraeducator proximity on students with disabilities is beginning to be a concern in inclusion programming. Giangreco, Edelman, Luiselli, and MacFarland (1997), in an article titled "Helping or Hovering? Effects of Instructional Assistant Proximity on Students with Disabilities," suggested that assigning an instructional assistant to a student with special needs in a general education class, though intended to be helpful, may sometimes result in problems associated with excessive, prolonged adult proximity.

Two other related sources of ethical dilemmas pertain to substitute teachers. Substitutes, like other teachers, have received little preparation to work with paraeducators. Whereas some substitute teachers are skilled in the subjects they are assigned to teach, others are not. Even when substitutes are skilled in the subject matter, they typically enter the classroom with little knowledge of the routines, procedures, and learning needs of students in the class. When a substitute teacher works in a classroom served by a paraeducator, many potential ethical dilemmas may arise. In this situation, it is clear that the paraeducator is more familiar with the routines, procedures, and learning needs than is the substitute teacher. The paraeducator may be inclined to assume the lead role, or the substitute may tacitly initiate such an arrangement. Either way, the outcome is that the substitute teacher passes the day without assuming the principal responsibility for the class.

In contrast, the paraeducator may fail to provide essential information to the substitute teacher about routines, procedures, and learning needs of students, expecting that a substitute teacher should know what to do. Or, the substitute teacher may fail to request such information from the paraeducator. In either case, the substitute is working at a distinct disadvantage, deprived of information that is readily available.

Of even greater ethical concern is the situation wherein no substitute teacher is employed and the paraeducator is placed in the position of substitute teacher. There are various reasons for this circumstance. For example, in some localities, few substitutes are available. In others, the cost of hiring substitute teachers strains the budget of the school or district. Whatever the reason, the paraeducator is placed in a role that may violate the codes of ethics for professionals and paraeducators.

Volunteers provide valuable contributions to schools throughout the country. Volunteers may be parents, community leaders, business personnel, or other individuals who want to help in schools. Some volunteers are very well prepared, some may even be former school professionals, and others are not well prepared and have only a sincere desire to help in the educational setting. When volunteers and paraeducators are in the same classroom, it is often difficult for a casual observer to differentiate one from the other. This apparent lack of differentiation gives rise to ethical dilemmas. Three clear distinctions, however, may be made between paraeducators and volunteers. First, the district does not employ volunteers, whereas paraeducators are school employees who are paid to perform specific duties at specific times. Second, school districts and school professionals have less control over the attendance, actions, and ethical behavior of volunteers than they do over the attendance, actions, and ethical behavior of paraeducators. Thus, some tasks that must be performed in specified ways, that require specific behaviors, or that must be performed at specific times are better performed by paraeducators than volunteers. Finally, volunteers have no right to access certain confidential information about students. Thus, some tasks that require knowledge of confidential information may not be safely assigned to volunteers and should be assigned instead to paraeducators. Teachers need to be aware of the distinctions in roles of volunteers and paraeducators in order to delegate appropriately and create appropriate plans for the duties of each. Without question, all school professionals should be prepared to recognize and understand the value and roles of paraeducators.

School professionals also need to know how the employment of paraeducators and use of volunteers may give rise to certain ethical dilemmas in their practice.

Another issue concerns family involvement in planning paraeducator services to implement the Individualized Education Program (IEP). Family members should be active participants in considering the need for paraeducator services in an IEP. If a student requires the services of a paraeducator to assist with the implementation of the IEP, family members need to contribute to the decision making and planning about how those services will be delivered. The Iowa Department of Education, Division of Early Childhood, Elementary and Secondary Education (1998), recommended that families ask the following questions:

1. What issues do family members and other IEP team members need to address when considering the needs of the student?
2. What accommodations or modifications are needed and who will provide those accommodations?
3. What services will be provided by the paraeducator?
4. What skills does the paraeducator need to work effectively with the child? How will the paraeducator be trained prior to starting services? What ongoing staff development will be provided to the paraeducator?
5. Where will the services be provided?
6. How much time will the paraeducator be working with the learner?
7. How long will the services be needed?
8. How will families know when the learner outcomes and objectives have been achieved?
9. Who is responsible for directing and monitoring the paraeducator?
10. Who should families call about programming issues such as my child's progress, class scheduling, instructional needs, or social interaction with peers?
11. How will information the paraeducator has about the child's experiences at school be shared with the family?

Finally, an ethical dilemma exists regarding the preparation and training of paraeducators. Various agencies and organizations with responsibilities for improving the quality of personnel preparation must work together to develop policies and standards for effective staff development. This must be done to ensure the availability of a highly skilled workforce. Unless the following questions are asked and answered, ethical dilemmas addressed in this chapter will continue.

1. Have knowledge and skills required by paraeducators and assistants to work in different positions, in various programs, and across disciplines been identified and developed?
2. Are there systematic competency-based opportunities for personnel development and career advancement
   - for paraprofessionals?
   - for administrators who manage paraprofessionals?
   - for educators and other professionals who supervise paraprofessionals?
3. Does the training content provide paraeducators and their supervisors with an understanding of the roles of professionals as team leaders, diagnosticians, program planners, and supervisors of paraprofessionals?
4. Have the team leadership and supervisory roles been identified and the knowledge and skill competencies developed to prepare the professionals for these roles?
5. Does the training content demonstrate respect for children and youth with disabilities and their families, as well as for those who come from diverse ethnic, cultural, and language backgrounds?
6. Does the training content include information on the ethical, legal, and team-based roles of professionals and paraeducators in the delivery of education and related services?
7. Do licensed or certified professionals involved in the training of paraeducators have knowledge of and respect for the distinction in professional and paraeducator roles?
8. Is sufficient time and opportunity provided for orientation, initial training, and continued competency development?

9. How can different constituencies (e.g., professional associations, provider agencies, institutions of higher education) contribute to the appropriate efforts to improve the quality of teacher–paraeducator staff development?

Paraeducator Ethical and Professional Dilemmas

Tymchuk (1982, p. 170) listed seven steps for making ethical decisions:

1. Describe the parameters of the situation.
2. Describe the potential issues involved.
3. Describe the guidelines already available that might affect each issue (e.g., values, laws, codes, practice, research).
4. Enumerate the alternative decisions for each issue.
5. Enumerate the short-term, ongoing, and long-term consequences, as well as the probability of their occurrence.
6. Present evidence (or lack thereof) for those consequences, as well as the probability of their occurrence.
7. Rank order and vote on the decision.

Using these steps, the reader is asked to analyze five ethical and professional dilemmas and answer a number of discussion questions related to each dilemma. Critical to the analysis is accurately assessing all elements of the situation evoking the dilemma. Please remember that situations are seldom simple and the more complex, the greater the need for accuracy in analyzing the situation.

Ethical and Professional Situations

SITUATION 1

Mary is a teacher of a primary classroom that includes two students who have learning and sensory disabilities. Mary grades the latter students on effort and they always receive A's based on their hard work. All the other children are graded on what they learn and, although they may work hard, most do not receive A's. The paraeducator feels Mary's grading procedure is unfair. She speaks to Mary and discovers they have very different philosophies. The paraeducator shares her concerns with one of her friends, who happens to be a parent of one of the students in that class.

Situation Discussion Questions

1. What should the paraeducator do if she believes a breach of ethics has occurred? What should the teacher do?
2. Are some things right for students with disabilities that may not be right for others?
3. Whose responsibility is it to assign grades to students in a classroom? Who is ultimately accountable, and can accountability be shared from the viewpoint of the employer and the school system?
4. Do you feel inclusion requires a different procedure for evaluating the performance of students with disabilities?
5. What are the major professional and ethical issues in this case?

SITUATION 2

The school professional, Raja, has planned a field trip for his class to a local restaurant's main offices to learn about business and management techniques. This chain has recently been criticized for sexual harassment of its employees and the paraeducator (Sharon) refuses to go. Raja notes that the criticism has never been validated and that the paraeducator's values have an impact on his ability to expand learning experiences for the students. The plans for the field trip continue on schedule. This is not the first time Raja and Sharon have had a discussion on values and differences of opinion.

Situation Discussion Questions

1. As an employee, what might the consequences of a refusal be? Do you feel a dismissal would be warranted if you were the principal of the school?
2. If ultimately ordered to go, does the order constitute sexual harassment?

3. Is the question of values relevant here and, if so, how does one deal with it professionally and ethically?
4. The paraeducator code of ethics indicates that the supervisor has ultimate responsibility for instruction. Is this an instructional issue or a relationship issue?
5. Should the paraeducator go? If yes, why? If no, why not?

SITUATION 3

John, a school professional, and Tashira, the paraeducator with whom he has worked for years, have had a major disagreement. John has taken a few days off as sick leave when he actually went to baseball games. Tashira knows what he did and has informed John that she will not cover for him anymore. This has happened several times before. Frequently he leaves class and allows her to take over. John tells Tashira that she is being disloyal and that others do it regularly. Tashira feels it is bad for the classroom because the substitute teachers are sometimes unsatisfactory and she feels uncomfortable when John is not there.

Situation Discussion Questions

1. If Tashira has known about the reasons for John's absences before and not reported them, what are the ethical implications?
2. Where does loyalty fit into a relationship, and what really constitutes loyalty?
3. Have you ever known of someone who called in sick but wasn't? What were your feelings?
4. Since John has Tashira as a paraeducator, do his absences have less of an impact than his absence might if he had no paraeducator? Should this be given consideration in determining the ethical implications?
5. What if Tashira was absent and John found out she was not sick? Is it as serious?
6. What will happen to this instructional team if Tashira follows through on her decision to report John's sick leave deception and her concerns about him leaving her with the class?
7. Can and should it be settled between John and Tashira and never reported to administration?

SITUATION 4

Juan, a teacher of a very diverse class of children with learning disabilities, had been ill for 2 days recently and Marci, the paraeducator, worked with a substitute teacher who delegated almost everything for the 2 days to her. In addition, the substitute teacher seemed to avoid the Hispanic children in the classroom and, when he did interact with them, was very rude and condescending. Juan has called in sick again and, although the paraeducator asked for a different substitute, she was informed that teacher selection was not within her purview. The substitute she previously had concerns about was the one selected to substitute again.

Situation Discussion Questions

1. If a substitute teacher is not a very confident teacher, would it not be better to let the paraeducator do the teaching?
2. Should paraeducators have a role in selecting and evaluating substitutes? If so, how should this role be fulfilled in terms of ensuring that personal differences are not conflicting with professional competence concerns?
3. If the substitute teacher feels uncomfortable teaching Hispanic children, would it not be acceptable for Marci to teach them?
4. Would it be justifiable for Marci to take personal leave and let another paraeducator work with the substitute?
5. Is there a point where commitment to children becomes secondary to one's personal integrity and survival? If so, how does one justify this within the stated parameters of any of the professional organization or the paraeducator codes of ethics?

SITUATION 5

Josephine is a first-year teacher and has never worked with a paraeducator. Marie, the paraeducator assigned to her classroom, has 15 years of experience and is only a few hours from having earned her own bachelor's degree via a career ladder program. Josephine is somewhat in awe of Marie and has essentially taken a backseat to her. Marie has a dominant personality, knows the children, knows the school system, and does not hesitate to assume any responsibilities Josephine might relinquish. The question to others, and especially to Josephine's induction year mentor, is who is really teaching the class?

Situation Discussion Questions

1. Are any of the professional organization or paraeducator codes of ethics principles being violated? If so, which one(s)?
2. If you were Josephine's mentor, what would you advise or how would you help Josephine?
3. What could Marie do to help Josephine without making it appear she is taking over or being too commanding?
4. Does the fact that Marie almost has her bachelor's degree make a difference in this situation? After all, the two women are almost identical in terms of preparation.

Summary

The purpose of this chapter has been to provide professionals with an understanding of ethics and professionalism as these relate to their work with paraeducators. More and more professional educators and others in related disciplines are emphasizing the study of ethics as a means of coping with serious dilemmas occurring in educational settings among and between professionals. Because education is a people-oriented activity, the need to establish and maintain effective ethical relationships and practice is critical. These relationships motivate not only professionals and support personnel, but also children, parents, and a variety of others. The concept of a team is predicated on relationships; eliminating ethical dilemmas, which impair the purity of these relationships, is crucial. The professional with no knowledge of ethics is a professional in trouble. The professional who knows ethics and practices in an ethical manner is a professional who will always be in demand and command of those relationships and experiences that foster success.

Discussion Questions

1. From an ethical perspective, discuss why teacher supervision is essential for working with paraeducators.
2. What do the school professional and paraeducator need to know about professionalism and ethics?

3. What are some important ethical considerations when planning to integrate a paraeducator into a team where he or she will be supervised by a number of teachers?
4. If the job of a paraeducator is to be considered a career choice, how do you feel about a nationally accepted code of ethics for paraeducators?
5. What are some possible ethical issues connected with the supervision of paraeducators?
6. Divide into groups and discuss the ethical issues involved in scheduling, conferencing, delegation, lesson planning, small and large group instruction, and paraeducator training.
7. Identify some of the professional and ethical considerations that should be discussed with paraeducators when they are employed.
8. Think about a time when you made a difficult decision regarding an ethical dilemma. Who were the stakeholders, and what were your obligations to each? What resources did you use to help you resolve the dilemma? What was the outcome and was it successful?

EXERCISES

1. The importance of confidentiality is paramount. If you were to develop a 1-hour inservice program for paraeducators on this topic, what would you include? Develop an inservice outline containing the content you think is important.
2. Ask your local school district for guidelines and standards (a code of ethics) for school professionals and other employees. How does the code relate to paraeducators?
3. Review the following guidelines developed by the state of Utah (Utah State Board of Education, 1995) that support ethical practice in involvement of paraeducators in education programs. Read each guideline and then discuss its implementation. Focus on ethical implications of the guideline.
   - Guideline 1—The paraeducator shall be considered and supported as a team member responsible for assisting in the delivery of education and related services.

- Guideline 2—The entire instructional team shall participate within clearly defined roles to provide an appropriate educational program for students' disabilities.
- Guideline 3—Paraeducators, whose primary responsibilities involve student contact in instructional or related services roles, shall have the job description, supervision, and career development support consistent with their instructional assistant role.
- Guideline 4—Differentiated staffing patterns should enhance the continuity and quality of services for students and the morale, training, and dignity of staff.
- Guideline 5—Paraeducators shall be provided with training commensurate with their responsibilities to ensure appropriate education for students with disabilities.
- Guideline 6—Professionals shall provide appropriate supervision to ensure that paraeducators deliver appropriate support in the education process.
- Guideline 7—Administrators shall resume a central role in the support and recognition of paraeducators as integral and permanent partners in providing an appropriate education for students with disabilities.
- Guideline 8—Paraeducators shall be recognized and supported for their expertise and contributions and shall receive ongoing opportunities for career development and advancement.

4. Discuss the following staff development workshop description. What are the problems associated with this description? Rewrite the description from an ethical perspective.

WORKSHOP DESCRIPTION 1

This informative workshop will provide paraeducators with practical strategies for selecting and designing small group instructional curriculum, teaching students, pacing lessons, and increasing student responses. It will also give you tips you can use to manage your students.

WORKSHOP DESCRIPTION 2

A special workshop is available for paraeducators in charge of computer labs. You will learn many innovative tips to manage your computer lab. You will learn to plan and design programs for computer use.

5. Review the following job description. Examine the description from an ethical perspective. What is missing from the job description? How can this job description be improved?

PARAEDUCATOR–SPECIAL EDUCATION
JOB DESCRIPTION

Title: Paraeducator—Special Education

Months: 9.0 months per year

Hours or FTE: 4.5 hours per day

Salary Range: $11.90 to $13.00 per hour

Minimum Qualifications: High school diploma or GED

Preferred Qualifications: Skills with behavior management and experience with special reading program implementation; first aid and CPR; experience with children.

Special Working Conditions: Will be working one-on-one with a male student. May require toileting, diapering, lifting, and health-related procedures.

Application Procedures: Completed applications and requests for consideration must be received during the posting period.

Interviews will be arranged through Human Resources only. Current and/or previous supervisors will be requested to provide information on your job performance.

Posting #139EA An Equal Opportunity Employer Classified Position

6. Review the following five case studies and discuss, in a group, the professional and ethical implications of each situation.

CASE STUDY 1

It is one o'clock in the afternoon and the third-grade teacher has an IEP meeting. The principal asks the paraeducator to be in charge of the class for the rest of the afternoon. The paraeducator was told to teach the lessons to the entire class as scheduled in the lesson plan book.

Case Study Discussion Questions

a. How do you feel about this situation?

b. Discuss this case from the perspective of the principal, teacher, and paraeducator.

c. What are the professional and ethical implications of this case?

CASE STUDY 2

Chris, a student with behavior problems, has disrupted the classroom several times this semester. The teacher has just about had it with him. Today, the teacher said to Jane, the paraeducator, "I'm assigning you to work only with him. I can't stand his behavior anymore."

Case Study Discussion Questions

a. How do you feel about paraeducators working with the most challenging students?

b. What should have been done differently?

c. What are the professional and ethical implications of this case?

CASE STUDY 3: INTRODUCTION

Karen Adams has been assigned to David Bowen's classroom. On the first day of school, Mr. Bowen introduces himself and the paraeducator by saying, "I am Mr. Bowen, your teacher, and this is Karen. Karen is a helping teacher for Tommy, Susan, and Mark."

Case Study Discussion Questions

a. How do you feel about Mr. Bowen introducing Karen by her first name?

b. Discuss the potential problems that could result by assigning the paraeducator to work with a child rather than a class or program.

c. How could this be handled differently?

d. What are the professional and ethical implications of this case?

CASE STUDY 4: CONFIDENTIALITY

Fred, a second-grade teacher, works with two paraeducators in his classroom, Jesse and Joann. Fred has decided he needs to talk with both of them about a problem that is developing. He has heard Jesse and Joann discussing students outside the classroom and believes that they are violating confidentiality. He wants to be clear in stating the guidelines about confidentiality without being punitive with the paraeducators.

Case Study Discussion Questions

a. What should Fred bring to the meeting that outlines confidentiality?

b. How should he begin the meeting so that Jesse and Joann feel that the meeting is friendly yet professional?

c. What material should he give to Jesse and Joann for future reference?

d. What can Fred do to make sure that Jesse and Joann understand the issues of confidentiality?

e. What are the professional and ethical implications of this case?

f. Think about a time when you made a hard decision regarding an ethical dilemma. Who were the stakeholders, and what were your obligations to each? What resources did you use to help you resolve the dilemma? What was the outcome and was it successful?

CASE STUDY 5: ROLES AND RESPONSIBILITIES

Several students in a class have very limited English. Helen, the paraeducator, is fluent in their native language. Because the paraeducator is very competent and understands the children's needs, the teacher asks the paraeducator to tutor these children. The paraeducator plans the lessons, translates classroom material, and adapts the curriculum when appropriate. The teacher and the paraeducator meet weekly to discuss how things are going. In addition to the instructional duties, the teacher asks the paraeducator to visit the parents of these children at their homes to strengthen the school–home relationship. The paraeducator feels comfortable with her job and enjoys the interaction with the students and families.

Case Study Discussion Questions

a. How do you feel about this situation?
b. Do you feel the assigned role is appropriate for this paraeducator since she understands the needs of the children and families?
c. What could be done differently?
d. What are the professional and ethical implications of this case?

Glossary of Terms Associated with Ethics

Code of ethics. A document that maps the dimensions of the profession's collective social responsibility and acknowledges the obligations that individual practitioners share in meeting the profession's responsibilities.

Core values. Commitments held by a profession that are consciously and knowingly embraced by its practitioners because they make a contribution to society. There is a difference between personal values and a profession's core values.

Ethical dilemma. A moral conflict that involves determining appropriate conduct when an individual faces conflicting professional values and responsibilities.

Ethics. The study of right and wrong, duty and obligation. Ethics involves critical reflection on morality.

Morality. Individuals' view of what is good, right, or proper; their beliefs about their obligations; and their ideas about how they should behave.

Principles of professional conduct. Rules included in a code of ethics that mark the line between acceptable and unacceptable professional behavior.

Professional ethics. The moral commitments of a profession. Professional ethics involve moral reflection that extends and enhances the personal morality that practitioners bring to their work. Professional ethics concern the kinds of actions that are right and wrong in the workplace and help individuals resolve the moral dilemmas that they encounter in their work.

Standards of practice. Agreed upon procedures for doing the work of a profession. A range of acceptable practices may be exercised in a particular situation.

Values. The qualities or principles that individuals believe to be intrinsically desirable or worthwhile, and that they prize for themselves, for others, and for the world in which they live (e.g., truth, honesty, justice, respect for people and the environment.)

References

American Association of School Administrators. (1960). *Professional administrators for American schools* (38th Yearbook). Washington, DC: Author.

Bateman, B. (1982). The special educator as a professional person. *Exceptional Education Quarterly, 2*(4), 57–69.

Copeland, J. R. (1928). *Natural conduct: Principles of practica–Ethics*. Stanford, CA: Stanford University Press.

Council for Exceptional Children. (1997). *CEC code of ethics and standards of practice*. Reston, VA: Author. Retrieved August 14, 2002, from the World Wide Web: http://www.cec.sped.org/ps/code.html

Darling-Hammond, L. (1990). Teachers and teaching: Signs of a changing profession. In W. R. Houston, M. Haberman, & J. Sikula (Eds.), *Handbook of research on teacher education* (pp. 267–290). New York: Macmillan.

Dewey, J. (1962). Reconstruction in philosophy: Reconstruction in moral conceptions. In W. T. Jones, F. Sontag, M. O. Beckner, & R. J. Fogelin (Eds.), *Approaches to ethics: Representative selections from classical times to the present*. New York: McGraw-Hill.

Education for All Handicapped Children Act of 1975, 20 U.S.C. § 1400 *et seq*.

Edwards, P. (1967). *The encyclopedia of philosophy* (Vol. 3). New York: Macmillan & Free Press.

Everett, W. G. (1918). *Moral values: A study of the principles of conduct*. New York: Henry Holt.

Feeney, S., & Freeman, N. K. (1999). *Ethics and the early childhood educator using the NAEYC code*. Washington, DC: National Association for the Education of Young Children.

Giangreco, M. F., Edelman, S. W., Luiselli, T. E., & MacFarland, S. Z. C. (1997). Helping or hovering? Effects of instructional assistant proximity on students with disabilities. *Exceptional Children, 64*(1), 7–18.

Goodlad, J. I., Soder, R., & Sirotnik, K. A. (1990). *The moral dimension of teaching*. San Francisco: Jossey-Bass.

Handelsman, M. M. (1986). Problems with ethics training by "osmosis." *Professional Psychology, 17*, 371–372.

Hartoonian, H. M. (1976). *The ethics of our profession: The student and schooling*. Washington, DC: National Council for the Social Studies Annual Convention. (ERIC Document Reproduction Service No. ED 132 083)

Heller, H. W. (1982). Professional standards for preparing special educators: Status prospects. *Exceptional Education Quarterly, 2*(4), 77–87.

Heller, H. W. (1983). Special education professional standards: Need, value, and use. *Exceptional Children, 50*(3), 199–204.

Howe, K. R., & Miramontes, O. B. (1992). *The ethics of special education: Professional ethics in education series*. New York: Teachers College Press.

Individuals with Disabilities Education Act of 1990, 20 U.S.C. § 1400 *et seq.*

Iowa Department of Education, Division of Early Childhood, Elementary and Secondary Education. (1998). *Guides for effective paraeducator practices in Iowa.* Des Moines: Author.

Kaufmann, J. M. (1992). Foreword. In K. R. Howe & O. B. Miramontes (Eds.), *The ethics of special education* (pp. xi–xvii). New York: Teachers College Press.

Kaufmann, J. M. (1993). How we might achieve the radical reform of special education. *Exceptional Children, 60*(1), 6–16.

Konnert, W., & Graff, O. B. (1976). The sine qua non of organizational effectiveness. *Educational Administration Quarterly, 12*(3), 1–8.

Leiberman, M. (1956). *Education as a profession.* Englewood Cliffs, NJ: Prentice Hall.

MacKenzie, J. S. (1925). *Manual of ethics* (4th ed.). New York: Noble and Noble.

Maple, C. C. (1983). Is special education certification a guarantee of teaching excellence? *Exceptional Children, 49,* 308–313.

Marlowe, L. (1971). *Social psychology: An interdisciplinary approach to human behavior.* Boston: Holbrook Press.

Moore, W. E. (1970). *The profession: Roles and rules.* New York: Russel Sage Foundation.

Myers, D. A. (1973). *Teacher power–Professionalization and collective bargaining.* Lexington, MA: Heath.

National Association for the Education of Young Children. (1997). *Code of ethical conduct and statement of commitment.* Washington, DC: Author.

National Education Association. (1975). *Code of ethics for the education profession.* Reston, VA: Author.

Pickett, A. L. (1999). *Strengthening and supporting teacher/provider–paraeducator teams: Guidelines for paraeducator roles, supervision, and preparation.* New York: National Resource Center for Paraprofessionals, Center for Advanced Study in Education, Graduate Center, City University of New York.

Reynolds, M. C., & Birch, J. W. (1982). Special education as a profession. *Exceptional Education Quarterly, 2*(4), 1–13.

Robbins, S. P. (1976). *The administrative process: Integrating theory and practice.* Englewood Cliffs, NJ: Prentice Hall.

Sarason, S. B. (1990). *The predicted future of educational reform. Can we change before it's too late?* San Francisco: Jossey-Bass.

Stephens, T. M. (1985). Personal behavior and professional ethics: Implications for special educators. *Journal of Medical Ethics, 11,* 47–53, 191.

Symonds, P. M. (1928). *The nature of conduct.* New York: Macmillan.

Turnbull, R. H., & Barber, P. (1984). Perspectives on public policy. In E. L. Meyen (Ed.), *Mental retardation: Topics of today–Issues of tomorrow* (Vol. 1, pp. 5–14, Serial No. 1). Reston, VA: Division on Mental Retardation of the Council for Exceptional Children.

Tymchuk, A. J. (1982). Strategies for resolving value dilemmas. *American Behavior Scientist, 26,* 159–175.

Utah State Board of Education. (1995). *Utah state standards for paraeducator roles and supervision.* Salt Lake City: Author.

Vasa, S. F., & Steckelberg, A. L. (1991). *Issues and responsibilities in utilizing, training, and managing paraprofessionals.* Lincoln: Department of Special Education and Communication Disorders, University of Nebraska.

Index

About the Editors

Anna Lou Pickett is the former director of the National Resource Center for Paraprofessionals in Education and Related Services (NRCP). She established the National Resource Center for Paraprofessionals as an operating unit of the Center for Advanced Study in Education located at the City University of New York. Currently she provides technical assistance to state and local education agencies and to professional organizations to help them build systems and practices to improve the employment, supervision, and preparation of paraeducators. Her travels as director of the NRCP and now as a consultant have taken her to The Netherlands, Canada, Guam, and all but three states. She is also the author of several journal articles, instructional programs, and resource materials concerned with enhancing the status, professional development, and performance of the paraprofessional workforce.

Kent Gerlach is a professor in the School of Education at Pacific Lutheran University in Tacoma, Washington. His research interests include paraeducator issues, inclusion, and collaboration. He has conducted numerous staff development workshops throughout the United States, Guam, Micronesia, Canada, and Australia.

He has received several teaching awards, and most recently received the Faculty Achievement Award for his work with the Washington State Legislature and the Washington State Education Association. He serves as a consultant to the National Education Association and the Council for Exceptional Children on issues affecting paraeducators and those who supervise them. Kent is the author of several journal articles and resource materials dealing with communication and team building and the ethical issues affecting the roles of paraeducators and their supervisors.